Dynamics of Foreign Policy and Law

Dynamics of Foreign Policy and Law

A Study of Indo-Nepal Relations

Surya P. Subedi

OXFORD
UNIVERSITY PRESS

OXFORD
UNIVERSITY PRESS

YMCA Library Building, Jai Singh Road, New Delhi 110 001

Oxford University Press is a department of the University of Oxford.
It furthers the University's objective of excellence in research, scholarship,
and education by publishing worldwide in

Oxford New York
Auckland Cape Town Dar es Salaam Hong Kong Karachi
Kuala Lumpur Madrid Melbourne Mexico City Nairobi
New Delhi Shanghai Taipei Toronto

With offices in
Argentina Austria Brazil Chile Czech Republic France Greece
Guatemala Hungary Italy Japan Poland Portugal Singapore
South Korea Switzerland Thailand Turkey Ukraine Vietnam

Oxford is a registered trade mark of Oxford University Press
in the UK and in certain other countries.

Published in India
by Oxford University Press, New Delhi

First published 2005

ISBN 019 5672011

Typeset in AGaramond
by Eleven Arts, Keshav Puram, Delhi 110 035
Printed in India by Roopak Printers, New Delhi 110032
Published by Manzar Khan, Oxford University Press
YMCA Library Building, Jai Singh Road, New Delhi 110 001

Dedicated to the generations of defenders of the sovereignty
and independence of Nepal
from Bir Amar Singh and Bir Bhakti Thapa
to
His Majesty, the late King Birendra Bir Bikram Shah Dev

Contents

APPENDICES

Treaties Relating to Indo-Nepal Relations

Other Treaties of Interest

Acknowledgments

This is a collection of my unpublished and published, but substantially revised and updated, essays written over almost two decades, and therefore I have a great many people to thank. For want of space it is not possible to list all of their names here; nevertheless, I would like to put on record my appreciation for the help, encouragement, and guidance that I have received from a number of people and institutions.

First and foremost, it was His Late Majesty King Birendra of Nepal who personally inspired and encouraged me to such a degree that without his support I would not have been able to acquire the ability to write many of the essays included in this collection. He was a monarch who had the foresight and wisdom to work for a national consensus and to stand for national interests when confronted by adverse conditions. I have decided to dedicate this book primarily to his loving and lasting memory, as his tragic death was not only a great loss to humanity and the people of Nepal but also a massive loss to me both personally and professionally.

I would also like to record my sincere appreciation to the publishers of various prestigious books and journals for their permission to use the material from my previous contributions published by them. Most of the published papers have been substantially revised and updated to reflect the changes that have taken place since their initial publication. There is a group of people who have been instrumental in shaping my career and I owe a great debt to them for their invaluable support. They include, Radheshayam 'Kamaro', former minister of state for law and justice, Nepal; Professor Scott Davidson of the University of Hull; Dr Christine Gray of the

University of Cambridge; Professor Ian Brownlie of the University of Oxford; Professor Nico Schrijver of the Institute of Social Studies, The Hague; and Professor Martin Ira Glassner of the University of Connecticut, USA.

I am grateful to His Majesty's Government of Nepal and the Foreign and Commonwealth Office of the UK for their support and recognition of my academic and professional work.

My thanks also go to the Oxford University Press (New Delhi) for publishing this book and to its editorial team for the patience and hard work that they have put into publishing this book. I would like to thank Ms Lee-Anne Robins and Ms Nkechi Ogbonna for their research assistance in the publication of this book.

Last, but not the least, my hearty thanks go to my eldest brother, Shree Komal Nath Subedi, for his support, guidance, and encouragement during my studies in Kathmandu; to my wife, Kokila, for being there as a solid pillar of support; and to my children, Pranay and Anita, for their love, support, and understanding.

London
January 2005

Surya P. Subedi

Introduction

India and Nepal are probably the closest neighbours in existence anywhere who share the greatest number of differences. Although they appear to have so much in common, they tend to have difficulties in resolving many vital issues, including border disputes, trade and transit issues, and matters relating to cooperation in the water sector. With cooperation and mutual understanding both stand to gain a great deal for the benefit of their respective peoples. Unfortunately, a succession of political leaders of both countries have been unable to demonstrate the degree of farsightedness and wisdom required to cultivate and nurture a relationship that does not really demand much hard work or major sacrifice for it to flourish. However, the problems persist; a small problem is allowed to exacerbate and then to become apparently intractable. In other words, they have been unable to successfully manage the process of change that has taken place in their relations since 1950.

India and Nepal share not only a long and open border but also cultural history. Although India is a secular state in terms of its legal and governmental structure, its population is predominantly Hindu. Nepal is officially the only Hindu kingdom in the world, albeit this status is contested by some sections of the population. There is a sizeable population of Indian origin living in Nepal and vice versa. That is one reason why the 1950 Treaty of Peace and Friendship accords nationals of India national status in Nepal and vice versa with regard to certain industrial, economic, and commercial activities. However, the nature and scope of this treaty has been the subject of the control controversy in Indo-Nepal relations ever since its conclusion.

Critics have argued that it is a treaty based on the 'Himalayan frontier policy' of India; fundamentally a policy pursued by the British during the height of their colonial expedition in South Asia, and should thus be altered to reflect the current reality.

While the spirit of cooperation between neighbours has brought about a great deal of prosperity in many parts of the world, Indo-Nepal relations are still not in tune with the times, as is the case with the state of economic development in each of these two countries. India has a rather old-fashioned patronizing attitude towards Nepal, and the latter in turn suffers from the syndrome of a small country unable to move forward in her relations with India. This unfortunate state of affairs has hindered Nepal's attempts at modernization and economic development and has also undermined India's image as a large democratic nation capable of coming to terms with the reality of prudent conduct of relations with her smaller neighbour. Given her location in the southern flanks of the Himalaya, Nepal is virtually a country landlocked with India, and therefore there is a tendency in New Delhi to regard Nepal as its own backyard. This has given Nepal a sensitivity about her geographical 'handicap'.

Indians are critical of the inclination of Nepalese leaders to adopt the role of an irritant neighbour, incapable of understanding the bilateral relations between them from a broader perspective. Nepal is an important but a relatively smaller factor in the much larger Indian canvas, but India is too large a factor in the much smaller Nepalese canvas. India has a regional view in her dealings with Nepal while the latter has a bilateral view vis-à-vis her relations with India. Consequently, there are a number of misrepresented and misguided differences in their respective views of each other that have hindered the prospect of meaningful cooperation between them. It is left to diplomacy to analyse both perspectives and employ appropriate legal techniques to fashion a solution.

However, there does not seem to be a balance in the interplay between diplomacy and law in shaping the relations between Nepal and India. Consequently, Indo-Nepal relations have become the perfect 'laboratory' for testing various principles of international law. While some treaties concluded between the two countries are lopsided, thereby inviting inevitable criticism from intellectuals; certain others, even those concluded ostensibly on the basis of equality, have yet to be implemented because they too have been tainted by the old mindset of 'unequal' treaties. For instance, Nepal as a landlocked country has a guaranteed right to free access to and from the sea through the territory of India under international law, but India has taken a long time to acknowledge this and is slow and often reluctant to honour this right in practice. What is more, there are treaties whose very existence is contested by the parties. Treaties have been concluded between the two countries without their being designated as such in order to avoid the parliamentary scrutiny that treaties require. All these complexities provide a worthy case study for an international lawyer. It is in this context that the essays presented in this book attempt to provide an insight into the dynamics of law and foreign policy in Indo-Nepal relations. A study of the key treaties concluded between Nepal and India provides interesting reading for those interested both in international law and international relations.

Currently, there seems to be some realization on the part of Indian leaders too that relations with Nepal have to be reviewed and revised in line with modern practices of international relations. What is required is to promote Indo-Nepal cooperation on the basis of mutual interests and sovereign equality. Far more can be achieved by pursuing more forward-looking policies such as those advanced by the former prime minister of India, I.K. Gujral. Both Nepal and India are poor countries and both of them have fallen behind in their efforts to reap the benefits and opportunities offered by globalization.

Nepal is a country with immense resilience. It has a huge potential, and that has to be realized. Nepal's hydroelectric power potential itself is a huge source of optimism. However, this resource has to be utilized to uplift the economic standards of the people and currently that is not happening at a satisfactory pace. Nepal needs huge investment, and experience shows that it is not likely to come readily from outside South Asia. The natural market for Nepal's hydroelectric power is India and the investment required for it could come from India.

If Nepal and India do not move rapidly to utilize the resources Nepal has to offer in the development of their respective economies, these resources may become redundant when new and cheaper forms of energy become available. There is still a great deal of mistrust, confusion, and dogmatism dominating Indo-Nepal relations. It is necessary to develop an environment in both Nepal and India that is conducive to meaningful cooperation between these two countries. For this, we need to study the nature of relations between the two countries, analyse the treaties that are in existence, point out the mistakes of the past, and draw lessons from these so that both countries can move forward in a spirit of cooperation. This is precisely the aim of this book.

The objective of this collection of essays is to provide a detailed analysis of the legal complexities that exist between Nepal and India and to analyse the major problems from an international legal perspective. It is hoped that this volume will fill the significant gap that exists in the literature on this subject. The extant literature on the subject is devoted more to political and economic issues than to legal ones. There is virtually no work thoroughly examining the major international legal issues relating to Indo-Nepal relations. This book is being published at a time when both India and Nepal are committed to reviewing some of the so-called 'unequal' treaties between the two countries. It is hoped that it will serve as a useful source of reference for diplomats and politicians of both India and Nepal, as well as for the academics and researchers of South Asia and beyond.

The book is divided into eight chapters and covers a wide range of topics relating to Indo-Nepal relations. The first chapter sets the stage for a discussion of several key issues in Indo-Nepal relations and the concluding chapter provides an outlook for the future. The other chapters deal with political, economic, and security matters between the two countries. This book also includes in the appendices the principal treaties concluded between Nepal and British India as well as those between Nepal and post-Independence India for the reader's convenience. This is because, while some of the treaties concluded by Nepal with British India still have a great impact on current problems existing between India and Nepal, they are not readily available. Also, some of the treaties that have been reproduced in their entirety in the appendices are ones that have been extensively referred to in the text.

London

Surya P. Subedi

1

Indo-Nepal Relations: The Causes of Conflict and their Resolution

Describing the nature of Indo-Nepal relations,[1] a scholar and a former foreign minister of Nepal rightly states that 'there are few countries in the world whose histories, cultures and traditions have been so closely interlinked for such a long time'.[2] Perhaps, this is one reason why the Indo-Nepal relationship is so very complex and governed by a number of treaties many of which are now outdated, undemocratic, and based on the colonial legacy of the Raj as well as the Cold War. Located between the two giants of Asia, Nepal understandably wants to have a balanced relationship with both.

However, as a landlocked country surrounded by India to the east, south, and west, Nepal is virtually dependent on the former for her access to the sea and the international market. Nepal constitutes a narrow strip across the northern frontier of India, with whom it shares a 500-mile border and this border remains open. That is why India maintains that the security interests of both countries are 'inevitably joined up'.[3]

This is one reason why, since the days of the Raj, the rulers of India, who have regarded the Himalaya as a second frontier under the so-called 'Himalayan frontier policy', have sought to keep Nepal, which lies on the southern slopes of the Himalaya, within the Indian sphere of influence. Consequently, India has used a variety of measures, including the grant of transit facilities, as political leverage, to ensure that Nepal remains under the broader Indian security framework. The resentment on the part of the Nepalese to this policy and India's insistence on maintaining it has been the principal reason for the frequent serious friction between these two states.

The climax was the 1989 economic embargo imposed by India against Nepal following the expiry of the term of Nepal's trade and transit treaties with India.

The crisis continued for over a year and ended only when a movement in Nepal overthrew the panchayat government, which had taken a strong nationalist stand with India. It was a movement against the partyless panchayat system of government organized by a number of political factions some of which had received the support of Indian political leaders in their design to topple the panchayat government. For instance, Chandra Shekhar, the leader of an Indian political party which was in the Janta Dal led coalition government of India, headed by V.P. Singh, led an 'illegal' rally organized by Nepali Congress party in Kathmandu in November 1989 which ended with a pledge to topple the panchayat government of Nepal. Chandra Shekhar was accompanied by other parliamentarians belonging to the ruling party of India.[4] The movement itself was partly sparked by the scarcity of essential commodities created by the Indian economic embargo against Nepal.

After the overthrow of the panchayat regime, a new government came to power in Nepal headed by Krishna Prasad Bhattarai of the Nepali Congress. One of the first steps taken by the new government was to normalize its relationship with India. Consequently, Bhattarai, the new prime minister, visited India, and at the conclusion of his visit in June 1990, he signed a joint communique that sought to limit Nepal's freedom of action in certain foreign and domestic matters. Of course, under this communique India agreed to restore the status quo ante to April 1987 in matters of trade and transit,[5] but this was only after Nepal had agreed to terms favourable to India in matters ranging from India's security concerns to granting national status to Indian nationals in Nepal in excess of any provisions in any existing treaty between the two countries.[6]

It is understandable that for a country like India, which has gone to war with China on territorial disputes which have not yet been resolved, to demand a degree of understanding of India's security concerns from a country bordering China but geographically part of South Asia with a 500-mile long open border with India. One however wonders what these Indian security concerns are, and how Nepal can avoid undermining such concerns without compromising its own sovereignty and freedom of action?

Three major bilateral instruments have been concluded by India with Nepal supposedly to protect the former's security concerns: the 1950 Peace and Friendship Treaty, the 1965 Arms Assistance Agreement, and the 1990 Joint Communique. It is interesting that India concluded these bilateral treaties with Nepal when the government in power there was either in crisis or about to fall or was merely a caretaker government. These are times when a government is less accountable to the people and has no mandate from them to conclude a treaty with other states on matters of vital concern to the country, and yet these are also times when such governments are keen to obtain foreign support either to remain in power or to win forthcoming general elections.

While India concluded the 1950 Peace and Friendship Treaty with an oligarchical government in Nepal which was about to be overthrown by a popular movement, the 1965 Arms Assistance Agreement was concluded with Nepal in the aftermath of certain insurgent activities carried out against Nepal from Indian soil by activists of the Nepali Congress Party living in exile in India. Similarly, the 1990 Joint Communique was concluded with Bhattarai's caretaker government of Nepal, which had no mandate to conclude any agreement of such gravity. It was an interim government not elected by the people nor appointed by any constitutional authority but propelled to power by a popular movement during the 1989/1990 crisis sparked partly by India's economic embargo imposed upon Nepal.

In short, India has concluded treaties with Nepal dealing with security matters when the government in Nepal, whether it be a panchayat government or Nepali Congress government, was weak. That is one reason why many people in Nepal are apprehensive not only of India but also of their own government as hardly any government of this country of the past, whether it be a Panchayat government or a Nepali Congress government, has cared to take the people in confidence or encourage public debate on vital matters of foreign policy. The principal areas of dispute between Nepal and India fall by and large into the following heads.

Problems Surrounding India's Security Concerns

The 1950 Treaty of Peace and Friendship[7]

The observance of the 1950 Peace and Friendship Treaty has been the matter of acute controversy between Nepal and India more or less since the late 1950s when a 'secret' letter exchanged with the treaty was made public. Prime Minister Mohan Shumsher, the head of an oligarchical government (the Rana regime) which was about to be overthrown by a democratic movement led by the Nepali Congress, signed this letter, together with the treaty between India and Nepal. In its last days in power that government was desperate for foreign assistance for its survival and was prepared to act in concert with New Delhi. Nehru, a shrewd politician, quickly grasped the situation and the opportunity it offered. That is how the Peace and Friendship Treaty was concluded between these two countries under which India managed to secure terms favourable to it. Muni, an Indian writer, states that 'the Ranas fully accommodated India's security and commercial interests'.[8] Soon after, that oligarchical regime in Nepal fell, but the treaty it concluded survived and survives to this day much to Nepal's discomfort.

The principal provisions of the treaty and the letter of exchange are as follows:

Defence and Security

(1) The two governments hereby undertake to inform each other of any serious friction or misunderstanding with any neighbouring state likely to cause any breach in the friendly relations subsisting between the two governments.[9]

(2) Neither government shall tolerate any threat to the security of the other by a foreign aggressor. To deal with any such threat, the two governments shall consult with each other and devise effective countermeasures.[10]

(3) Any arms, ammunition, or warlike material and equipment necessary for the security of Nepal that the government of Nepal may import *through* the territory of India shall be so imported with the *assistance and agreement* of the government of India ...[11]

(4) Both governments agree not to employ any foreigners whose activity may be prejudicial to the security of the other ...[12]

Economics and Commerce

(5) Each government undertakes, in token of the neighbourly friendship between India and Nepal, to give the nationals of the other, in its territory, national treatment with regard to participation in the industrial and economic development of such territory and to the grant of concessions and contracts relating to such development.[13]

(6) The two governments agree 'to grant, on a reciprocal basis, to the

nationals of one country in the territories of the other the same privileges in the matter of residence, ownership of property, participation in trade and commerce, movement, and other privileges of a similar nature'.[14]

(7) If the government of Nepal should decide to seek foreign assistance in regard to the development of the natural resource of, or of any industrial project in, Nepal, the government of Nepal shall give first preference to the government or the nationals of India, as the case may be, provided that the terms offered by the government of India or Indian nationals, as the case may be, are not less favourable to Nepal than the terms offered by any other foreign government or by other foreign nationals.[15]

Nepalese View of the Treaty

Successive Nepalese governments have every now and again claimed that the 1950 treaty is now outmoded and derogations from it are commonplace.[16] As both countries have let many of its provisions fall into disuse in the last 40 years, the time has come to review the treaty and replace it by a new one. One of the arguments advanced by Nepal to make its case against the 1950 treaty is that the government in New Delhi remained silent when Nepalese were forced to leave certain north-eastern Indian states, e.g. Assam and Meghalaya, in the late 1980s. Given the agreements reached by the central government in New Delhi with various nationalist movements in Indian states, it is difficult for India to ensure that Nepalese nationals enjoy national treatment in all parts of India. India should not expect Nepal to conform to a treaty to which India itself is unable to conform. Nepalese officials complain that Indian political leaders tend to forget the sensitivity showed by Nepal to India's territorial integrity and security by maintaining silence during the Gorkhaland movement and the eviction of thousands of Nepalese from north-eastern India.

Many Nepalese complain about the influx of Indian labourers into Nepal. It is said that once they enter, it is difficult to distinguish them from the Nepalese people of the Terai region. This unchecked immigration is creating unemployment and brewing resentment within Nepal. It was against this background that the panchayat government had introduced the work permit scheme for Indian nationals. Analysts have suggested that this move was suspected by India to be a move to identify the vast number of ethnic Indians living in the Terai belt of Nepal. Many Nepalese were unhappy too with the Nepali Congress government's 'soft' stand on India, particularly in relation to letting cheap, untaxed Indian goods undercut local products. India must realize that these are some of the problems which any government in Nepal will have to deal with.

The government of Nepal states that it is difficult for a small country like it, with a population of 23 million, to accord national status to the Indians who number over a billion. Nepal has therefore enacted laws barring foreign nationals, including Indians, from owning land in Nepal. As Nepal borders on some of the poorer parts of India, there is a continuous flow of Indian immigrants and labourers into Nepal in search of work. Some Nepalese have argued that this treaty places an unfair burden on Nepal and gives unreasonable say to India in the conduct of Nepal's domestic affairs: the privileges accorded to Indian nationals in Nepal under the treaty are not amenable to the present day realities because they are likely to pose a threat to the sovereignty of Nepal and disturb its internal social harmony.

A number of arguments have frequently been raised in Nepal claiming that the 1950 treaty has never acquired validity.[17] Among them are the contentions that it is an unequal treaty;[18] India has materially breached some its provisions;[19] and that a fundamental change of circumstances warrant the suspension of the application of the treaty, etc.

Indian View of the Treaty

India, however, regards the 1950 treaty as valid and insists upon full compliance of its provisions by Nepal. Nevertheless, it emerged from the debate during the 1989 stalemate between India and Nepal that the former, too, was prepared to enter into negotiations with the latter on the whole gamut of mutual relations, including the 1950 treaty. However, what India was saying was that because of its 'special relationship' with Nepal it had been very 'generous'[20] to its neighbour in many matters and now, as the latter was intent on changing this 'special relationship', in New Delhi's view, Nepal was merely another neighbour like Bangladesh and Pakistan, and, thus, not worthy of 'generous' treatment from India. A former foreign minister of state of India, Natwar Singh, who was one of the key players in shaping India's policy towards Nepal during the 1989 crisis, stated that

> With Nepal, India has a very special, even unique, relationship ... The treaty of friendship of 1950 emphasizes this special and unique relationship. For quite some time the Nepali authorities have been uneasy about some clauses of the

treaty and would wish to modify parts of it. By all means. Let both sides sit down and have a second look at it. At the same time, we, as sincere well-wishers of Nepal, should put the facts and realities of life before our Nepali friends. This is precisely what Mr Rajiv Gandhi did when he met King Birendra in Belgrade in September 1989 at the time of the non-aligned summit. Without violating confidentiality, I can say that what the former prime minister impressed on the king was that it was not the question of one or two or three treaties or even of the 1950 treaty, or the king's proposal for a zone of peace. The real issue was what kind of relationship did Nepal want with India. That to use an overworked but nevertheless useful Americanism was the bottom-line.

The choice was to maintain the spirit of the treaty of 1950 after making mutually acceptable modifications in it or go in for a relationship envisaging trade on the most-favoured nation (MFN) basis as with other countries. Nepal could not abandon the treaty and still enjoy the economic advantages of a special relationship which are not inconsiderable.[21]

He then concluded that 'both countries must evolve a strategic plus security understanding without any reservations'. This sums up the position held by India during the 1989 Indo-Nepal stalemate. At first sight, this appears to be a fair and frank proposition. A closer examination of this statement however shows us that he was using a language of threat: if Nepal did not opt for a 'special relationship' with India, the latter would sever not only the facilities granted under the 1950 treaty, but also the transit facilities enjoyed by Nepal; facilities accorded by international law to landlocked states.[22] This is what actually happened during the 1989 crisis. He stated that if Nepal abandoned the 'special relationship' with India it would have

very adverse immediate and long-term effects, e.g. the advantages of economic, trade and transit and financial aid would evaporate. Fifty lakh [five million] Nepalese living, working, owning property and business, and facing no discrimination would become aliens. Railway freight would go up. Port charges could shoot up. These are just the most obvious examples.

He should have remembered that by becoming aliens the Nepalese would not ipso facto forfeit their property and business and lose their jobs in India. Even in the event of abrogation of the 1950 treaty, India would still be under an obligation under international law to treat the aliens fairly and protect their property. It would not be able to deprive the Nepalese of their property and business merely by virtue of the abrogation of any treaty with Nepal,[23] but would continue to have an obligation to provide minimum international standard of treatment to Nepalese nationals.[24]

Shrivastava is more blunt in narrating and echoing India's threat:

> In Belgrade Rajiv Gandhi asked the king what he would like to do about various agreements. In trade, if he desired the most-favoured nation treatment, the Government of India would agree to that. But in that case all the special arrangements will have to go ... Rajiv Gandhi also asked the king about the 1950 Treaty and said that if Nepal wanted to change the treaty, it could. But with that everything else will stop. Even their property will have to be confiscated ... With the abrogation of the Treaty all its provisions, which favour Nepal and its citizens, will cease to exist. [25]

He claims that in purchasing certain weapons, Nepal had violated a defence treaty with India: 'Even though there was a defence treaty with us in force, they [i.e. Nepal] did not inform India about it'.[26] This is an example of how certain so-called Nepal experts associated with the South Block attempt to misinterpret the situation. Nepal had no defence treaty with India in 1989 and was under no obligation to inform India of its actions in acquiring arms.

What is more, during the climax of the 1989/90 crisis, it was believed that India had proposed a 'secret' draft treaty designed to severely restrict Nepal's independence and sovereignty and to strengthen India's position in relation to it. Had the draft agreement been accepted by Nepal it would have required Nepal to repeal those laws unfavourable to Indian nationals, including the provision of the Civil Code of Nepal which bars foreign nationals, including Indians, from acquiring and owning land in Nepal. Also, India seems to have sought to explicitly mention 'employment' in the provision dealing with Nepal's treatment of its nationals. This attempt was to further to tighten up the provision of the 1950 treaty, which does not include employment in the provision concerning the treatment of Indian nationals in Nepal.

Apparently, the 'secret' draft agreement would have required Nepal to cooperate with India in military matters too. It would in effect have been a military alliance that India had long been seeking. It would have expanded and perpetuated the provision of the 1965 Agreement and brought Nepal firmly within India's grip with regard to Nepal's acquisition of arms and ammunition as well as to the training of military personnel. It would have required Nepal to consult India on matters relating to the training of military personnel in third countries. The draft agreement would have also given India significant, even blanket, control over the utilization of the waters of Nepalese rivers and excluded third country involvement in the development of water projects in Nepal.

When the king and the then prime minister, Marich Man Singh, refused to be coerced into this draft treaty, India started its covert 'game plan' of overthrowing the nationalist panchayat system of government. The king was wise to sense India's broader aims and was able to defuse the situation by giving powers to his own people rather than agreeing to India's draft agreement designed to limit Nepal's freedom of action. However, the irony is that when Krishna Prasad Bhattarai visited India in the aftermath of the democratic movement of Nepal in 1990, he finally agreed through the 1990 joint communiqué, to most of India's core positions initially advanced in the secret agreement. Thus, this visit was one of the most damaging for Nepal in terms of her relations with India. Although K.P. Bhattarai, too, rightly rejected the idea that Nepal had to purchase weapons necessary for its defence from India, thereby negating the existence of the 1965 Arms Agreement, he actually conceded on other vital issues.

The 1965 Agreement on Arms Assistance[27]

In the aftermath of the Sino–Indian border war of 1962 as well as the insurgent activities carried out from Indian soil against Nepal by some Nepalese political activists who were living in exile in India (who were opposed to the panchayat system of government in Nepal), Nepal and India had concluded an Arms Assistance Agreement under which India undertook to 'supply arms, ammunition, and equipment for the entire Nepalese Army' and to 'replace the existing Nepalese stock by modern weapons as soon as available and also to provide the maintenance of and replacement for the equipment to be supplied by them'.[28] Nepal was, nevertheless, 'free to import from or through the territory of India arms, ammunition, or warlike material and equipment necessary for the security of Nepal. The procedure for giving effect to this arrangement shall be worked out by the two governments acting in consultation.'[29]

From the Indian standpoint, this freedom, however, did not extend to the import of weapons by Nepal from or through China because it was India that was responsible for the supply of weapons to the entire Nepalese army and to replace the existing stock with modern armaments.

However, for Nepal, this 1965 agreement no longer has any validity. According to the then Nepalese prime minister, K.N. Bista, the agreement was cancelled by Nepal after consulting India some time in 1966.[30] He has said this loudly and clearly more than once. He claimed that India had agreed to the cancellation, a claim not refuted by India. India has however said nothing about the agreement until friction erupted between these two countries in 1989. After 20 years of silence, the Indian foreign ministry reportedly circulated the 'secret' agreement to the Indian media to arouse public support for the actions taken by New Delhi against Nepal.

The 1990 Joint Communiqué

As stated earlier, this Joint Communiqué was signed in the aftermath of the 'Cold War' of 1989/90 between Nepal and India. The principal provisions of the communiqué on security matters read as follows:

> Nepal and India will fully respect each other's security concerns. In this context, neither side will allow activities in its territory prejudicial to the security of the other. The two countries shall have prior consultations with a view to reaching mutual agreement on such defence related matters which, in the view of either party, could pose a threat to its security.

Other principle commitments undertaken by Nepal under the communiqué are as follows:

> Restoration of tariff preferences to Indian goods by, *inter alia*, exemption of additional customs duty.
>
> Exemption of basic customs duty on imports of primary products from India as provided for similar products from Nepal imported to India.
>
> Tariff preferences for third country goods should not be such as to be detrimental to the tariff regime for Indian exports.
>
> Removal of Indian nationals from the ambit of the Work Permit Scheme.

Thus, India managed to include in this communiqué most of what it had in the draft secret agreement presented to King Birendra. Krishna Prasad Bhattarai had little understanding or the ability to understand the gravity of such matters. Although India also undertook certain commitments with regard to Nepalese exports and imports, what India actually did was to restore more or less the same trade and transit facilities that it had been according Nepal prior to the 1989/90 economic embargo, in return for new concessions from Nepal. This shows how India has manipulated Nepal's freedom of transit—a freedom guaranteed under international law. Nepalese leaders were happy just to get the same facilities restored by India without realizing that the implications of other provisions of the communiqué tended to tie the hands of Nepal in many matters of vital concern, including security. For instance, the 1990 Joint Communique describes Nepalese rivers as 'common rivers', a concept which is different from the concept of international rivers and could seriously weaken Nepal's bargaining power with India when it comes to negotiating economic cooperation projects regarding the exploitation of Nepalese rivers to generate hydroelectric power or other projects concerning flood control and irrigation, etc.

Similarly, the national treatment provisions of the 1950 treaty had not included employment within the ambit of national treatment to be accorded to the nationals of each country. However, the 1990 Joint Communique requires Nepal to remove Indian nationals from the ambit of the Nepalese Work Permit scheme. This is an extra concession secured by India from a weak Nepali caretaker government in the aftermath of the 1989/90 crisis.

With regard to the provisions of the communiqué on India's security concerns, it is not clear what is meant by the term 'full respect for each other's security concerns' in the provision quoted above. Would India not object to Nepal's decision to import weapons from other countries or to conclude defence arrangements with other countries designed to strengthen its security? Alternatively, does it simply mean that 'neither side will allow activities in its territory prejudicial to the security of the other'? or does it mean the following which seems to have been the position of India during the 1989/90 crisis with Nepal:

(a) Firstly, joint Indo-Nepal surveillance of the border between Nepal and Tibet (which really means China).

(b) All training of Nepalese military personnel to be conducted by India alone.

(c) Thirdly, no foreign aided project along the open 500 mile Indo-Nepal border to be implemented without Indian concurrence.

(d) Nepal must respect property rights of Indians in Nepal and shall not deprive Indians of these rights except under the due process of law; and

(e) Lastly, all Nepali laws that are not in conformity with the 1950 Treaty of Peace and Friendship will be terminated.[31]

These proposals, as described by Sen Gupta, serve to demonstrate a long-standing Indian insensitivity to Nepal's national pride. He rightly poses a series of relevant questions: How would China react if Nepal permitted Indians to keep an eye on Nepal's border with China? Would they not ask for a similar right of a joint Nepal–Chinese eye on Nepal's border with India? What is the justification for the demand for an Indian zone of influence along the 500-mile Indo-Nepal border? On what democratic basis can India demand that Nepal not send her military personnel for training to any country other than India? Who is going to determine which Nepali laws violate the 1950 treaty, an ambiguous and poorly drafted document?[32]

Since the 1990 Joint Communiqué includes certain provisions similar to those of the 1950 Treaty, was this communiqué intended to replace the 1950 treaty? The communiqué states that '(p)ending the finalization of a comprehensive arrangement covering *all aspects* of bilateral relations, the two prime ministers agreed to restore *status quo ante* to April 1, 1987 in the relations between the two countries'. This indicates that the communiqué was meant to be valid for a provisional or temporary or transitional period. Thirteen long years have passed since the signing of this provisional Joint Communiqué and no such single comprehensive arrangement, as envisaged in the communiqué, has as yet been concluded between these two countries. Then the question to be asked in this context is: Is this temporary or transitional communiqué still valid, especially after the conclusion of separate bilateral treaties on trade and transit in 1991 or the conclusion of the Mahakali River Treaty in 1996? What is the legal status of this communiqué?

From an analysis of the events leading up to the signing of the communiqué as well as its provisions themselves one could arrive at three possible conclusions.

First, as the Joint Communiqué included all major issues covered by the 1950 treaty, both India and Nepal implicitly acknowledged that the 1950 treaty was now outmoded. It should be noted that both countries had stated during the 1989/90 crisis that they were willing to enter into a dialogue to review the treaty. According to Article 59 of the Vienna Convention on the Law of Treaties, a treaty should be considered as terminated if the parties to it conclude a later treaty, or it is otherwise established that the parties intended that the matter should be governed by that treaty. This is the case here. Let us take a provision of the 1950 treaty and its counterpart in the 1990 Joint Communiqué as an example: Paragraph 1 of the letter exchanged with the 1950 Treaty:

> Neither Government shall tolerate any threat to the security of the other by a foreign aggressor. To deal with any such threat, the two governments shall consult with each other and devise effective countermeasures.

A similar provision is included in the 1990 Joint Communiqué:

> The two countries shall have prior consultations with a view to reaching mutual agreement on such defence related matters which, in the view of either party, could pose a threat to its security.

Are both of these provisions valid and necessary? If not, which one of these is valid? Which one was meant to govern matters covered by these provisions? A logical answer to these questions would be that it is the 1990 Joint Communiqué that prevails over all other arrangements made before it on the matters covered by it. Consequently, one would have to presume that those provisions of the 1950 treaty similar to those of the 1990 communiqué are no longer in operation.

One could argue that the Joint Communiqué was designed merely to reiterate and strengthen the provisions of the 1950 treaty. If that was the case, the Joint Communiqué should have mentioned the treaty somewhere in the text and the Joint Communiqué should not have envisaged the conclusion of 'a comprehensive treaty covering all aspects of bilateral relations'.

Second, it is also arguable that as the 1990 Joint Communiqué was meant to be valid for only a short transitional or temporary period, it is no longer valid, especially after the conclusion of two separate treaties on trade and transit in 1991 as well as the Mahakali River Treaty of 1996, as the communiqué had included provisional measures not only on security matters but also on trade and transit facilities and other matters of cooperation between the two countries.

A third conclusion that could be said to flow from the first and second conclusions is that at present there is no bilateral treaty between Nepal and India concerning security or defence matters, e.g. to inform each other of any frictions with other states or to consult each other on security matters with a view to devising countermeasures or to reach any other mutual agreement on such defence-related matters which, in the view of either party, could pose a threat to its security. In short, it can be argued that the provisions of the 1950 treaty concerning security matters were replaced by the 1990 Joint Communiqué which in turn has now lost its validity because of its provisional or temporary character.

However, India is unlikely to accept this mere legalistic interpretation of the situation. One might say that treaties are treaties; they remain valid unless terminated in accordance with their provisions. Further, a considerable weight of public opinion holds the view that for the sake of maintaining the goodwill that Nepal enjoys among the people of India, she should show certain understanding on matters relating to India's security concerns so long as it does not mean compromising her own sovereignty and freedom of action on defence and security matters.

The Problem of Free Access to and from the Sea

The principal international instruments concerning landlocked states are the Barcelona Convention and Statute on Freedom of Transit of 1921,[33] the High Seas Convention (HSC) of 1958,[34] the Convention on Transit Trade of Landlocked Countries of 1965[35], and the Convention on the Law of the Sea (LOSC) of 1982.[36] Both Nepal and India are party to the Barcelona Convention and Statute. Nepal is also a party to the 1958 High Seas Convention and the 1965 Convention on landlocked states, but India is not a party to these conventions. However, India has just become a party to the 1982 Convention, which guarantees the right of free access for landlocked states. In view of the mandatory character of Article 125 (1) of this convention and the approval of this provision by consensus during the Third United Nations Conference on the Law of the Sea, the right of free access, as embodied in the 1982 Convention, could now be regarded as part of customary international law,[37] binding on all states, including India.

Moreover, a substantial weight of authority supports the view that the right of free access to and from the sea to landlocked states and the principle of freedom of transit are now a part of customary international law, binding on all states.[38] This may be one reason why India acknowledged during the 1989/90 crisis that, as a landlocked country, Nepal had a right of free access to and from the sea under international law even in the absence of a bilateral transit treaty, although the question concerning the number of transit points required by Nepal remained controversial.

Narasimha Rao, the then Indian minister of external affairs, speaking in the lower house of the Indian parliament on 26 April 1989, stated that in 'the field of transit, a landlocked country *has a right* only to one transit route to the sea under International Law' (emphasis added).[39] This was evidenced by the fact that even in the absence of a transit treaty India allowed Nepalese exports and imports to and from third countries, albeit under very restrictive conditions and only through two of the 15 transit routes that were in use prior to the expiry of the old treaty. As Nepal had launched a publicity campaign to gain support and sympathy from the outside world with regard to its problem with India, Indian officials were making strenuous efforts to convey the message that India did not intend to deny Nepal its right of transit even in the absence of a transit treaty.[40]

It should be said at the outset that the new transit treaty, i.e. that concluded in 1991, repeats, with minor alterations, the provisions of that of 1978. The preamble to the treaty recognizes that 'Nepal as a landlocked country needs access to and from the sea to promote its international trade'. This recognition is however diluted in the treaty by the inclusion of the principle of reciprocity. Article I makes the transit right of Nepal subject to reciprocity, which is not consistent with the very concept of a right of free access of landlocked states. According to Article 125 of the 1982 Convention, the right of free access to and from the sea is not subject to reciprocity; this right is unilaterally and solely available to landlocked states.

Thus, on the surface, Nepal seems to have achieved a satisfactory transit treaty with India as the latter conceded to the Nepalese demand for a separate treaty on transit and for 15 transit routes, in contrast to the stance taken by New Delhi during the Indo-Nepal stalemate that under international law Nepal was entitled to only one transit route; India also agreed to continue to provide overland transit facilities through Radhikapur for Nepal's trade with or via Bangladesh. Nevertheless, the fact remains that the entire exercise relating to the right of landlocked states during the Third United Nations Conference on the Law of the Sea and the incorporation in the resulting 1982 Law of the Sea Convention of the right of free access of landlocked states does not seem to have influenced any of the transit treaties concluded by Nepal with India. Nor, apparently, has account been taken of other provisions of the 1982 Convention on the Law of the Sea on landlocked states. For instance, the Transit Treaty of 1991 disregards not only Article 125(1), but also Article 126 of this convention. Nepal has secured neither simplified exports and imports procedures[41] nor India's recognition of Nepal's 'right' of free access to and from the sea. Most striking of all is the incorporation of the principle of reciprocity in the treaty. The elimination of the requirement of reciprocity in the 1982 Convention represented a major breakthrough for landlocked states, but if bilateral transit treaties concluded even after the coming into force of the 1982 Convention on the Law of the Sea still embody the principle of reciprocity, it could be regarded, from the international law point of view, as disastrous.

At first glance, Kathmandu's grant of reciprocal transit facilities to India does not sound disastrous so long as India is interested merely in securing general transit facilities in the event of need. In fact, India too is entitled to certain transit facilities under the general principle of the freedom of transit.[42] The reality however is that Nepal's exercise of the right of free access to and from the sea should not be made dependent on Nepal's granting similar facilities to India which is not landlocked. It is hardly justifiable to ask Nepal to offer similar facilities in return for something that is available to Nepal by virtue of the fact that it is landlocked. As the 1991 treaty is intended to provide transit facilities to Nepal for her access to the sea, the reciprocity requirement seems, in practical terms, meaningless, as landlocked Nepal, by definition, lacks the means to reciprocate. In fact, India's transit trade through Nepal is non-existent; it does not actually need to use Nepalese territories for its international trade. India seems to have employed this reciprocity clause merely as political leverage. So far as the Indo-Nepal relationship is concerned, the concept of reciprocity raises numerous issues. As stated earlier, India wishes to tie Nepal's transit right to other issues like bilateral trade, treatment of Indians living in Nepal, India's strategic interests, etc. Nepal can only hope that India will not again in the future attempt to pressurize Nepal by mixing her transit facilities with other bilateral matters. In that case, Nepal's right of access will have been strengthened as a legal right rather than as facilities dependent on India's goodwill.

Exploitation of Nepal's Water Resources for Mutual Benefit

There is yet another dimension to Indo-Nepal relations. Numerous rivers originate in the Himalayas and flow through Nepal to India and ultimately to the Bay of Bengal; they could provide a great deal of hydroelectric power, a cheap and durable form of energy much needed by both states. It is estimated that Nepalese rivers could generate up to 83,000 MW of hydroelectric power,[43] which is more than the combined total hydroelectric power currently produced by the USA, Canada, and Mexico. For instance, a single hydroelectric power project, the Karnali Project, would have an installed capacity of 10,800 MW, the second largest in the world.[44] India has developed considerable interest in these projects[45] but views the third party investment in Nepal with suspicion, fearing that Nepal may become a back door for the entry of multinationals into India's domestic economy.[46] Obviously, New Delhi would like to see Kathmandu acting in a way that would also benefit India if any gigantic projects like Karnali were to be implemented.

However, many Nepalese take the view that India is keen to exploit Nepal's hydro-power potential to its advantage. Their opinion is based partly on Nepal's experience with the Kosi and Gandak projects in the early 1960s under which India secured disproportionate benefits to Nepal's detriment. It was as a result of this hang-up of the past that led to the insertion of a clause, at the insistence of all nationalist forces within Nepal, in the new Constitution of Nepal of 1990 requiring a two-thirds majority in parliament to ratify a treaty dealing with the exploitation of Nepal's water resources. The people of Nepal wished to insert a safeguard in the constitution to prevent successive governments in Nepal from succumbing too easily to external pressure in matters of vital concern. This provision makes it necessary for a party in power to take all other major political parties in confidence before concluding such treaties. This was the mistake made by the Nepali Congress government led by G.P. Koirala, when he concluded the Tanakpur Agreement with India in 1992. He tried to conduct everything very discreetly, not informing the people or parliament of what he had done or what he was going to do. His attempt to defend the agreement was rejected by Nepal's Supreme Court.

India and Nepal concluded yet another comprehensive treaty concerning the sharing and exploitation of the water resources of the Mahakali River in 1996. However, for a number of reasons arising from the mistrust that exists between the two countries, the treaty is now basically defunct. Many people in Nepal felt in hindsight that she was once again the overall loser. India, on her part, tried to secure as much as possible at Nepal's expense before and after the conclusion of the treaty. Indeed, India had secured, through the Mahakali Treaty, protection of her existing uses of the waters of the river, a goal she had set to achieve from the time of the 1989/90 crisis. It was believed that a secret draft treaty, which India sought to impose on Nepal, during the crisis, had included provisions designed to secure India's existing uses on the Nepalese rivers. India finally achieved this goal through the 1996 treaty, at least with regard to the waters of the Mahakali River.

India has a clearly defined agenda in its dealing with Nepal; the executors of Indian foreign policy maintain continuity and do their homework better than their Nepalese counterparts. Consequently, Nepal ends up signing treaties without fully realizing the far-reaching implications of the treaty. India has a systematic approach in its dealing with Nepal but the latter acts in an adhoc fashion as and when confronted by a given situation and comes out a loser at the end of the day.

Resolution of Indo-Nepal Problems

The first and foremost act that appears to be necessary to resolve all outstanding problems surrounding the Indo-Nepal relationship is to democratize it and develop it on the basis of equality, openness, mutual respect, and trust. It is necessary to replace certain antiquated colonial style treaties between the two countries. Indeed, the provisions of the 1950 Treaty of Peace and Friendship and the 1965 Arms Assistance Agreement on security matters are very similar, some even identical, to those of the 1923 treaty concluded by Nepal with British India. If Indo-Nepal relations are democratized, it would be difficult for Nepalese political parties to win elections on the basis of anti-India policy and the Indian leaders will also be unable to interfere in the domestic politics of Nepal for their own party-political purposes.

Legal arguments apart, one should not lose sight of the fact that the relationship envisaged in 1950 under the Peace and Friendship Treaty of that year has undergone substantial changes over the years. Sunanda Datta-Ray, an Indian writer, rightly advises his government that Nepal knows that

> access to or from a landlocked country is no longer a favour. It knows, too, that colonial style treaties cannot forever inhibit a sovereign nation's foreign policy options or choice of arms supplier. Since there is nothing India can do about these legal entitlements, it might do so with good grace so that at least friendship and influence survive. Ultimately, these will remain our best weapons in the Himalayan

Kingdom. We cannot afford to blunt them through the antics of busybodies whose phoney idealism or cynical calculation threatens to spoil the climate for a reconciliation.[47]

Therefore, it is necessary for both countries to commit themselves to ushering Indo-Nepal relations into a new era of cooperation based on the generally accepted principles of international law, the tenets of non-alignment, and the principles of equality and mutual respect for each other's vital national interests. After reading the 1990 joint communiqué one arrives at the conclusion that it was supposed to be a new starting point in Indo-Nepal relations. It was designed to usher this relationship into a new era of cooperation, as it envisaged the conclusion of a new comprehensive treaty covering all aspects of bilateral relations. However, no negotiations are under way for the conclusion of such a comprehensive treaty and no provisional arrangement can last for more than a short period of time. Both India and Nepal should prepare themselves to face the challenges of the new millennium when most regions of the world will have their own trading blocs and stronger economic relations. Therefore, what can be stated in conclusion is that the time has come for both Nepal and India to take a careful look at the whole range of treaties concluded between them, and to revise them in the light of the changed circumstances in both domestic and international fronts in accordance with the norms of international relations of the twenty-first century.

Notes and References

1. An earlier version of this chapter was published by me in Subrata K. Mitra and D. Rothermund (eds), *Legitimacy and Conflict in South Asia*, New Delhi: Manohar, 1997, pp. 220–45.

2. Rishikesh Shaha, 'Himalayan Impasse: Need for New Perspectives', *Times of India*, 7 June 1989.

3. Nehru's speech in the Indian Parliament on 17 March 1950. See A.S. Bhasin, *Documents on Nepal's Relations with India and China 1949–66* (Bombay: Academic Books, 1970), p. 23.

4. See Sunanda K. Datta-Ray, 'Living with Nepal: Must Busybodies Queer the Pitch?', *Statesman Weekly* (Calcutta), 17 Feb. 1990.

5. 'India agrees to lift trade blockade from Nepal', *Daily Telegraph* (London), 9 June 1990. Complete text of the Nepal–India Joint Communiqué is reproduced in *Rising Nepal*, 12 June 1990, p. 3.

6. For instance, Nepal agreed to remove Indian nationals from the ambit of the work permit scheme and to grant a number of other concessions to Indian nationals in matters not covered even in the 1950 treaty.

7. See, for text of the treaty, A.S. Bhasin, *Documents on Nepal's Relations with India and China 1949–66* (Bombay: Academic Books, 1970), p. 32. See, for a letter exchanged with the treaty, R. Shaha, *Nepali Politics: Retrospect and Prospect* (Delhi: OUP, 1978), p. 252.

8. S.D. Muni, *Foreign Policy of Nepal* (New Delhi: National Publishing House, 1973), p. 22.

9. Art. II of the 1950 Treaty.

10. Para. 1 of the Side Letter.

11. Para. 2 of the Side Letter.

12. Para. 5 of the Side Letter.

13. Art. VI of the 1950 Treaty.

14. Art. VII of the 1950 Treaty.

15. Para. 4 of the Side Letter.

16. Speaking to the press on 18 May 1989, the chief spokesman of the government of Nepal stated that 'HMG is also carefully considering the observation made by India's External Affairs Minister P.V. Narasimha Rao that, instead of accusing each other of violating the 1950 peace and friendship treaty, it would be wise for both India and Nepal to devise ways and means to remove the distortions or anachronisms of the treaty. As regards Nepal's position, we have clearly stated that we are willing to review the 1950 peace and friendship treaty with a view to making it in tune with the time. It may be recalled that the treaty was concluded by India with the last Rana Prime Minister four decades ago in different political, economic and social setting.' See *Nepal and India: Facts and Chronology of the Problem* (Kathmandu: Department of Press Information, Government of Nepal), p. 78.

17. See the views of a leading Nepali lawyer, Ganesh Raj Sharma, with *Janamach Weekly*, Jestha 5–11, V.S. 2051, Kathmandu.

18. H.L. Shrestha, *Some Unequal Treaties* (Kathmandu: Jhilko Publication, 1980), pp. 12–14.

19. An example cited in this regard is India's imposition of a permit system in 1976 for Nepalese nationals intending to visit Darjeeling, Sikkim, and Meghalaya. The new regulation placed Nepalese visitors to these districts on a par with other foreign nationals, *Times of India*, 13 Oct. 1976. This was an example of clear violation of Art. VII of the 1950 treaty, which accords national treatment to each other's nationals in several matters, including movement.

20. See the editorial in the *Statesman Weekly* (Delhi), 20 Jan. 1990.

21. K. Natwar Singh, 'An Agenda for Talks with Mr Bhattarai', *Times of India*, 7 June 1990, p. 8.

22. This issue is discussed in greater detail below.

23. See Article 43 of the Vienna Convention on the Law of Treaties of 1969. This article reads as follows: 'The invalidity, termination or denunciation of a treaty, the withdrawal of a party from it, or the suspension of its operation, as a result of the application of the present Convention or of the provisions of the treaty, shall not in any way impair the duty of any State to fulfil any obligation embodied in the treaty to which it would be subject under international law independently of the treaty.'

24. See generally, C.F. Amerasinghe, *State Responsibility for Injuries to Aliens* (1967); Eagleton, *The Responsibility of States in International Law* (1928). Article 9 of the Montevideo Convention on Rights and Duties of States reads that 'Nationals and foreigners are under the same protection of the law'. See also draft Article 5.1 proposed in 1957 by the Special Rapporteur of the International Law Commission on State Responsibility in the *Yearbook of the International Law Commission* (1957), vol. II, 104. The draft Article provided that rights of aliens shall not be less than the 'fundamental human rights' recognized and defined in international instruments.

25. L.P.S. Shrivastava, *Nepal at the Crossroads*, New Delhi: Allied Publishers, 1996, pp. 108–9.

26. Ibid., p. 109.

27. See D.P. Kumar, 'Chinese Anti-Aircraft Guns: Nepal Violated Secret Agreement with India', *Statesman* (Delhi), 27 May 1989.

28. Para. 3 of the agreement.

29. Para. 5 of the agreement.

30. *Rising Nepal*, 25 June 1966.

31. As summarized in a comment on Indo-Nepal relations by Lt General M. Thomas in the *Indian Defence Review* of July 1990, pp. 14–15. His summary is based on Bhabani Sen Gupta's article on Indo-Nepal relations in *Hindustan Times*, 14 May 1990. Gupta seems to have seen a comprehensive draft treaty containing these points which was proposed by India to Nepal during the 1989/90 crisis outlining India's position.

32. Ibid.

33. *League of Nations Treaty Series*, vol. 7, nos. 1–3, p. 11 ff.

34. 450 *United Nations Treaty Series*, pp. 11–113.

35. 597 *United Nations Treaty Series*, pp. 42–63.

36. UN Doc. A/CONF. 62/122, 7 Oct. 1982.

37. The Preamble to the HSC states that its provisions are 'generally declaratory of established principles of international law'.

38. See generally, UN, UNCLOS I, *Official Records*, vol. I, UN DOC. A/CONF. 13/29 and Add. 1, pp. 311 ff; M.I. Glassner, *Access to the Sea for Developing Land-Locked States* (1970); V.C. Govindraj, 'Land-locked States and their Right

of Access to the Sea', *Indian Journal of International Law* (1974), p. 190; A.M. Sinjela, *Land-Locked States and the UNCLOS Regime* (1983).

39. *Foreign Affairs Record*, vol. 35, no. 5, May 1989, New Delhi, pp. 131–3.

40. See *Times of India*, 17 April 1989. However, what India was saying was that because of its 'special' relationship with Nepal it had been very 'generous' to its neighbour in extending transit facilities and now, since Nepal was intent on changing this special relationship, in the view of New Delhi, Nepal was merely another neighbour like Bangladesh and Pakistan, and, thus, not worthy of 'generous' treatment by India.

41. See, for a discussion on cumbersome customs and transit procedure, S.P. Subedi, *Land-Locked Nepal and International Law* (Kathmandu: 1989), ch. 3. Pilferage of Nepalese goods on Indian railways increases Nepalese export costs. According to a survey, transit costs consume 8 per cent of Nepal's GDP. See *Far Eastern Economic Review*, 8 March 1990, 24.

42. Article 2 of the Barcelona Statute on Freedom of Transit provides a general freedom of transit for all states party to it.

43. 'Only 0.64 per cent of that potential is now harnessed. Foreign consultants say 25,000 MW are easily exploitable if and when India and Nepal reach some agreement on pricing', *Far Eastern Economic Review*, 8 March 1990, 26.

44. *Foreign Affairs Record*, vol. 37, no. 3 (March 1991), p. 35, Ministry of Foreign Affairs, Government of India.

45. See, for certain developments in this direction, an understanding between India and Nepal, *Nepal Gazette*, pt. IV, vol. 41, no. 36 (1992), 7–10.

46. James Clad, 'GDP set to Slump in Wake of Transit Dispute: Gasping for Breath', *Far Eastern Economic Review*, 8 March 1990, 25–7.

47. See S.K. Datta-Ray, 'Living with Nepal: Must Busybodies Queer the Pitch?', in *Statesman Weekly*, 17 Feb. 1990, 11.

2

India-Nepal Security Relations and the 1950 Treaty

Introduction

Indo-Nepal relations are very old and date from ancient times, long long before 1950 or the Treaty of Peace and Friendship. However, the 1950 Treaty is a uniquely significant landmark in the relationship because it goes far beyond the standard diplomatic format of relationship and seeks to concretize a grand vision handed down from centuries. This was the vision cherished by the great leaders of both countries, Prime Minister Jawaharlal Nehru and His Majesty King Tribhuvan. It was a vision of a Nepal and an India, both independent, sovereign and free, but indissolubly linked by unbreakable bonds.

[P.V. Narasimha Rao, speech in the Lok Sabha,
26 April 1989]

Wedged between China and India, each with its respective social, economic, and political systems, Nepal has since its unification in 1769 sought to maintain a stance of political neutrality—a very independent line—in its foreign relations.[1] Such a policy was propounded by King Prithvinarayan Shah, the founder of modern Nepal;[2] owing chiefly to its observance, Nepal has survived great upheavals in South Asia and no colonial flag has ever flown over the kingdom. It is a member of the Non-Aligned Movement (NAM) and is non-aligned and neutral in its relations with its two giant neighbours. The policy of political neutrality has been central to the foreign policy initiatives of successive Nepalese governments.

Nepal's attempt to pursue an independent and neutral policy has often come under severe scrutiny from India, which regards Nepal as part of a broader Indian security framework envisaged under the Peace and Friendship Treaty of 1950 concluded between the two countries.[3] This treaty deals with several matters, including certain questions of defence and the treatment of each other's nationals. In view of the treaty's provisions, India claims a 'special relationship' with Nepal. Although none of the provisions imply that India has any role in the conduct of Nepal's foreign affairs, New Delhi has tried to use the treaty to ensure that Kathmandu does not compromise India's 'security concerns' in Nepal's relations with China.

The Indian government seems to have taken the view that Nepal's attempts to pursue a totally independent and neutral policy runs counter to the 1950 treaty and undermines the 'special relationship'. Certain Nepalese scholars also have subscribed to the view that changes in the treaty relationship are necessary for Nepal to pursue an independent foreign policy.[4] The scope of the treaty provisions was a highly controversial issue during the 1989 India-Nepal controversy over trade and transit, and both countries raised the issue of the revision of the treaty. However, even though the crisis ended with the conclusion of the two separate treaties on trade and transit demanded by Nepal, the fundamental issues surrounding the crisis were not tackled.

So far, no serious and comprehensive attempt has been made to analyse the provisions of the 1950 treaty. The controversy in 1989 revealed that both countries are unhappy with the treaty as it stands and with the manner in which it is observed in practice; while Nepal insisted it was outmoded, India accused Nepal of violating it.[5] It is in this context that this chapter examines the provisions of the 1950 treaty concerning security matters and presents a case for its revision.

Political Background and Issues Arising from the 1950 Treaty

In the aftermath of the Second World War, India gained independence and the communists came to power in China. With the aim of preventing communist influence from spilling over into the neighbouring Himalayan kingdoms, India sought to strengthen the 'Himalayan frontier policy' of British India under which the Himalaya were regarded as a second frontier. For this, India concluded three treaties of peace and friendship with three small neighbouring kingdoms—Nepal, Bhutan, and Sikkim—in order to bring them within its sphere of influence. Although the 1950 treaty with Nepal was concluded with the head of the oligarchical Rana regime in its last days in power, it has survived to this day, much to the discomfort of some Nepalese. The whole process was conducted so discreetly that most of the provisions that could have aroused objections in Nepal were included in letters exchanged on the day the treaty was signed, and the existence and contents of these letters were kept secret for nine years. The letters were not attached to the treaty when it was registered with the United Nations.[6]

Many changes have taken place in both Nepal and India since the conclusion of the 1950 treaty, and both sides have intermittently derogated from several of its provisions. Nevertheless, India has been reluctant to alter these provisions because, in its view, opening a formal debate on the matter may give rise to numerous problems, with India in the end losing the privileges it currently enjoys. In the past, Nepal has both formally and informally indicated that it is not satisfied with the treaty and seeks changes in its terms. Although the treaty can be terminated by either party with one year's notice, the Nepal government lacks the courage to do so as the consequences of a unilateral abrogation are unpredictable. Consequently, serious frictions have frequently arisen between the two nations, and reached a climax in March 1989 at the expiration of the trade and transit treaties.

> Nursing a long-time grievance that Nepal has observed 'neither the letter nor the spirit' of the 1950 treaty with India which was meant to guide the relationship between the two countries, India has decided to look afresh at the ties with its strategically placed neighbour in the north-east.[7]

That was how the 'cold war' between Nepal and India began in the latter part of 1988; it culminated in March 1989 in the closure of all but two of the 21 bilateral trade routes between Nepal and India and in the closure of 13 of the 15 transit routes through India used by Nepal for its international trade under a 1978 transit treaty. India had refused to renew the separate treaties on trade and transit and wanted to negotiate new arrangements.

The Issues

Importing arms. Although on the surface, the dispute seemed to be concerned with relatively straightforward trade and transit issues, one of the real problems was rooted in the importation of certain weapons by Nepal from China in June 1988. In New Delhi's view, Nepal had a duty to consult with India before purchasing such weapons from China. Although the purchase was small, consisting mainly of anti-aircraft guns, India took the matter very seriously. The provision in the 1950 treaty concerning the importing of weapons by Nepal reads:

> Any arms, ammunition or warlike material and equipment necessary for the security of Nepal that the Government of Nepal may import *through* the territory of India shall be so imported with the assistance and agreement of the Government of India [emphasis added].[8]

Although this provision makes it clear that the government of Nepal would have to seek India's agreement to import weapons *through* Indian territory, Delhi insisted that importation of arms from China amounted to a violation of the *spirit* of India's treaties with Nepal. A party to a treaty which cannot establish claims on the basis of the letter of the treaty and resorts to the spirit of the treaty has a difficult task in proving its claim, as different people with varying perspectives may glean a different spirit of the treaty, which is a subjective matter.

India also invoked a 'secret' Arms Assistance Agreement concluded between the two countries in 1965 to support its stand.[9] Under the agreement, concluded in the aftermath of the Sino–Indian border war of 1962, India undertook to 'supply arms, ammunition, and equipment for the entire Nepalese Army', and to 'replace the existing Nepalese stock by modern weapons as soon as available and also to provide the maintenance of and replacement for the equipment to be supplied by them'. Nepal was, nevertheless, 'free to import from or through the territory of India arms, ammunition, or warlike material and equipment necessary for the security of Nepal. The procedure for giving effect to this arrangement shall be worked out by the two governments acting in consultation.'[10]

From the Indian standpoint, however, the agreement did not extend to the import of weapons by Nepal from or through China because it was India's responsibility to supply weapons for the entire Nepalese army and replace the existing stock with modern armaments. Here again the Indian argument is not tenable. Does Nepal by implication relinquish its right to import weapons from other countries by agreeing to receive Indian help in the reorganization and modernization of its army? Nowhere in the 1965 agreement is anything of the kind suggested. Of course, were Nepal to import weapons from any other country *through* India, Nepal would have to consult India, but if Nepal is importing the weapons from China or through China, it is under no obligation to consult India. The agreement does not limit Nepal's freedom of action so far as Nepal's dealing with other countries is concerned.

The 1950 treaty was concluded at a time when neither state envisaged the possibility that weapons could be imported from China across the Himalaya, as there was no road, rail, or air link between Nepal and China. At the time of the conclusion of these accords, the Indian government may well have thought that Nepal's freedom was effectively limited without clearly saying so, and the 1965 agreement represents a follow-up to the 1950 treaty in this respect. However, over the years things have changed; Nepal now has a road link with China and could easily import weapons through it. Moreover, according to the then Nepalese prime minister, K.N. Bista, the agreement was cancelled by Nepal after consulting India some time in 1969.[11] He claimed that India had agreed to the cancellation, a claim not refuted by Delhi. India however said nothing about the agreement until friction erupted between the two countries in 1989. Then, after 20 years of silence, the Indian Foreign Ministry reportedly leaked the 'secret' agreement to the Indian media to arouse public support for actions taken by New Delhi against Nepal.

Work permits. Prime Minister Rajiv Gandhi said during the 1989 crisis that India had taken a strong position with Nepal because 'two or three recent happenings upset' India. He stated that most upsetting were the two questions of work permits for Indians and certain new taxes imposed on Indian goods. Although Rajiv Gandhi claimed that these things were 'totally against the spirit' of India's relations and the treaty India had with Nepal,[12] they were not in clear contravention of any bilateral treaty in force. This is because it is obvious from the provisions of Article VII of the 1950 treaty that granting national treatment in certain matters by one contracting party to the nationals of the other does not also imply national treatment in employment. Article VII reads as follows:

The Governments of India and Nepal agree to grant, on a reciprocal basis, to the nationals of one country in the territories of the other the same privileges in the matter of residence, ownership of property, participation in trade and commerce, movement and other privileges of a similar nature.

If those instrumental in bringing about the treaty had intended to include employment within the scope of national treatment they would have clearly said so. A topic as important as granting equal employment opportunities to foreign nationals cannot be covered by the term 'other privileges of a similar nature'; the doctrine of *expressio unius est exclusio alterius* (express mention of one thing is the exclusion of the other) suggests that employment does not fall under the ambit of national treatment as provided in the treaty. Of course, a large number of Nepalese work in India without being required to obtain work permits and vice versa, but that does not mean that either state is under a treaty obligation to accord national treatment in matters of employment opportunities to the nationals of the other.

However, from New Delhi's perspective, importing Chinese weapons and introducing a work permit scheme by Kathmandu amounted to 'blatant violation' of the 1950 treaty from which flowed special terms in the areas of trade, economy, education, and culture. That is why India wanted to discuss the entire gamut of its relations with its neighbour and negotiate a *single* comprehensive treaty dealing with both trade and transit matters as they were, in India's view, interrelated. This row continued for over a year and ended only with a change of government in Nepal. At the end of a visit to India by the new Nepalese prime minister in June 1990, a joint communiqué was signed under which New Delhi agreed to restore the status quo ante to April 1987 in matters of trade and transit.[13]

The agreement came after Nepal and India had consented, inter alia, to fully respect each other's security interests, which was understood by many to mean that Nepal would not buy any weapons from China without consulting India nor have any defence dealings with the former to the detriment of the latter. Nepal also agreed to remove Indian nationals from the ambit of the work permit scheme and to grant them a number of other concessions. In fact, it was believed that during the 1990 crisis India had proposed a draft agreement which sought to make a clear and specific mention of 'employment' within the ambit of the national treatment. India was trying to insert a provision that was not included in the 1950 treaty. The caretaker prime minister of Nepal, K.P. Bhattarai, gave India what it could not secure during the panchayat system by imposing an economic embargo or other methods of coercion.

Common Defence. It is doubtful whether the 1950 treaty, basically a political document, provides for common defence. Article II merely requires the exchange of military information: 'The two Governments hereby undertake to inform each other of any serious friction or misunderstanding with any neighbouring State likely to cause any *breach* in the friendly relations subsisting between the two Governments' (author's emphasis). This requirement in no way indicates that the treaty provided for common defence, as it requires neither regular nor immediate supply of information. It is up to each side to judge whether its frictions with third countries are likely to cause any breach in the friendly relations with the other contracting party; the friction or misunderstanding must be serious and likely to cause a breach in, and not simply affect, the friendly relations subsisting between the two countries in the view of the government concerned.

Moreover, the requirement is limited to information that is likely to breach the friendly relations *between the two contracting parties*, i.e. neither is required to inform the other of any friction or misunderstanding with other states that is unlikely to affect Indo-Nepal relations. Thus, India did not inform Nepal when it twice went to war with Pakistan and once with China after the conclusion of the 1950 treaty. Certain Nepalese writers and officials have overlooked this and asserted that India's failure to inform Nepal during these wars amounted to non-observance of the treaty.[14]

Paragraph one of the letters exchanged with the 1950 treaty has often been cited to show that the treaty is a military pact:

> Neither Government shall tolerate any threat to the security of the other by a foreign aggressor. To deal with any such threat, the two governments shall consult with each other and devise effective countermeasures.

Although this section appears to provide for a common defence, a closer examination reveals it as no more than a poorly formulated provision that suffers from a number of deficiencies. First, one cannot infer a clear meaning from this paragraph, under which the threat must come from a foreign aggressor. However, under the unanimously adopted resolution of UN General Assembly of 1974 on the Definition of Aggression, widely regarded as the most authoritative definition, aggression is the *use of armed force* by a state against another state in contravention of international law. A state, which merely threatens another state or is using armed force in self-defence, is not an aggressor, although a threat of force is illegal under international law.

To regard paragraph one of the letters of exchange as providing for the use of force also seems inconsistent with the provisions of Article 103 of the Charter of the UN. Both multilateral military pacts and bilateral alliances provide for collective military measures only in the event of a breach of peace or an armed attack by a foreign aggressor against the contracting parties.[15] A mere threat by a foreign power does not activate the right of self-defence under Article 51 of the UN Charter. If a UN member state perceives a threat from a foreign aggressor it should not resort to self-help: it is obliged to follow the provisions of the charter under which the Security Council has been designated as the authority to determine the existence of any threat to the peace and decide on the measures necessary to maintain or restore international peace and security (Article 39).

Pointing to paragraph one of the letters and the phrase 'devise effective counter-measures', Rishikesh Shaha claims that this provision 'implies nothing short of a military pact between Nepal and India'.[16] However, his assertions seem based only on the phrase 'devise effective counter-measures'. In international law, 'countermeasures' means both forcible and non-forcible actions. After analysing several peace, friendship, and mutual assistance agreements concluded by the former Soviet Union with other countries, Imam states that all such treaties 'commit the signatories to regular consultation, meetings and contacts on vital issues of the day affecting the interests of both the parties'.[17] The 1950 treaty lacks the entire essential characteristics of a treaty of alliance,[18] and is not a military pact. Such has been the position of both India and Nepal. For instance, Nehru said in 1959 that the 1950 treaty was 'not a military alliance by any means'. His counterpart in Kathmandu, B.P. Koirala, affirmed in 1960 that he did not envisage joint defence between India and Nepal, as military alliances were 'worse than useless', especially between Nepal and India.[19] Nepal's 1950 treaty with India does not even resemble the somewhat modest 1971 Indo-Soviet 'friendship treaty', in which Article 9 states: 'In the event of either party being subjected to an attack or a threat thereof, the High Contracting Parties shall *immediately* enter into mutual consultations in order to remove such threat and to take appropriate effective measure to ensure peace and the security of their countries'[20] (emphasis added). Nepal's treaty with India requires neither *immediate* consultation nor *joint measures* to repel the aggressor.

Therefore, Shaha's assertion that the 1950 treaty 'has more teeth to it than the Indo–Soviet Treaty of 1971'[21] is not correct. The 1950 treaty has no teeth at all, and if any teeth are seen in it, they are obsolete. The consultation that is required of the two governments under the Indo-Nepal treaty is to deal with any threat, but not to expel the aggressor. The same is true of the requirement relating to devising effective countermeasures. If devising countermeasures is to expel the aggressor, one could plausibly argue that the term 'effective countermeasures' generally means military measures, although military measures may not always be 'effective countermeasures'. Besides, the requirement envisaged in the letters of exchange is not to repel an aggressor but to deal with any threat to the security of the parties. Such a threat may be dealt with in a number of ways, including diplomatic and economic measures that may be more effective in countering a threat than provocative military ones.

Paragraph one of the letters has a number of other weaknesses. First, it seems to go beyond the scope of article two of the treaty, which merely requires the exchange of military information. However, according to the opening paragraph of the letters, the two governments agreed to regulate certain matters through the exchange of letters. Second, before invoking paragraph one of the letters, a contracting party must establish that there is a threat to its security by a foreign power, and the other state must believe that such a threat exists. One state's perception of the existence of a threat may not coincide with that of the other.

Thus, it seems to be an unfounded claim that the 1950 treaty provides for common defence. In fact, India did not consult with Nepal when it went to war with China and Pakistan after the conclusion of the treaty. Paragraph one of the letters of exchange remains riddled with ambiguities and problems. One may argue that under the 'object and purpose' principle of the interpretation of treaties (Article 31 (1) Vienna Convention on the Law of Treaties), or under the principle of effectiveness, an accepted canon of treaty interpretation, a reasonable meaning would have to be accorded to paragraph one, the principal purpose of which seems to be to provide legal ground for India's intervention in the event of a direct Chinese threat to Nepal, a country referred to by Nehru, as 'almost geographically a part of India'.[22] Even in that case, however, such help may come only if *all of the following* conditions are met:

(1) Nepal itself decides that a threat to its security by a foreign power exists;

(2) Nepal of its own free will decides to consult with India in its own time to deal with such threat; and

(3) Nepal proposes during the consultation that devising effective countermeasures is necessary to deal with such threat.

Under no circumstances can India unilaterally decide to take action to deal with any threat to the security of Nepal. Further, since it is the UN Security Council that has the competence to determine the existence of any threat to the security of UN members and can take the necessary steps to deal with such a threat (Article 39 of the UN Charter), India cannot unilaterally decide to take action to deal with any threat to the security of Nepal. Under Article 103, the obligations undertaken by member states prevail over any other obligations undertaken under any other international agreement.

Legal Status of the 1950 Treaty

Nepal insists that the 1950 treaty is now an outmoded document, derogations from which are commonplace. Both countries have let it fall into disuse over the past forty years. A number of arguments have frequently been raised in Nepal to make its claim. Baral argues that '[i]n practice the treaty has been modified to a considerable extent'.[23]

It should be clarified at the outset that contentions by a party to a treaty—such as those raised in Nepal—that it is an unequal treaty do not per se provide valid ground for the termination or denunciation of the treaty, the suspension of its operation, or the withdrawal of a party from it; nor do the non-observance of any normal diplomatic protocol during the conclusion of the treaty, nor its non-registration with the UN secretary-general. The only legal effect of such non-registration is that the treaty cannot be invoked by the states party to it before any organs of the UN, including the International Court of Justice. Moreover, as there is no time limit prescribed for such registration, India could register it at any time if it deemed it necessary to do so.

The argument based on the effect of desuetude does not seem to be tenable in this context, as both India and Nepal have continued to honour many of the treaty's provisions, but such partial derogation or non-observance may not be invoked to argue that the entire treaty has fallen into disuse and thus become obsolete. Allegations of violations alone are insufficient to assert that the treaty is no longer valid. Nepal has not officially claimed such a material breach by India, and even failed to do so during the 1989 crisis which offered it the opportunity of doing so.

Nepal has expressed its willingness to review the 1950 Peace and Friendship Treaty with a view to bringing it in tune with the times. If so, Nepal should formally notify India of its intention to bring about modifications in the treaty or to abrogate it. A mere change of government does not ipso facto invalidate a treaty concluded by the former government, however autocratic it may have been; the new government must still exercise the power of termination provided for in the treaty or in the international law of treaties. Under Article 10, Nepal can terminate the treaty by giving one year's notice. As long as Nepal does not do this and both countries continue to honour the treaty with some derogations and exceptions, it is difficult to maintain that the *rebus sic stantibus* (fundamental change of circumstances) rule, reflected in Article 62 of the Vienna Convention, applies in this case. As the circumstances of international life are always changing, a mere demonstration of changes in bilateral relations is not a ground for the termination of a treaty under this rule. Even if one were to accept that enough significant shifts have taken place in Indo-Nepalese relations since 1950 to warrant amendments to the treaty, the changes have not resulted in a radical transformation of the extent of obligations Nepal still must fulfil. Even a clear need for revision of a treaty does not invalidate it.

Status of the 1965 Agreement on Arms Assistance

So far as some Nepalese are concerned, the 1965 'secret' Agreement on Arms Assistance no longer stands following Nepal's denunciation of it. When Nepal notified India of its intention to cancel the agreement, India raised no objection, which amounted to India's acquiescence to termination. However, Nepal's unilateral denunciation is somewhat controversial because the agreement contains no provision regarding termination, denunciation, or withdrawal. Paragraph 6 provides that it 'may be reviewed, from time to time, by consultations' between the two governments, suggesting that the agreement was not of a provisional or temporary character and that Nepal did not have the authority to unilaterally denounce it. Nevertheless, some of the provisions suggest that they, if not the entire agreement, are of a provisional character. For instance, India undertook 'to supply arms, ammunition, and equipment for the entire Nepalese Army on the basis of a total strength of about 17,000 men, comprising four reorganized brigades'.[24] This provision does not imply that India would keep supplying such resources even if Nepal were to increase the number of brigades or the number of soldiers in excess of the 17,000 men mentioned in the agreement.

One must not, however, lose sight of the developments that took place after Nepal's unilateral denunciation. This, along with its assertion that the 1950 Treaty of Peace and Friendship had fallen into disuse, offended India, and in an effort to dilute the impact of Nepal's denunciation, King Mahendra implied in an interview given to an Indian newspaper in 1970 that the 1965 agreement continued to be operative on a de facto basis.[25] This reading was however possibly based on assumptions rather than facts. The king did not state that the 1965 agreement was valid, but as such interpretations suit India, it seems to regard that the king had indirectly repudiated Nepal's earlier unilateral declaration concerning the agreement. The king reportedly said that the two states had arrived at a 'full understanding on the exchange of "military" information on developments harmful to either country'. As there was already a provision to that effect in the 1950 treaty, the king's interview did not add anything new; he was simply reaffirming the treaty provision.

The king of course appeared to have agreed to India's proposal to station senior Indian military personnel at its embassy in Kathmandu for an agreed upon period and responsibilities. This did not however add anything significant to Indo-Nepalese military ties, as it is quite normal for states to have senior military personnel at their embassies in countries with whom they share a strong military and security relationship. The king carefully distanced himself from any arrangements the Indian government might make inside the Indian embassy as that was no concern of Nepal. If Nepal had entered into any significant accord with India on military cooperation, the king could not have possibly stressed during the interview that Nepal would never agree to compromise its sovereignty and neutrality in any manner.

Conclusion

The above discussion shows that Nepal has a very complex bilateral relationship with India governed by a number of treaties. While India expects Nepal to be sensitive to its security interests, Nepal, as a landlocked country, expects India to be liberal with regard to its trade and transit problems. Hence, a great deal of understanding and goodwill is required from both sides in order to make the bilateral treaties work in the interests of both countries. Understanding and goodwill could be made long-lasting if both countries approached the problems surrounding the 1950 treaty and the treaties on trade and transit within the framework of the South Asian Association for Regional Cooperation (SAARC) and in conformity with the principles of the Charter of the UN.

Treaties should reflect the current nature of relations between states; they should be revised simultaneously with changes in bilateral and international relations. India should not expect the Nepal of the twenty-first century to abide by the outmoded treaty provisions, such as those designed to forbid Nepal from employing any non-Indian foreigners. It is simply not feasible for Nepal to give first preference to Indian nationals when developing her natural resources. Although Nepal has long disregarded these provisions, India has nonetheless cited them in her efforts to block Nepal's attempts to acquire significant foreign assistance for the development of her natural resources. Through various means, whether it be through the Side Letter of 1950 or the draft 'secret' agreement of 1989 or the 1990 joint press communiqué, India has made it clear that she wishes to retain firm control over the exploitation of Nepal's natural resources, principally water resources. For this purpose, India has used all the influence it can summon internationally to block Nepal's attempts to have her natural resources exploited and utilized with third-party involvement.

Unless the fundamental disputes surrounding the 1950 treaty are resolved in a spirit of cooperation and persuasion rather than control and coercion, history may repeat itself when any misunderstanding between Nepal and India over operation of their treaties arises. It therefore seems that the time has come for both countries to take a careful look at the provisions of the 1950 treaty and revise them in the light of changes that have taken place over the past four decades, rather than merely ignore them. In fact, both Nepal and India appear to have agreed during the Indian Prime Minister I.K. Gujral's visit to Nepal in June 1997 to review the 1950 treaty; they directed the foreign secretaries of the two country to meet in two months' time to discuss all matters of bilateral interest, including issues related to the 1950 treaty. Accordingly, the foreign secretaries of Nepal and India met in New Delhi in August 1997, but little progress was made. During the visit to India of the then Nepalese Foreign Minister, Kamal Thapa, in September 1997, the foreign secretary of Nepal was reported to have handed over to his Indian counterpart a non-paper or informal paper on possible elements of a new treaty. According to the Nepalese Ministry of Foreign Affairs, the proposed elements of the new treaty were as follows:

- to strengthen further the already strong bonds of friendship that exist between Nepal and India on the foundations of sovereign equality and mutuality of benefits;
- to remove the existing anomalies in the treaty;
- to fully reflect the universal principles and norms that govern modern inter-state relations; and
- to have an equitable new treaty which fully respects sovereign equality and also reflects the present realities.[26]

However, it is not clear what Nepal was attempting to achieve by presenting such a general, timid, and vaguely couched proposal to India, without identifying and pinpointing those provisions of the treaty that are inconsistent with the principles of sovereign equality and mutuality of benefits or the norms of modern inter-state relations. As India has agreed to discuss the issues related to the 1950 treaty, Nepal can afford to be bold in presenting to it a concrete list of provisions that are in need of revision and suggest a concrete set of alternative provisions. In the absence of such an approach, Nepal cannot expect to achieve any amelioration from a reluctant India. In fact, the time has come for these two countries to conclude a new treaty to replace the outmoded one rather than merely try to amend minor details of the virtually obsolete original. A visionary, thoroughly thought-through, and professional new treaty will be accorded due respect and could achieve the results desired (though not yet formulated) by Nepal.

Notes and References

1. An earlier version of this chapter was published by me in the *Asian Survey* issue of March 1994, vol. 34, 273–84. I am grateful to the Regents of the University of California for their permission to use my article in this book. See also Surya P. Subedi, 'The Himalayan Frontier Policy of British–India and the Significance of the 1923 Treaty of Friendship between Great Britain–Nepal', 27 *Journal of the Britain–Nepal Society* (London, December 2003), 35–9.

2. He said 'the kingdom is like a yam between two stones. Maintain friendly

relations with the Emperor of China. Great friendship should also be maintained with the Emperor beyond the Southern Seas (i.e. the British), but he is very clever. He has kept India suppressed and is entrenching himself on the plains. One day that army will come. Do not engage in offensive acts. Fighting should be conducted on a defensive basis.' Quoted in R. Shaha, *Nepali Politics: Retrospect and Prospect* (Delhi: OUP, 1978), p. 104.

3. Text of the 1950 treaty is in A.S. Bhasin, *Documents on Nepal's Relations with India and China 1949–66* (Bombay: Academic Books, 1970), n.5, p. 32; for letters exchanged with the treaty, see Shaha, *Nepali Politics*, p. 252 (hereafter Exchange of Letters).

4. For instance, see R. Shaha, *Nepali Politics*, op. cit., n. 2, ch. 7.

5. Narasimha Rao accused Nepal of eroding over the years the vision of the 1950 treaty: 'Its spirit has been weakened, its content whittled away practically in every sphere of the Indo-Nepal relationship', *Foreign Affairs Record*, 35:45 (New Delhi, May 1989), pp. 131–4.

6. United Nations Treaty Series 3.

7. *Times of India*, 7 Oct. 1988, p. 1.

8. Para. 2 of Exchange of Letters.

9. *Statesman* (India), 27 May 1989.

10. Paras. 3 and 5 of the 1965 Agreement.

11. *Rising Nepal*, 25 June 1969.

12. *Times of India*, 17 April 1989, 1. It is worth noting that even in Gandhi's view, Nepal had not violated any actual treaty provisions but rather the *spirit* of bilateral relations and bilateral treaties, a difficult thing to ascertain.

13. The complete text of the Nepal–India joint communiqué was published in *Rising Nepal*, 12 June 1990, 3.

14. For instance, an interview with Prime Minister Bista in *Rising Nepal*, 25 June 1969, 1.

15. For example, see an analysis of a number of bilateral treaties concluded by the former USSR in Z. Imam, *Towards a Model Relationship: A Study of Soviet Treaties with India and Other Third World Countries* (New Delhi: ABC Publishers, 1983), pp. 105–78.

16. R. Shaha, 'Himalayan Impasse: Need for New Perspectives', *Times of India*, 7 June 1989, 4.

17. Imam, *Towards a Model Relationship*, op. cit., n. 15, p. 81.

18. The provisions of the 1950 treaty could be compared with the 1948 Treaty of Friendship, Cooperation and Mutual Assistance between Finland and the former Soviet Union. Nepal's obligations under the 1950 treaty with India are significantly less exacting than Finland's obligations under the Soviet–Finnish treaty. Nepal is under no obligation to fight any war jointly with India or to assist India in a war, not even to expel an aggressor.

19. Nehru's statement in a press conference, New Delhi, 3 Dec. 1959, in

Bhasin, *Documents on Nepal's Relations,* op. cit., n. 3, p. 28, Koirala's remarks, pp. 49–50.

20. *International Legal Materials*, 10 (ILM), 1971, p. 904.

21. Shaha, *Nepali Politics*, op. cit., n. 2, p. 121.

22. Nehru's statement in Parliament (Bhasin, *Documents*, op. cit., n. 3, p. 23).

23. L.R. Baral, 'Nepal in the Non-Aligned Movement', *in* G.R. Agrawal et al., *Fundamentals of Nepalese Foreign Policy* (Kathmandu: CEDA, Tribhuvan University, 1985), pp. 93–118, at 106; B.C. Malla, 'Nepal a Zone of Peace: National Perspective', ibid., pp. 11–9, at 15.

24. 1965 Agreement on Arms Assistance, para. 3.

25. See D. Mukerjee's report under a somewhat misleading heading, 'India, Nepal Accord on Military Tie', *Times of India*, 21 Oct. 1970, 1.

26. The proposed elements of the non-paper presented by Nepal have been published in the Nepalese media. Although the proposals are in the public domain, I was able to obtain an authentic version of the elements of the proposal from the Nepalese Ministry of Foreign Affairs and it is on file with me.

3

The Concept of a Zone of Peace: The Vision of a Country at Peace with Itself and at Ease with her Neighbours

Introduction

Nepal was the envy of South Asia until the late 1980s. Unlike many other South Asian states, Nepal did not have an active ideological insurgency, nor any spiralling ethnic or communal conflicts. The political system in the country was not fully democratic, but there was at least peace. Its citizens enjoyed the benefits of law and order offered by the system led by the king. Money-launderers, drugs-dealers, corrupt politicians, and bureaucrats feared the king. The traditional national institutions commanded respect from the people. The economy was somewhat stagnant but there were signs of improvement. In fact, prior to the 1989 crisis with India on trade and transit issues, Nepal's GDP annual growth rate was 5.7 per cent.[1] Tourists poured into the country from all over the world, bringing in much-needed foreign currency for Nepal's economic development.

If there was any threat to Nepal's peace and prosperity, it came from external sources. This was one reason why the king had sought to insulate the country from outside interference by proposing in 1975 that the country be declared a Zone of Peace; his proposal gained support from an ever-increasing number of states. The country was confident and was beginning to assert greater freedom in the conduct of its domestic and foreign policies. It was seeking to free itself from the so-called 'Indian security umbrella', i.e. India's Himalayan frontier policy. The peace zone proposal was a manifestation of that desire to free Nepal from the Indian sphere of influence, and a skilful exercise of Nepalese diplomacy.

However, after the political changes of 1990, the political leaders of the country appeared to have decided to abandon the policy of a zone of peace, apparently to placate India, which was against the proposal in the first place. This move on the part of the new political leaders to squander the diplomatic wealth accumulated over a long period of time, has not been explained either to the people of Nepal or to those foreign powers who supported the proposal. The political leaders would have gained a great deal of tangible and intangible benefits for Nepal had they put democracy, human rights, and the policy of a zone of peace high on their internal and external agendas. All of these three concepts are complementary.

Recent events, both at home and those relating to Indo-Nepal relations, have demonstrated how unwise it was on the part of Nepal's political leaders to abandon its proposal to be a zone of peace. In fact, the events of the recent past vindicate the reasons behind the proposal. The idea of a zone of peace was very consonant with the policy of non-alignment; a policy continued by the successive governments since 1990. There is no choice for Nepal but to adhere to the policy of neutrality and non-alignment; the proposal for a zone of peace would have further strengthened this policy. Should some sense prevail among the leaders of the country, it is still not too late for Nepal to revive the proposal and make it the flagship of her foreign policy serving as a valuable instrument of statecraft, which will help both to insulate her from outside interference and to create conditions of peace within the country. Perhaps the time has come to revive the idea of a zone of peace, which King Birendra proposed in 1975, as a tribute to him following his death in 2001. The reasons why the proposal was first mooted are still valid and perhaps even more urgent today than ever before.

Whether small or big, every state has to take some new initiatives in the conduct of their international relations so as to command respect from other states. Not many states have a high regard for a state that fails to demonstrate a vision or any imagination in the conduct of its foreign policy. This is what is happening with regard to Nepal today: she does not seem to have a clearly defined goal for her foreign policy, and indeed seems to be virtually bankrupt of any ideas. All the country seems to be doing is either crisis management: dealing with immediate problems at hand in its relations with India or Bhutan or embellishing the strategy designed to attract greater amounts of foreign aid. Such limited vision is symptomatic of under-expectation on the part of her political leaders and underestimation on the part of foreign ministry officials. It thus reinforces the impression that Nepal indeed has no clearly defined foreign policy and is simply responding to events.

Both intellectually and ideologically, the concept of a zone of peace is an interesting phenomenon. Politically speaking, it is a sensible policy for a small country such as Nepal. Diplomatically, it would convey the impression to the outside world that Nepal is able to take certain policy initiatives and has a foreign policy agenda that it wishes to pursue. In legal terms, Nepal would have gained much in terms of her freedom of action without amending or abrogating the 1950 Treaty of Peace and Friendship. The political leaders have not only squandered the benefits gained in the twelve years that have elapsed since the restoration of democracy in 1990; they have also squandered the diplomatic capital Nepal could have accumulated over these years. In this context, this chapter analyses the nature of the proposal and the policy options available to Nepal, should wisdom and foresight prevail upon the political leaders of Nepal's various political parties.

Historical Background

Nepal is a country with a long history of independence, political stability, and an ancient culture and civilization. It also had a long history of peace. That is not to say that Nepal has never been engaged in war. Nepal of course came into being through wars unifying many petty kingdoms and city-states. After this unification, Nepal advanced on other states: Nepalese forces also crossed the River Ganges in the south, and reached as far as Punjab in the West. Nepal fought two victorious wars with Tibet in 1788 and 1791, and between 1814 and 1816 fought a two-year-long war with the then mighty British Empire in India, ended by the Treaty of Sugauli of 1816.[2]

Since then, Nepal has maintained a peaceful relationship with Britain. Through the 1923 treaty,[3] Nepal's first bilateral treaty registered with the League of Nations Secretariat, Britain fully recognized Nepal as a sovereign and independent state. Nepal was at war with Tibet again between 1855 and 1856, which ended with the signing of the Treaty of Kathmandu in 1856.[4] Thus, after signing peace treaties with both of her neighbours, Nepal had lived in peace for nearly one-and-a-half centuries. Internally, it is a country noted for religious harmony among its people. As one observer correctly says, 'Nepal is a land where a host of cultures have met, fused, and continued to thrive'.[5] Both the principal religions of the country, Hinduism and Buddhism, teach the lessons of peace and friendship. Lord Buddha, born in Nepal, preached wholly the cause of peace; ahimsa (non-violence) which is one of the fundamental principles of Buddhism. Nepal is committed to the policies of the Non-Aligned Movement. This policy is dictated by her size, economy, and geo–political situation, as well as by her experience and culture. Nepal's desire for peace and neutrality, coupled with the tension in and around Nepal created by certain national and international events of the early 1970s, seem to have inspired Nepal to propose that she be declared a zone of peace.

International Events

After the Second World War, many changes took place in the Asian region. India gained independence in 1947. Many small entities agreed to join the Union of India while a few others were annexed by force. The Communists came to power in China in 1949. India wanted to make the Himalaya a strong natural border with China.[6] For this, India concluded lopsided treaties of peace and friendship in and around the 1950s with her three small neighbouring Himalayan kingdoms—Nepal,[7] Bhutan,[8] and Sikkim[9]—in order to bring them within her sphere of influence. Parts of Jammu & Kashmir fell into the hands of India and Pakistan. The Chinese took over Tibet. Full-scale war broke out twice between India and Pakistan, and once between China and India. East Pakistan emerged as an independent state, Bangladesh. The US came to aid Pakistan, and also to establish a powerful base in Diego Garcia. India's changed foreign policy brought her closer to the former Soviet Union.[10] India tested a nuclear device in 1974. In that same year she annexed Sikkim. The relationship between the major countries of the region remained unsettled, which led to a localized arms race.

While all of these events were pushing South Asia into a more complicated phase, Nepal was very keen on maintaining an equilibrium with her neighbours. Chadwick and Thompson write that 'wedged between two colossal powers—India ... and China ... Nepal maintains a careful stance of political neutrality'.[11] An unbalanced policy could at any time endanger Nepal's sovereignty. This delicate policy had to be made clear to the rest of the world so that no country could make the excuse of misunderstanding Nepal's neutral and peaceful policy.

The Domestic Situation

The domestic situation, too, was tense before the zone of peace proposal. Nepal had her first elected parliament and an elected government in 1960. However, after a short period of the multiparty system, King Mahendra suspended the constitution and dissolved the government as well as parliament. He then promulgated another constitution which established the Partyless Panchayat System. The constitution banned political parties:

no political party or any other organization, union or association motivated by party politics shall be formed or caused to be formed or run.[12]

Opposition to the partyless panchayat system came from those who sought the reestablishment of the multiparty system. As the years passed under the new system, its opponents in exile in India used various methods to achieve their demands. Meanwhile, a young king, Birendra, succeeded to the throne in 1972 after his father's death. Opponents of the partyless panchayat system intensified their activities, pressurizing the new king in order to gain concessions to their demands. Some examples of the pressure are the hijacking of an RNAC plane,[13] and the explosion of a hand-grenade at Biratnagar on 16 March 1974, which killed two people and injured 37 just a few hundred yards away from where the king was meeting officials and representatives of the people.[14] There occurred other domestic events that caused certain controversial international repercussions. The Khampas, who fled Tibet with the Dalai Lama, were residing in the hilly regions of Nepal from where they used to carry out raids against the Chinese in Tibet. It was reported that during the king's visit to China in November 1973, His Majesty was asked personally by Chairman MaoTse-tung to disarm the Khampas who were said to have received arms and money from Taiwan, India, and the American CIA.[15] Nepalese forces had to disarm the Khampas in order to prevent them from using Nepalese territories as bases for their attacks against a neighbour. The annexation of Sikkim, a small neighbour, by India was a very sensitive issue in Nepal. In September 1974, an anti-Indian demonstration took place in Kathmandu against the association of Sikkim with the Indian Union, creating a certain amount of tension between the two countries. The Indian ambassador was summoned home and did not return for some weeks.[16]

This was the scene of national and international events that surrounded Nepal before the peace zone proposition was made. Although such events might not be serious to a larger country, they were sufficient to cause anxiety regarding Nepal's independence and her neutral stance. Such was the situation faced by a young king who seemed determined to lay greater emphasis on developing the economy of Nepal than on political issues,[17] yet the country was still unwillingly drawn more into political issues than into development works.

To summarize:

- the situation of South Asia was becoming increasingly tense and the superpowers became involved in the region;
- the small state of Nepal was not able to take part in the arms race, as were other regional powers, or to defend the country through military strength;
- the superpowers and regional powers did not appear reluctant to undermine the sovereignty of smaller states if they deemed it necessary for their strategic interests;
- to avoid any misunderstanding of Nepal's neutral and peaceful policy by neighbouring powers it became increasingly necessary for Nepal to declare a clear, permanent policy of neutrality not only in times of war but also in times of peace;
- as the rules of neutrality are narrowly defined and designed principally for the time of war, Nepal needed a wider-reaching device applicable to all situations;
- although the principles of the UN Charter and Panchsheel were in force, Nepal needed a more *specific regime* convenient and suitable for her *unique geo-political position*;
- being a least-developed country, Nepal needed a stable political environment and unhampered peace in order to develop her economy without being involved in the power politics of the region, and without suffering from fears for her independence.

Nepal could have been inspired by all of these given factors to put forward an appropriate solution, that of being declared for all time a zone of peace. This may have been considered an excellent proposal for disposing of unwanted and avoidable problems; it was an easier way of obtaining a guarantee of her sovereignty and recognition of her policy from other states without any military alliances and without surrendering any of her sovereign rights to any foreign power.

The Proposal

Addressing a farewell reception for visiting royalty, presidents, prime ministers, and other foreign guests in Kathmandu who attended the king's coronation in February 1975, His Majesty King Birendra said:

> As heirs to one of the most ancient civilizations in Asia, our natural concern is to preserve our independence, a legacy handed down to us by history ... We need peace for our security, we need peace for our independence, and we need peace for development ... And if today, peace is an overriding concern with us, it is only because our people genuinely desire peace in our country, in our region, and everywhere in the world. It is with this earnest desire to institutionalize peace that I stand to make a proposition—a proposition that my country, Nepal, be declared a Zone of Peace.[18]

The king went on to reason:

> we wish to see that our freedom and independence shall not be thwarted by the changing flux of time when understanding is replaced by misunderstanding, when conciliation is replaced by belligerency and war.[19]

Aftermath

The proposal was very well received: many states supported it immediately and no objections to the proposal were raised. By 1988, 97 states had registered their support. The wide support came from states of every social, political, and economic group and region of the world. Apart from the then Soviet Union, all the major powers, all industrial and economic powers and, except India, most of Nepal's neighbouring countries, supported the proposal. India and the former Soviet Union, however, did not oppose the proposal while maintaining that they were studying it. The proposal also received nationwide support from within Nepal, even from certain noted opposition leaders. In compliance with this national support, the proposal was incorporated into the panchayat constitution of Nepal. The Third Amendment to the constitution provided:

The objective of the foreign policy of the Panchayat System shall be to endeavour to make Nepal a zone of peace by adhering to the basic values of the United Nations and the principles of non-alignment.[20]

Various efforts were made at national and international level to clarify the nature of the proposal. The then prime minister of Nepal, Surya Bahadur Thapa, explained seven principal features of the proposal during an address to the Nepal Council of World Affairs; he said that Nepal was prepared to assume the following obligations on a reciprocal basis with those countries that supported the proposal:

1. Nepal will adhere to the policy of peace, non-alignment and peaceful co-existence and will constantly endeavour to develop friendly relations with all countries of the world, regardless of their social and political system, and particularly with its neighbours, on the basis of equality and respect for each other's independence and sovereignty.
2. Nepal will not resort to the threat or use of force in any way that might endanger the peace and security of other countries.
3. Nepal will seek the peaceful settlement of all disputes between it and other state or states.
4. Nepal will not interfere in the internal affairs of other states.
5. Nepal will not permit any activities on its soil that are hostile to other states supporting this proposal and, in reciprocity, states supporting this proposal will not permit any activities hostile to Nepal.
6. Nepal will continue to honour the obligations of all existing treaties which it has concluded with other countries as long as they remain valid.
7. In conformity with its policy of peace and non-alignment, Nepal will not enter into military alliance nor will it allow the establishment of any foreign military base on its soil. In reciprocity, other countries supporting this proposal will not allow the establishment of a military base on their soil directed against Nepal.[21]

Addressing the 24th Session of the AALCC in Kathmandu in 1985, the secretary of the Nepalese Ministry of Law and Justice said that the proposal had three principal objectives:

a) to preserve traditional independence and to ensure Nepal's security;

b) to accelerate the pace of national development in a peaceful atmosphere; and

c) to work in concert with all nations of the world for the maintenance of international peace.[22]

Evaluation

As King Birendra made clear, Nepal's proposal was not 'prompted out of fear or threat from any country or quarter'.[23] In fact, Nepal's relationship with both its neighbours was well balanced: she was in no way involved in the wars between India and Pakistan or China and India, and her policy of neutrality was respected by these countries during the wars. However, Nepal was directly influenced by the dramatically changing situation of South Asia. The Indo–Pakistan war of 1971 was one of the bloodiest in the post-Second World War period. The Pakistani army was on the rampage, indiscriminately killing thousands of its own civilian population of East Pakistan (now Bangladesh).

The loss of thousands of human lives during this period shocked the whole of South Asia. Several million people were made homeless and poured into India as refugees. These events were taking place in the vicinity of Nepal. The Indo–Soviet alliance,[24] the division of Pakistan, the growing implicit alliance among Pakistan, China, and the US,[25] and the loss of the independence of Sikkim[26] were events that greatly influenced Nepal. In sum, the feeling that 'in the whirligig of time, when the fierce winds of change blow with fury, there is no guarantee that the flickering light of peace may not blow off a nation'[27] seems to be one of the principal reasons why Nepal needed the status of a zone of peace: as a guarantee of her independence.

This proposal was an excellent innovation. It had a good beginning, yet it was not as efficiently pursued as it was proposed. Soon after the king made the proposal, the government of Nepal should have made every effort to transliterate it into legal instruments, thus making it a strong institution with legally-binding force. This could have been effected either through bilateral treaties accommodating the principles of the zone of peace or through a multilateral treaty which would have given a legal character to the proposal. Those states that supported Nepal's proposal could have also been persuaded into entering into a bilateral or a multilateral treaty. Yet, the Nepalese government was simply seeking support from as many countries as possible irrespective of the form of support. Of course, many states supported the proposal but the legality of such support was somewhat controversial. This is because some states extended support in principle, some lent general or political support, etc. For instance, the UK extended support in principle to Nepal's proposal. The Foreign and Commonwealth Office of the UK maintained that

> HMG's *general* approach to Zone of Peace proposals is well known. We support them providing they enjoy the support of all countries concerned. Consequently, we support the Nepalese proposal *in principle* and view it with much sympathy and interest.[28] [Emphasis added.]

This support is not unqualified. Cyprus[29] and Japan[30] also lent 'principled' support. Sri Lanka's was in general terms. J.R. Jayawardhane, the president of Sri Lanka, said that he supported the concept of zones of peace '*in all parts of the world*, including Nepal'[31] (emphasis added). Thailand considered Nepal's proposal 'in line with ASEAN's proposal'.[32] The French government said that it 'considers favourably the proposition'[33] of Nepal. The US's position was spelt out by President Reagan: 'We Americans support the *objectives* [of Nepal's proposal and] we endorse it'[34] (emphasis added). Spain said that 'Spain, which recognizes the right of all states to their independence and to freely choose their political option, welcomes all initiatives to promote peace and, therefore, gives its support [to the Nepalese proposal]'.[35]

Although these expressions of support represented in large measure state practice, many states seemed to have supported Nepal's proposal as a gesture of a friendly relationship rather than as a legal institution. Moral support, in other words, support not coupled with *opinio juris*, cannot bind the supporting states, general statements of political ideals have no legal value. In the absence of any treaty law, peace zones have to achieve the status of customary rules, which are neither easily created nor easily identifiable. This is highlighted by the ICJ in the *Nicaragua* v. *USA* case: the court distinguished between the processes of establishing a rule through treaties and through custom. In the latter situation, 'the shared view of the parties' as to a rule 'is not enough' and the court would look for *opinio juris*.[36]

Although certain states' support, e.g. that of China,[37] Pakistan,[38] Chile,[39] etc. was couched in legal terms, that of many other states' was loosely worded. In the event of any legal dispute, these countries might contend that their support was only a statement of political intention and not a formulation of law. This was the position maintained by the US in relation to the UN General Assembly Resolution 2131 (XX), although the US voted in favour of it.[40] States support and oppose many claims and propositions in their day-to-day work and international relations. Not all of these can be considered state practice. For instance, the General Assembly passes numerous resolutions every year. If all of them were to be considered international rules, as Lauterpacht wrote, 'how many rules of international law can there be said to be in effective existence?'.[41]

The US distinguishes its support of any proposal between the legal and the political, the latter being of negligible legal value. While voting against the general assembly resolution declaring the South Atlantic a zone of peace and cooperation, the US also made it clear that it opposes the resolution because it 'attempts to create an internationally recognised zone of peace through the adoption of a UN resolution rather than through multilateral negotiations',[42] a method opposed by the US, who usually favours a legalistic position with regard to such a proposition. Her view appears to be that a proposition considered as a matter of policy does not bind her unless she has explicitly agreed to undertake any commitment through treaties. This was reflected in the US's recognition of Austria's neutrality.[43]

From these circumstances it was not clear whether or not the US considered bilateral support of Nepal's proposal capable of creating an internationally recognized zone of peace. This fundamental issue raised doubts on the legal nature of international support obtained by Nepal to its proposal. Under such circumstances Nepal would have faced considerable difficulties in awarding legal status to its proposal. She might well have maintained that, while supporting the proposal, these states have not said that their support had political intentions. However, these states might also say that, as the proposal was not treated as a legal rule by Nepal, the proposee itself, there was no need to make it clear whether or not the support had political intentions. This lack of clarity was the problem associated with Nepal's proposal.

As many states maintained in their deliberations before the UN Ad Hoc Committee on the Indian Ocean as a Zone of Peace, a clearer understanding of certain 'fundamental matters, such as the scope, definition, and meaning of the zone of peace, was necessary' in pursuing such an intention.[44] Every proposal should have a precise definition, effective measures of realization, and procedures for follow-up and verification. In the absence of such elements, every proposition becomes merely decorative, simply a statement of ideals. Nepal's proposal does not seem to have satisfied certain of these requirements. In the nearly decade and a half of its existence, Nepal's proposal had neither been clearly defined nor incorporated into a single piece of its legislation. Incorporating the proposal into the Constitution of Nepal was a step forward, yet the provision was placed in Part IV under the Directive Principles of the Panchayat System, which, of course, had no legally binding force. The seven principal features of the proposal spelt out by Nepalese Prime Minister Thapa were an exemplary formulation of the components of peace zones, but the end result was neither a complete definition of a peace zone nor a statement of legal significance.

Conclusions

The political leaders who were propelled to power by the popular movement of the 1990s were not able to fully comprehend the benefits of the institution of a zone of peace for Nepal, seeing it simply as a policy of the panchayat system. They were too keen to placate India by abandoning the policy rather than persuading India to support it, as India too actually stands to gain by Nepal's being a zone of peace. For instance, India had to obtain from Sri Lanka, through the Agreement of July 1987, a guarantee that there would be no foreign military presence in Sri Lankan territories to the detriment of India's security interests.[45] By contrast, Nepal had unilaterally bound herself to the fact that in no event would there be any foreign military presence in Nepal against the interests of other countries. By supporting the zone of peace proposal, India would have automatically obtained the assurance that she needs. An internationally recognized peace zone between India and China is an advantage for both these countries. A significant part of India's northern frontier would be secured, and India could thus significantly reduce her armed forces on this frontier. By supporting Nepal's proposal, India would be entitled to certain rights too, e.g. to complain if Nepal's activities were not compatible with the principles of its being a peace zone. In fact, India seems to have proposed in its 'secret' draft agreement presented to Nepal during the height of the Indo-Nepal 'cold war' of 1989/1990, a provision similar to that which Nepal was offering through the institution of a zone of peace: that is to say, that both countries should undertake not to enter into any military alliance with any other state to the detriment of each other. The difference here is that the idea of zone of peace sought to preclude Nepal from entering into *any* military alliance, while the Indian draft proposal sought to require some form of a military alliance between Nepal and India while forbidding any other military alliance with any other states.

Notes and References

1. 'Gasping for breath', *Far Eastern Economic Review*, 8 March 1990, 25.

2. See in A.S. Bhasin, *Documents on Nepal's Relations with India and China 1949–66* (1970), pp. 13, 14.

3 Ibid., pp. 10–12.

4. Gisbert H. Flanz (eds), *Constitutions of the Countries of the World: Nepal*, vol. x (1985), pp. 1–2.

5. Douglas H. Chadwick and W. Thompson, 'At the Crossroads of Kathmandu', 172(1), *National Geographic* (1987) pp. 32, 65.

6. See, generally, T.S. Rama Rao, 'The Himalayan Frontier Policy of India: A Historical Perspective', *Indian Yearbook of International Affairs*, xv–xvi (1966–7), p. 558.

7. The 1950 Treaty of Peace and Friendship.

8. The Treaty of 8 Aug. 1949 between India and Bhutan.

9. The Treaty of 6 Dec. 1950 between India and Sikkim.

10. India and the Soviet Union concluded a 21-year treaty in 1971 incorporating certain security matters. See Keesing's, vol. xviii (1971–1972), p. 24773 for the Treaty of Peace, Friendship and Cooperation of August 1971 between India and the Soviet Union.

11. Chadwick and Thompson, op. cit., p. 62.

12. Flanz, op. cit., n. 4, p. 12.

13. *Keesing's Archives of Contemporary World Events*, vol. xxi (1975), p. 27062.

14. Ibid.

15. Ibid., vol. xx (1974), p. 26778.

16. Ibid., vol. xxi (1975), p. 27062.

17. The king reorganized the National Planning Commission, established the National Development Council, set up a committee to recommend on constitutional reforms, etc.

18. B. Rana, *HM King Birendra's Peace Proposal for Nepal* (Kathmandu: HMG/ Ministry of Communications, 1983), pp. 1–2.

19. Ibid.

20. Flanz, op. cit., p. 15.

21. Rana, op. cit., n. 18, pp. 3–4.

22. Personal communication.

23. Rana, op. cit., n. 18, p. 20.

24. Ibid.

25. China and the US supported Pakistan in its war with India. This is described as one of the factors that brought China and the US closer than before. Dr Henry Kissinger visited Beijing in 1972, paving the way for President Nixon's subsequent visit to China.

26. The Himalayan state of Sikkim was an Indian protectorate. Sikkim and India concluded a treaty of peace and friendship in 1950 which included provisions similar to those between India and Bhutan. See *Keesing's* vol XX (1974), pp. 26794, 26795.

27. From King Birendra's statement at the Fifth Non-Aligned Summit Conference in Colombo on 17 August 1976. See Rana op. cit., n. 18, p. 7.

28. Rana, op. cit., n. 18, p. 17.

29. Ibid., p. 18.

30. Ibid., p. 13.

31. S.C. Regmi, *The Peace Zone Proposal of Nepal* (1985), p. 47.

32. Rana, op. cit., n. 18, p. 14.

33. Rana, op. cit., n. 18, p. 28.

34. Ibid., p. 30.

35. Rana, op. cit., n. 18, p. 21.

36. Keesing's *supra*, n. 26, p. 1065.

37. Rana, op. cit., n. 18, p. 12.

38. Ibid.

39. Ibid., p. 14.

40. Official Records of the General Assembly Twentieth Session, First Committee, UN Doc A/c 1 SR 1423, p. 436.

41. Lauterpacht, *The Development of International Law by the International Court* (1958), p. 191, as cited in A D'Amato 'On Consensus' VIII, *The Canadian Yearbook of International Law* (1970), 104, 108.

42. Supra, pp. 47–50. Black et al., *Neutralization and World Politics* (Princeton, New Jersey: 1968), pp. 49–50.

43. UN Doc., A/AC 159/l80, 16 April 1988, para. 31.

44. T. Sagnier, 'Educating the "most beautiful children in the world"', *UN Chronicle*, vol. XXIV, no. 4, Nov. 1987, p. 74.

45. Regmi, op. cit., n. 31, pp. 40–1.

4

The Role of the United Nations in Resolving Trade and Transit Problems of Landlocked States and their Implications for Indo-Nepal Relations

Introduction

Of the total of 187 or so states in the world, 42 are landlocked,[1] and their number[2] has grown steadily over the past five decades with the increase in membership of the United Nations.[3] This has been followed by a considerable growth of interest in the trade and transit problems of landlocked states, and this is likely to accelerate in the future, owing to the increase in the volume of international trade and economic activities in these states as well as the acute problems faced by them in this process.[4]

While many landlocked states in Africa and Asia are still fashioning their trade and transit relations with their neighbouring transit states, a dozen new landlocked states have emerged in Europe, Africa, and Central Asia following the break up of the Soviet Union. Several of these states appear to be in the process of reshaping their trade and transit relationships with their neighbouring transit states in order to secure freedom of transit and free access to and from the sea through the territory of their coastal and other transit neighbours. Indeed, one of the key rights that all parties sought to secure in the Dayton Peace Agreement of 1995 concluded between the former Yugoslav republics was the unfettered right of access to and from the sea and freedom of transit for them.[5]

International settlements, redrawing of international boundaries, the creation of new states out of a single state and, most significant of all, the de-colonization process, have all contributed to the emergence of new landlocked states. They vary in size, in political, economic, and military strength, and in economic development. Although some of them are tiny enclave-type states such as San Marino and Lesotho, others are relatively large states such as Ethiopia, Mali, Kazakhstan, and Bolivia. Similarly, while landlocked states such as Nepal and Switzerland are strategically located, some others, such as Zambia and Kazakhstan, have the potential of themselves becoming regional powers. In terms of their economic development, most are developing, and sixteen of them are among the world's least developed countries. At the same time, a few landlocked states, such as Austria and Switzerland, enjoy a very high level of per capita income and are ranked among the most advanced developed countries.

All of them, however, have one aspiration in common. Their common characteristic is their lack of a seacoast, and their common aspiration is to secure and preserve freedom of transit across their neighbour countries and a right of free access to and from the sea for their third-country trade (trade with countries other than their neighbours). This is because these states feel that their landlockedness has a negative impact on their economic and social development since they have to depend on their neighbouring states for most of their external economic activities, including the export and import of goods. It is in this context that this chapter examines the role played by the UN during the past five decades or so, not only in resolving the problems of landlocked states, but also in helping them to develop their economies, as they are among the most geographically disadvantaged states in the world. In doing so, it will highlight the implications of the law developed by the UN for Indo-Nepal relations.

The Problem of being Landlocked

Unlike islands, atolls and peninsulas, which are natural features of the earth's surface, being locked is the result of political processes. National borders are drawn by people and not by nature. Contrary to popular belief, the problem of being landlocked is political and legal rather than geographic, requiring political and legal initiatives and solutions to the problem. Nepal's being landlocked state is a case in point. Although Nepal's border with Tibet runs largely through the Himalayas, the rivers originating there continue through the plains of Nepal to the Indo-Gangetic plains of India and ultimately reach the Bay of Bengal. Geographically, there is no reason for the division of this land mass into different states.

In ancient times, when the life of coastal people was made difficult by the seaborne forces of nature as well as by invading aliens and pirates, being landlocked was perhaps an advantage for the people living in the continental interiors. Later, when the world experienced phenomenal growth in international trade, landlocked states began to feel handicapped. Being landlocked can have a tremendous negative impact not only on commerce but also on other economic activities, as well as on the political independence of the state concerned. For instance, if foreign investors have to please state A in order to invest in state B, they will think twice before investing in state B. That is what is happening with regard to many landlocked states.

States have to become competitive to succeed economically. One way of becoming competitive is by offering efficient, cost-effective, and speedy transport. However, landlocked states can determine neither the suitability nor the availability of transport facilities beyond their borders. As stated in a recent UN conference on trade and development (UNCTAD) report on the problems of landlocked states,

> The existence of an efficient, flexible and well-managed transit system is a necessary condition for the international competitiveness of most outward-orientated enterprises in landlocked developing countries. Moreover, the costs and risks of transit aggravate the foreign-exchange problems of landlocked developing countries by reducing the volume and value of exports and inflating the costs of imports. This situation is compounded by the fact that landlocked countries generally have to pay for transit services in foreign exchange.[6]

The report goes on to give specific examples of the magnitude of such foreign exchange squeeze and states that the export trade of many landlocked developing states 'is partly reduced because resources that could profitably be transformed into export commodities are left un-utilized as a result of transit cost disadvantages'. As Sinjela points out,

> The long distance to and from the sea also raises transport costs for these states. For example, all things being equal, if two people—one in a landlocked state and the other in a coastal State—engage in a similar business enterprise, the person in a landlocked State would realize less in profits than the other because of the high transport costs incurred—costs which sometimes frighten away potential investors.[7]

This is one reason why most of the landlocked states of Asia, Africa, and Latin America have remained far behind in their efforts to develop their economy and why many of them belong to the category of least-developed states. This aspect of the plight of landlocked states was rightly captured by UNCTAD in 1976 in the following passage:

> Landlocked developing countries are generally among the very poorest of the developing countries. The lack of a territorial access to the sea, compounded by the remoteness and isolation from world markets, appears to be an important cause of their relative poverty, and constitutes a major obstacle to their development. Indeed, all but four of the 20 landlocked developing countries are on the list of countries identified by the United Nations as the least developed.[8]

This situation, described some 20 years ago, is still valid. Perhaps it has become even worse for many of these states with their increasing economic marginalization, internal environmental degradation, and the fall in the prices of their primary commodities in the world market. There was some hope for these states in the 1970s and 1980s when many people were euphoric about the idea of a New International Economic Order (NIEO) and the highly publicized potential benefits of the resources of the sea not only for coastal states but also for landlocked ones. However, all these expectations evaporated in the late 1980s and early 1990s as the ideas of distributive economic justice and a new world economic order were effectively shelved and the world was driven in the direction of greater marketization, liberalization, and privatization. This has resulted not only in less government within states but also in less international concern for or action on behalf of the less fortunate ones, including the landlocked states.

Even some of the gains made by these countries in the 1960s and 1970s have gradually been diluted or eroded altogether in the recent past. The NIEO is now virtually dead, and even the spirit of the 1982 UN Convention on the Law of the Sea (LOSC, 1982 Convention) was eroded by the 1994 Agreement Relating to the Implementation of Part XI of the Convention, which deals with deep seabed mining. First, the convention itself represented, as rightly described by Glassner, 'a disastrous loss for them [i.e., the landlocked states] in its provisions for access to the resources of the sea'.[9]

This is because the 1982 convention allowed the coastal states to claim a 200-mile exclusive economic zone (EEZ), an area that hitherto was part of the high seas and rich in resources, thereby leaving only the 'biological desert' of the deep sea for exploitation by all states, including the landlocked.

In effect, the introduction of the EEZ dramatically increased the distance between the high seas and landlocked states, making these countries more remote from the high seas. Second, whatever was achieved for developing countries in terms of its provisions relating to deep seabed mining under the 1982 convention was considerably watered down by the 1994 agreement.

What is more, international organizations dealing with development activities have gradually been forced out of business, and developing states, including some of the least-developed landlocked ones, have been told to compete on an equal footing with developed states in accordance with the spirit of the 'free play for all' rule established by the General Agreement on Tariffs and Trade (GATT) and the World Trade Organization (WTO) and supported by other international financial institutions such as the World Bank. These are the challenges that lie ahead for developing landlocked states. In order to be able to compete on an equal footing with other countries, the landlocked states need suitable infrastructures and liberal treatment from their transit states for their international trade. That is principally why landlocked states have long sought to have their freedom of transit and right of free access to and from the sea firmly established in international law and strengthened by the UN and its specialized agencies.

The Pre-UN Period

Early Writings

The origin of the freedom of transit concept can be traced to the writings of the seventeenth-century publicists. They believed that people had a natural right to traverse the territory of all countries for commercial purposes. The following statement of Grotius in his classic work *De Jure Belli ac Pacis* is an example:

> Lands, rivers and any part of the sea that has become subject to the ownership of a people, ought to be open to those who, for legitimate reasons, have need to cross over them; as for instance, if a people ... desires to carry out commerce with a distant people.[10]

Vattel held a similar view. He stated that the right of passage over foreign territory belonged to the category of 'rights which remain to all nations'.[11]

However, neither the writings of the publicists nor the multilateral treaties of the eighteenth and nineteenth centuries acknowledged any distinct status for landlocked countries. This situation was to remain unchanged until the post-First World War period in spite of the creation or recognition of some landlocked states by the Congress of Vienna of 1815 and the Treaty of Versailles of 1919. However, through Article 23 (e) of the Covenant of the League of Nations, the member states of the League undertook to 'make provision to secure and maintain freedom of communications and of transit and equitable treatment for the commerce of all members of the League'.

The Barcelona Statute on Freedom of Transit of 1921

In accordance with an undertaking specified in its Covenant, the League of Nations convened an international conference in Barcelona on 10 March 1921. On 20 April 1921, the Conference adopted, inter alia, two important instruments: (1) the Convention and Statute on Freedom of Transit (commonly known as the Barcelona Convention), and (2) the Barcelona Declaration Recognizing the Right to a Flag of states Having no Sea Coast. Thus, for the first time in the history of international relations, the Barcelona Statute established a general freedom of transit for all states parties to the Barcelona Convention. This freedom was available whether the purpose of the exercise of this freedom was to reach the sea or another inland territory. Article 1 of the Barcelona Statute adopted the following definition of the term *traffic in transit* entitled to freedom of transit:

> Persons, baggage and goods, and also vessels, coaching and goods stock, and other means of transport, shall be deemed to be in transit across territory under the sovereignty or authority of one of the contracting states, when the passage across such territory, with or without trans-shipment, warehousing, breaking bulk, or change in the mode of transport, is only a portion of a complete journey, beginning and terminating beyond the frontier of the state across whose territory transit takes place.

Article 2 of the Statute provides for free and non-discriminatory transit across the territory of the contracting parties:

> Subject to the other provisions of this Statute, the measures taken by Contracting States for regulating and forwarding traffic across territory under their sovereignty or authority shall facilitate free transit by rail or waterway on routes in use

convenient for international transit. No distinction shall be made which is based on the nationality of persons, the flag of vessels, the place of origin, departure, entry, exit or destination or on any circumstances relating to the ownership of goods or of vessels, coaching or goods stock or other means of transport.

In order to ensure the application of the provisions of this Article, contracting states will allow transit in accordance with customary conditions and reserves across their territorial waters.[12]

Evaluation of the Barcelona Convention and Statute

As outlined in a UN report, the Barcelona Statute views transit 'as a non-self-executing right, since its existence and its extent are subject not only to the consent of but also to an arrangement with the transit states'. Moreover, although the statute appears to regard transit as a 'right' as opposed to a 'privilege' granted unilaterally by the transit state, 'it is, however, clear that such a right is subject to reciprocity'. The UN report sums up the deficiencies of the Barcelona Statute as follows:

(a) One such deficiency was inherent in the Statute itself, in that most of the participants originated from Europe, thus ignoring similar problems which could be encountered in other parts of the world, such as in the colonies of the European Powers. In fact, Article 14 of the Statute stipulates that as a matter of principle the provisions of the Statute do not apply 'where a colony or dependency has a very long frontier in comparison with its surface and where in consequence it is particularly impossible to afford the necessary customs and police supervision';

(b) Proceeding in part from the previous argument, it appears that the right of transit, as it was viewed in the Barcelona Statute, was not a universal principle established once and for all but was rather the result of a temporary agreement between a few states;

(c) Being limited to two modes and means of transportation, namely railways and waterways, the Barcelona Statute did not take into account other means of transportation such as road, sea, lake, and river craft, as well as porters and pack animals.[13]

What is more, the statute gives quite broad discretionary powers to the transit state for the protection of its legitimate interests without defining what this term means. However, in spite of such deficiencies, the Barcelona Statute can be considered a landmark document for institutionalizing the right of transit of all states and in particular of those that are landlocked.

Furthermore, it was the Barcelona Conference, which recognized through a separate declaration the right of landlocked states to sail ships under their own maritime flag, and some have done so.

The United Nations Era

In the early years of the UN, the Barcelona approach lingered on, and international instruments dealing with freedom of transit draw no distinction between the needs of landlocked and other states. Yet, soon the international community began recognizing the special needs of landlocked states and dealing with this topic as such. A great deal has been done within the UN framework for the landlocked countries during the past four decades. It is no longer just an international legal issue. It has been considered within a broad spectrum of activities of the UN, its specialized agencies, and other international organizations and fora, ranging from international trade and aid to transportation, shipping, and the Law of the Sea. Therefore, it is proposed to deal with the developments of the past five decades under a number of headings and subheadings.

Freedom of Transit for International Commerce

International Economic Cooperation under the UN Charter

Two major issues dominated the thinking of those instrumental in creating a new international order in the aftermath of the Second World War. One was to avoid another catastrophic war, the other to promote universal economic and social progress for all states. Whereas the first objective was to be achieved through the collective security system envisaged in the UN Charter, the other was to be achieved through economic cooperation among the members of the UN in accordance with Chapter IX of the charter. Article 55 states that with a view to the creation of conditions of stability and well-being which are necessary for peaceful and friendly relations among nations, the UN shall promote, inter alia, conditions of economic and social progress and development for all states. All member states of the UN pledged themselves in Article 56 of the Charter 'to take joint and separate action in cooperation with the organization for the achievement of the purposes set forth in Article 55'.[14]

Freedom of Transit within GATT

It was in this spirit that the Bretton Woods institutions (the International Bank for Reconstruction and Development (IBRD or World Bank) and the International Monetary Fund (IMF), and the GATT were created in the immediate aftermath of the establishment of the UN. The 1947 General Agreement on Tariffs and Trade (outside but linked to the UN system) deals with freedom of transit in its Article V:

> 1. Goods (including baggage), and also vessels and other means of transport, shall be deemed to be in transit across the territory of a contracting party when the passage across such territory, with or without trans-shipment, warehousing, breaking bulk, or change in the mode of transport, is only a portion of a complete journey beginning and terminating beyond the frontier of the contracting party across whose territory the traffic passes. Traffic of this nature is termed in this article 'traffic in transit'.
>
> 2. There shall be freedom of transit through the territory of each contracting party, via the routes most convenient for international transit, for traffic in transit to or from the territory of other contracting parties. No distinction shall be made which is based on the flag of vessels, the place of origin, departure, entry, exit or destination, or on any circumstances relating to the ownership of goods, of vessels or of other means of transport.[15]

Although the provisions of the GATT do not depart significantly from those of the Barcelona Statute on Freedom of Transit, there are two principal differences. The Barcelona Statute includes persons as well as goods in the definition of traffic in transit, but the GATT definition is restricted to the passage of goods. Insofar as means of transportation is concerned, the GATT article, unlike the Barcelona Statute, includes not only traffic along railways and navigable watercourses, but also all means of land transportation. However, like the Barcelona Statute, there is no mention of our special consideration for the needs of landlocked states in Article V of GATT. All parties to the GATT enjoy this freedom of transit on the basis of reciprocity.

The Havana Charter

The Havana Charter for an International Trade Organization, adopted in 1948, was the next international instrument dealing with international trade after the GATT. Although the charter never came into force, it contained provisions recognizing the special situation of landlocked states, the first ever in an international instrument. Articles 10 and 33 of the Havana Charter dealt with freedom of transit of landlocked states. Although Article 33 closely followed the language of Article V of GATT, an interpretative note attached to it contained some interesting elements:

> If, as a result of negotiations in accordance with paragraph 6, a Member grants to a country which has no direct access to the sea more ample facilities than those already provided for in other paragraphs of Article 33, such special facilities may be limited to the landlocked country concerned unless the Organization finds on the complaint of any other Member, that the withholding of the special facilities from the complaining Member contravenes the most-favoured-nation provisions of this Charter.[16]

Moreover, Article 10 stipulated that 'facilities and special rights accorded by this convention to landlocked states in view of their special geographical position are excluded from the operation of the most-favoured-nation clause [MFN]'.[17]

The Role of ECAFE

Direct involvement of the UN and its specialized agencies in the problem of being landlocked began in the mid-1950s. A 1956 report of the Committee on Industry and Trade of ECAFE (the United Nations Economic Commission for Asia and the Far East) recommended that 'the needs of landlocked member states and members having no easy access to the sea, in the matter of transit trade be given full recognition by all member states and that adequate facilities therefore be accorded in terms of international law and practice in this regard'.[18] The General Assembly of the UN heeded this message and adopted a resolution in 1957 endorsing and reiterating the recommendation of the committee.[19]

As we shall see later, it was actually the work of ECAFE that led to the adoption of an international convention devoted solely to the transit trade problem of landlocked states in 1965. Meanwhile, a resolution adopted at the Ministerial Conference on the Asian Economic Cooperation held in 1963, recognized the 'right of free transit for landlocked countries and the special considerations which apply to their transport and transit problems and the importance of the relationship of these problems to questions of regional cooperation and expansion of intra-regional trade'.[20]

The Role of UNCTAD

Chiefly as a result of the efforts made within ECAFE, a subcommittee on landlocked countries was established at the UN Conference on Trade and Development (UNCTAD) held from 23 March to 16 June 1964 'to consider the proposal for the formulation of an adequate and effective international convention, or other means, to ensure the freedom of transit trade of landlocked countries and to formulate recommendations on this matter for consideration by the committee'.[21]

Once the subcommittee's work had been completed, UNCTAD adopted a set of eight principles for landlocked states, which provided the basis for a separate convention on their transit trade and was adopted in 1965. In Principle I, UNCTAD stated that 'the recognition of the right of each landlocked state of free access to the sea is an essential principle for the expansion of international trade and economic development'. Principle IV dealt with freedom of transit:

> In order to promote fully the economic development of the landlocked countries, the said countries should be afforded by all states, on the basis of reciprocity, free and unrestricted transit, in such a manner that they have free access to regional and international trade in all circumstances and for every type of goods.[22]

The same conference also adopted a recommendation on the preparation of a convention relating to transit trade of landlocked states and called upon the UN to convene an international conference on the subject in 1965. Accordingly, an international conference was convened at the UN Headquarters under the auspices of UNCTAD from 7 June to 8 July 1965. The Conference adopted a landmark Convention on Transit Trade of Landlocked States.

The United Nations Convention on Transit Trade of Landlocked States

The 1965 United Nations Convention on Transit Trade of Landlocked States significantly strengthened the freedom of transit of such states. Its preamble restates and reaffirms the eight UNCTAD principles of 1964 mentioned above. The main text includes quite a few other innovative provisions relating to landlocked states. For instance, Article 1 includes not only the passage of goods but also the passage of unaccompanied baggage in the definition of 'traffic in transit'. Similarly, it provides for quite a broad definition of the term *means of transport* to include, conditionally, even pipelines. Perhaps the most important of all is the guarantee in Article 2: 'Freedom of transit shall be granted under the terms of this Convention for traffic in transit and means of transport'.

There are two other noteworthy provisions in the convention. One is Article 4, which requires states parties 'to provide, subject to availability ... adequate means of transport and handling equipment for the movement of traffic in transit without unnecessary delay'. The other is Article 7, which requires states parties to take all measures 'to avoid delays in, or restrictions on, traffic in transit'. It goes on to state that 'Should delays or other difficulties occur in traffic in transit, the competent authorities of the transit State or States and of the landlocked State shall cooperate towards their expeditious elimination'. Last but not least important is the compulsory dispute settlement provision of Article 16: 'Any dispute which may arise with respect to the interpretation or application of the provisions of this Convention which is not settled by negotiation or by other peaceful means of settlement within a period of nine months shall, at the request of either party, be settled by arbitration.'

In many other respects, however, this convention repeats the language and substance of the Barcelona Statute and GATT Article V. It, too, accepts the principle of reciprocity, does not define the 'legitimate interests' of transit states, and requires a bilateral agreement with the transit state on the actual modalities of transit. Moreover, the effectiveness of this convention is rather limited as only very few transit states have ratified it. Thus, it is difficult to state that this convention created an unfettered universal right of landlocked states to freedom of transit across the territory of transit states.

The Right of Free Access to and from the Sea

As landlocked states are handicapped by not having seacoasts, their primary concern has long been to secure the right of free access to and from the sea. Although the 1921 Declaration Recognizing the Right to a Flag of States Having no Sea Coast adopted by the Barcelona Conference and the 1923 Geneva Convention and Statute on the International Regime of Maritime Ports deal with certain maritime rights of landlocked states, their main efforts to secure the right of free *access to and from the sea* have taken place within the context of the developing international Law of the Sea.

This was only natural as they need not only international trade but also the other freedoms of the high seas and the exploitation of the resources of the deep seabed to which they have rights equal to those of coastal states. Accordingly, it is within the context of the Law of the Sea that both the rights of access and freedom of transit have been dealt with since freedom of transit has been viewed as a natural corollary of right of access.

The difference is that whereas freedom on transit as found in the Barcelona Statute and GATT is a substantive principle in its own right, the freedom of transit designed to realize the right of free access to and from the sea has been viewed only as a procedural rule. Accordingly, the efforts of landlocked states in various Law of the Sea fora have been to secure the *right* of free access to and from the sea in the belief that once this right has been secured, freedom of transit will naturally flow from the right of free access.

The other reason for this emphasis on the right of access is that as freedom of transit has traditionally been viewed as a freedom available to all states on the basis of reciprocity, a claim by landlocked states to the right of free access to and from the sea by virtue of their being landlocked would not raise the issue of reciprocity. This would be a right available unilaterally to landlocked states as they need this right not only for international commerce but also to enjoy other freedoms of the high seas and to be able, at least in principle, to take part in the exploitation of the natural resources of the deep seabed.

The First United Nations Conference on the Law of the Sea

For the first time in the history of the UN, the General Assembly in its Resolution 1105 (XII) of 21 February 1957 convoking a UN Conference on the Law of the Sea recommended that the forthcoming conference 'should study the question of free access to the sea of landlocked countries, as established by international practice of treaties'. Accordingly, the conference assigned this subject to its Fifth Committee for consideration, and the result of the deliberations during the conference is Article 3(1) of the UN Convention on the High Seas, which reads as follows:

> In order to enjoy the freedom of the seas on equal terms with coastal states, states having no seacoast should have free access to the sea. To this end states situated between the sea and a state having no seacoast shall by common agreement with the latter, and in conformity with existing international conventions, accord:

(a) To the state having no seacoast, on a basis of reciprocity, free transit through their territory; and

(b) To ships flying the flag of that state treatment equal to that accorded to their own ships, or to the ships of any other states, as regards access to seaports and the use of such ports.[23]

This provision marked the first recognition of the special needs of landlocked states in an international treaty of universal character (indicated by the preamble, which states that the provisions of this convention are declaratory of customary international law). However, the weak language coupled with the word 'should', the requirement of reciprocity, and the explicit requirement of a bilateral agreement with the transit state to make the right of free access effective attracted criticism from landlocked states. It broadly reflected the various provisions of previous treaties dealing with such states. The weaknesses outlined above with regard to the Barcelona Statute were not remedied by this convention. The rights of landlocked states still remained non-self-executing and dependent on the goodwill of transit states.

For these reasons, the landlocked states sought a separate convention dealing with their problem, and the result of that effort was the 1965 UN Convention on Transit Trade of Landlocked States, discussed above. As even this document did not fully satisfy the concerns of landlocked states, they kept pressing for a more satisfactory international legal regime dealing with their rights during the nine years of negotiations in the Third UN Conference on the Law of the Sea (UNCLOS III).

The Third United Nations Conference on the Law of the Sea

As the Second UN Conference on the Law of the Sea held in 1960 failed to achieve anything significant, we pass directly to the third such conference, for which preparatory work was entrusted to the UN Committee on the Peaceful Uses of the Seabed and the Ocean Floor beyond the Limits of National Jurisdiction (the Seabed Committee) established in 1968. It was in this Committee that the problems of landlocked states were discussed after 1970. The famous Common Heritage Declaration of the UN General Assembly (Resolution 2749 (XXV) of 17 December 1970) stated in Paragraph 5 that the deep seabed 'shall be open to use exclusively for peaceful purposes by all states whether coastal or landlocked without discrimination'.

This was followed by a number of General Assembly resolutions, various studies of the secretary-general and several reports of various committees on the problem of landlocked states and their participation in the future mining of deep seabed resources. There were other activities that occured throughout the 1970s within other UN agencies such as ECAFE and UNCTAD relating to landlocked states, which sought to supplement and complement the activities of the committees and sub-committees of UNCLOS III.[24]

During the nine years of negotiations in UNCLOS III, a number of proposals were put forward by individual states, both landlocked and transit, as well as by groups of states, outlining their negotiating positions. While the landlocked states were keen to secure an unfettered right of free access to and from the sea, many transit states were anxious to have their sovereignty and territorial integrity preserved and not affected by the demands of landlocked countries. One other strongly contested issue between the landlocked and transit states was the question of reciprocity. The landlocked states insisted that reciprocity must be the basis for any cooperation between them and transit states. For instance, a document submitted to the conference by a group of landlocked states made the following comments on this question:

> As is known, the 1958 Convention on the High Seas in its Article 3, and in similar terms the 1965 New York Convention on the Transit Trade of Landlocked States in its Article 15, have secured to landlocked states the freedom of transit 'on a basis of reciprocity'. These provisions were apparently based on a wrong supposition that both the landlocked countries and the transit states have comparable positions and identical needs for transit. This is however not the case, for the purpose of free transit of landlocked countries is just that of ensuring them the exercise of their right of access to and from the sea.
>
> In Article XVI, the present draft declares therefore that 'reciprocity shall not be a condition of free transit of landlocked states' the fulfilment of which might be required by transit states in favour of their own transit to any other country, for it would not be necessitated by the need for access to the sea. Such conditions would not be just, in particular, in relation to those landlocked countries which are surrounded by several transit states'.[25]

However, as the aim of UNCLOS III was to adopt a convention on the Law of the Sea by consensus, it was necessary for all individual states as well as various groups of states to adopt a 'give and take' policy during the negotiations. The negotiated provisions on landlocked states of the 1982 UN Convention on the Law of the Sea are contained in Part X, Articles 124–32. Perhaps the most important of these articles is Article 125:

> 1. Landlocked States shall have the right of access to and from the sea for the purpose of exercising the rights provided for in this Convention including those relating to the freedom of the high seas and the common heritage of mankind. To this end, landlocked States shall enjoy freedom of transit through the territory of transit States by all means of transport.
>
> 2. The terms and modalities for exercising freedom of transit shall be agreed between the landlocked States and transit States concerned through bilateral, sub-regional or regional agreements.

This article does four important things. First, it guarantees the right of free access to and from the sea to landlocked states. Second, it also guarantees to them freedom of transit without any qualification if this freedom is to be exercised in relation to the right of free access to and from the sea. Third, it does not require a bilateral treaty with the transit state to be able to exercise the right of free access and freedom of transit. Only the detailed provisions of a technical character regarding the terms and modalities for exercising freedom of transit have to be agreed upon with the transit state. However, the actual right to exercise this freedom is itself no longer dependent on a bilateral agreement with the transit state. Fourth, breaking from the Barcelona tradition, it eliminates the requirement of reciprocity.

Part X of the 1982 Convention contains yet other provision with a positive and progressive character. Among them are Articles 126, 127, 130, and 131 which deal with exclusion from the application of the MFN clause in arrangements relating to the exercise of the rights of landlocked states, prohibition on imposition of customs duties, taxes, and other charges on landlocked states' traffic in transit, imposition of a duty to avoid delays and other difficulties in traffic in transit and equal treatment of ships flying the flags of landlocked states in the maritime ports of coastal states.

Not all the provisions of the convention on landlocked states are however trouble-free. For instance, it still leaves undefined the concept of the legitimate interests of transit states. Under the pretext of the protection of 'legitimate interests', transit countries can seriously undermine the rights and freedoms of landlocked countries. The term *legitimate interests* can be and has been interpreted by transit states according to their convenience. For instance, during UNCLOS III, India stated that in endorsing the rights of landlocked states, 'the legitimate interests of the coastal or transit state should also be borne in mind. Such interest might relate to the determination of routes and the protection of the security interests of the transit state'.[26] Accordingly, India used this approach to seriously impede Nepal's access to and from the sea in 1989 when Nepal and India had some differences on other trade and political issues that had very little to do with the exercise of Nepal's transit rights.[27]

Although the claim of landlocked states to freedom of transit has been significantly advanced and strengthened by the 1982 UN Convention on the Law of the Sea, this freedom concerns the exercise of the right of free access *to and from the sea* by landlocked states. Insofar as the *freedom of transit* of landlocked states *across the territory of transit states* to reach other states or other inland territory is concerned, the last legal word is the 1965 Convention under which this freedom is, as stated earlier, available on the basis of reciprocity and subject to a number of other qualifications.

Nevertheless, the 1982 Convention establishes once and for all the right of free access to and from the sea for landlocked states—a right of universal character—in international law. This is perhaps the UN's greatest contribution to the cause of landlocked states. The LOSC, which has been signed by 159 states and entities, has already entered into force. Even before this occurred, many of its provision were widely regarded as representing custom. This is particularly true with regard to the provisions on landlocked states.

Rights of Landlocked States to the Resources of the Sea

When the UN was established, the maximum area of the sea that coastal states could lawfully claim as their territorial sea was no more than 12 nautical miles from their baselines, the rest being open to all states, whether landlocked or coastal. However, the changes that have taken place in the Law of the Sea since the establishment of the UN have allowed the coastal states to appropriate for themselves a vast area of the sea under the concepts of the continental shelf and a 200-mile exclusive economic zone (EEZ) with little regard for the interests of landlocked states.[28]

The richest areas of the sea, both in terms of living and non-living resources, are the areas now claimed by coastal states under these two concepts. What is more, as a result of the very liberal method of drawing baselines under the Law of the Sea and due to the acceptance of new concepts, such as historic bays and archipelagic waters, large additional areas of the sea have actually come under the direct control of coastal states. During this scramble for the sea, coastal states have dramatically expanded their jurisdiction over an area that was part of the global commons until the establishment of the UN, and the landlocked states have become silent victims of the entire process and have been unable to do much about it.

The UN Convention on the Law of the Sea leaves nothing for landlocked states in the continental shelf extending up to 200 miles, the area of the sea richest in mineral resources. Only if the continental shelf of a coastal state extends beyond 200 miles is that state required to make payments or contributions in kind through the International Seabed Authority for the exploitation of the non-living resources of that extended area. The relevant provisions of Article 82 of the LOSC to this effect are as follows:

> 1. The coastal state shall make payments or contributions in kind in respect of the exploitation of the non-living resources of the continental shelf beyond 200 nautical miles from the baselines from which the breadth of the territorial sea is measured.
>
> 2. The payments and contributions shall be made annually with respect to all production at a site after the first five years of production at that site. For the sixth year, the rate of payment or contribution shall be 1 per cent of the value or volume of production at the site. The rate shall increase by 1 per cent for each subsequent year until the twelfth year and shall remain at 7 per cent thereafter. Production does not include resources used in connection with exploitation.
>
> ....
>
> 4. The payments or contributions shall be made through the Authority, which shall distribute them to States Parties to this convention, on the basis of equitable sharing criteria, taking into account the interests and needs of developing states, particularly the least developed and the landlocked among them.[29]

Similarly, the provision relating to the access of landlocked states to the fisheries resources of the exclusive economic zone of their neighbouring coastal states is very weak and may mean very little in practice. This is because the landlocked states' access is limited to 'an *appropriate* part of the *surplus* of the living resources' of the EEZ of a neighbouring coastal state (emphasis added). Article 69(1) of the convention reads:

Landlocked States shall have the right to participate, on an equitable basis, in the exploitation of an appropriate part of the surplus of the living resources of the exclusive economic zones of coastal States of the same sub-region or region, taking into account the relevant economic and geographical circumstances of all the States concerned and in conformity with the provisions of this article and of Articles 61 and 62.[30]

Articles 61 and 62 require the coastal state to, inter alia, determine the allowable catch of the living resources in its EEZ and promote the objective of optimum utilization of the living resources in such a zone. As can be seen from Article 69(1), the access of a landlocked state to the EEZ of a neighbouring coastal one is somewhat limited and subject to a number of qualifications.[31] For instance, according to Article 71, coastal states can deny this right altogether to landlocked countries if the former's economy is overwhelmingly dependent on the exploitation of the living resources of its exclusive economic zone.

What is left for landlocked states to exploit with other coastal states is the 'biological desert' of the deep sea and the mineral resources of the deep seabed under an international regime established by the 1982 Convention. However, as stated earlier, the significance of the deep seabed-mining regime created by the convention was diluted by an agreement concluded in 1994.

Landlocked states were joined by a group of 'geographically disadvantaged states' during UNCLOS III in their pursuit of a claim for preferential treatment for them in the distribution of the proceeds from the mining of deep seabed resources. However, the coastal states, the majority at UNCLOS III, did not concede this with regard to the mining of the deep seabed, let alone the mineral resources of the continental shelf. However, a few provisions in the deep seabed-mining regime of the convention seek to secure effective participation of landlocked states together with other developing countries in mining activities in the International Seabed Area. For instance, Article 148 provides that

The effective participation of developing States in activities in the Area shall be promoted as specifically provided for in this part, having due regard to their special interests and needs, and in particular to the special need of the landlocked and geographically disadvantaged among them to overcome obstacles arising from their disadvantaged location, including remoteness from the Area and difficulty of access to and from it.[32]

Similar provisions can be found in other articles dealing with the Area (i.e., the deep seabed), especially in Articles 152 and 160 (2)(k). However, such statements are rather vague representing no more than rhetoric and can do very little to help the landlocked states to overcome the difficulties that they face because of their geographically disadvantaged position.

Efforts Made to Address the Practical Problems of Landlocked States

UNCTAD

Parallel to the international legal developments outlined in the preceding paragraphs, efforts have been made within UNCTAD since its establishment to address the problems of landlocked states at a more practical level. In other words, these efforts have focused on devising effective means of materializing in practice the rights secured internationally by landlocked states. Quite early on it was realized that the problems of these states are such that they warrant detailed practical measures to enable them to benefit from the rights and freedoms secured by law. As most developing landlocked states gained their independence during the first three decades of the UN, they needed assistance in different forms to improve their economies. In addition to needing technical assistance to develop the best routes and modes of transit for their exports and imports, they also needed a fairer international trading system to enable them to compete with other countries. It is in these areas that the assistance of UNCTAD has played a crucial role.

Although developing an international legal framework for their transit was a common effort of *all* landlocked states, whether developed or developing, for the long-term benefit of all of them, the activities within UNCTAD have been principally designed to promote the interests of *developing* landlocked states. Owing to their economic strength as well as to the foresight and wisdom of their neighbouring coastal states, most *developed* landlocked countries had managed to secure satisfactory arrangements with their coastal neighbours by the time the 1982 Law of the Sea Convention was concluded. Accordingly, what follows is an examination of UNCTAD's role in promoting principally the interests of *developing*, and in particular, the least developed landlocked states rather than enhancing the interests of all landlocked countries in general.

UNCTAD has indeed played a very important role in advancing the cause of developing landlocked states, especially the least developed.[33] Its efforts have ranged from preparatory work for the 1965 New York Convention on Transit Trade of Landlocked States to identifying problems of developing landlocked states in regard to invisibles, including shipping, to studying and producing basic data on developing landlocked states and their transit neighbours, to examining transport networks, and transit and transport costs, and physical accessibility to foreign markets for landlocked countries.

In addition, it has also proposed special measures, various programmes of action designed to alleviate the problems faced by developing landlocked states and prepared or commissioned country reports on individual ones. In doing so, UNCTAD has recommended measures for the improvement of transit transport infrastructures and services for landlocked developing countries. It has also organized, beginning in 1993, biennial meetings of governmental experts from landlocked and transit developing countries, representatives of donor countries, and financial and development institutions.

The 1995 meeting adopted a Global Framework for Transit Transport Cooperation between Landlocked and Transit Developing Countries and the Donor Community, which, inter alia, outlines a wide range of recommendations for further appropriate action to improve transit transport systems.[34] It spells out the measures necessary to resolve the problems of landlocked states, including a strategy for mutually supportive and beneficial actions by the landlocked and transit developing countries in all areas of the transit transport sector. This Global Framework has widely been regarded as a significant contribution of UNCTAD to the UN's development objectives.[35]

Moreover, UNCTAD has committed itself to playing a leading role and to acting as a focal point in the UN system on issues relating to landlocked developing countries. A 1993 report by the UNCTAD Secretariat states that 'UNCTAD will continue to provide technical assistance to support the landlocked and coastal states in their efforts to improve the transit systems and will thus make its contribution in the various areas mentioned [in the report]'. Such areas include:

(a) Accumulating, evaluating and disseminating information on transit matters, drawing lessons from experiences in different regions and sub-regions with regard to the design and improvement of transit systems;

(b) carrying out transit-related studies which help decision-makers, particularly with a view to identifying critical bottlenecks which could be removed quickly at minimum cost;

(c) organizing training programmes tailored to the needs of transit policy-makers, managers, and operators;

(d) monitoring the progress in the implementation of action by the international community related to the transit needs and problems of landlocked developing countries;

(e) formulating measures to be adopted at the national, sub-regional, and international levels to improve the transit systems in the light of changing economic and political environments.[36]

Indeed, these are precisely the types of activities that many landlocked developing countries would like to see carried out by UN bodies and other international organizations. As stated earlier, UNCTAD has already done a great deal to help the developing landlocked states in these areas. What remains to be seen is whether UNCTAD will be provided with necessary resources to continue and accelerate its very desirable work in this field.

The UN General Assembly

As a result of the work of UNCTAD, the specific actions required on the part of the international community have often been taken up by the UN General Assembly itself. For instance, in its Resolution 46/212 of 22 December 1991, the General Assembly recognized that 'the lack of territorial access to the sea, aggravated by remoteness and isolation from world markets, and prohibitive transit costs and risks impose serious constraints on the overall socio-economic development efforts of the landlocked developing countries'. In the same resolution, it invited the secretary-general of UNCTAD to carry out specific studies in the following areas:

(a) Implications of high transit costs on the overall development of the landlocked developing countries;

(b) identification of specific areas in the context of sub-regional and regional cooperation for the promotion and integration of transit infrastructure and services and harmonization of transit transport policies and legislation and the assessment of regional trade possibilities for the expansion of the trade sector of landlocked developing countries;

(c) improvement of current transit insurance regimes;

(d) application of new information technology to improve transit services;

(e) identification of specific training needs to improve the managerial capacities and the skills of personnel involved in transit operations to ensure effective utilization of transit transport facilities;

(f) development and expansion of all other alternatives and/or complements to ground transportation in order to improve the access of landlocked countries to foreign markets.

The resolution appealed to all states, international organizations, and financial institutions and its implementation was viewed as a matter of urgency and priority. The specific actions related to the particular needs and problems of landlocked developing countries envisaged in resolutions of UNCTAD and other documents such as the Programme of Action for the Least Developed Countries for the 1990s, and the International Development Strategy for the Fourth United Nations Development Decade. The same appeal was reiterated in General Assembly Resolutions 48/169 of 21 December 1993 and 50/97 of 20 December 1995.

Other UN Bodies

Many other UN bodies and specialized agencies support and supplement the activities of UNCTAD concerning the problems of landlocked states. Among them, the most active have been the UN Development Programme (UNDP), the UN Economic and Social Commission for Asia and the Pacific (ESCAP, formerly ECAFE), the UN Economic Commission for Africa (ECA), the UN Economic Commission for Latin America and the Caribbean (ECLAC or CEPAL), and the UN Economic Commission for Europe (ECE). For instance, the ECA is currently involved in coordinating and facilitating the consolidation and establishment of a network of transport corridors with appropriate mixes of transport modes, including those that serve the interests of the landlocked states of Africa. It is also going to conduct a survey of transit costs for transit transport. Similarly, ESCAP has focused its assistance for the Asian landlocked and transit states on land transport, transit arrangements, environment and natural resource management, technical development and trade promotion. The ESCAP project on Asian Land Transport Infrastructure Development (ALTID), for example, is expected to be a major contribution to the development of transport infrastructure in the Asian region.[37]

Other International Treaties

A number of other international treaties deal with various aspects of transit transport. Among them are the 1972 Customs Convention on Containers, the 1975 Customs Convention on the International Transport of Goods under TIR Carnets (TIR Convention), the Kyoto International Convention on the Simplification and Harmonization of Customs Procedures, the 1982 International Convention on the Harmonization of Frontier Controls of Goods, the International Convention concerning the Carriage of Goods by Rail, and the Convention on the Contract for the International Carriage of Goods by Road.[38]

The TIR Convention is designed to enable vehicles or containers carrying the TIR Carnet to journey from their point of departure to their point of destination without having to undergo any customs examination when crossing intermediate boundaries. The Kyoto Convention, currently being revised, provides a comprehensive guide to the major customs procedures. Similarly, the 1972 Customs Convention on Containers was designed to facilitate the use of containers by granting temporary admission to a country, without customs documents being required on their importation and re-exportation, and without furnishing a form of security. However, the participation of developing transit and landlocked states in these treaty regimes has not been encouraging. If these states were to accede to these treaties and implement their provisions in practice, transit transport of goods to and from landlocked states would be less cumbersome, more efficient, and less time-consuming.

From Norm-setting to Implementation

As the process for firmly establishing the rights and freedoms of landlocked states in international law, especially those relating to freedom of transit and right of free access to and from the sea, has brought about a generally satisfactory outcome for landlocked states, attention is now focused on implementing these rights and freedoms in practice. Indeed, the adoption of the Law of the Sea Convention and its entry into force in 1994 have not left much room for the time being for further strengthening of the position of landlocked states in international law. It is now natural to pay more attention to the economic problems faced by developing landlocked states in the face of their worsening economic situation, growing trade imbalance, and increasing economic marginalization.

As stated earlier, of the 42 landlocked states, 31 or so are developing countries, among which 16 are least developed countries. That is one reason why the problem of landlocked states has been considered within a wide spectrum of UN activities dealing with developing and least developed countries. Leading in these activities has been UNCTAD. This agency has played a very important role in enhancing the cause of the developing landlocked states. However, forces at play within and outside the UN at this juncture in history are seeking to undermine the work of such agencies. In the name of restructuring and reorganization of the UN system, agencies such as UNCTAD seem to have been subjected to cut after cut in their budget and personnel. While the UN General Assembly is asking UNCTAD to do more for developing landlocked states year in year out, the diminishing resources at the disposal of this body do not seem to allow it to undertake the tasks assigned to it.

Unfortunately, this seems to be the situation for many UN agencies involved in development activities. Most of the developed states wish to see a diminished role for the UN in development activities in order to help resolve the financial difficulties faced by this world body, even as the political leaders in these states are advocating less government in their own countries and less action internationally on such issues. What is more, globalization, marketization, liberalization, and privatization have taken hold in more or less every area of economic activity, be it global or local, and private actors rather than public ones have become more influential in today's international economic climate.

Currently, the principal concern of developed states appears to be to fight an economic battle to maintain their present level of prosperity rather than to extend a helping hand to less fortunate states. The idea of South–South cooperation has withered away in this process of globalization and liberalization. Overwhelmed by the forces of change, the developing states themselves are in disarray and are no longer capable of maintaining their solidarity to secure a fairer collective deal for them. Most of them are competing individually for prosperity and accelerating their efforts for industrial development. Left behind are those countries that are less developed among the developing states, and especially the least developed landlocked states who are geographically disadvantaged, economically weak, and are sorely in need of support from the UN and other international organizations.

If the developed countries of the world were to halt the decay in their morality and revive the idea of a fairer international economic system for all, they would have to help the UN create a system designed to enable the landlocked states to compete on an equal footing in accordance with the GATT/WTO ideals of 'free and fair play for all'. The efforts of UNCTAD and other bodies have been geared to enabling the landlocked states to prosper on their own feet. These agencies should be allowed to continue and accelerate their efforts to this effect. What is needed is an efficient, cost-effective, and speedy system of transportation for these geographically disadvantaged states. They need help to modernize the existing infrastructure and build new facilities for their exports and imports as the international community has recognized that the 'geographical situation of landlocked countries is *an added constraint* on their overall ability to cope with the challenges of development' (emphasis added).[39]

Regional and Sub-Regional Cooperation

One of the ways the UN can help in this direction would be to bring the landlocked and transit states together to create sub-regional or regional regimes for cooperation to improve transport facilities for all participants. The UN has played a rather encouraging role in promoting regional cooperation in other areas such as environmental protection through the Oceans and Coastal Areas Programme of the UN Environment Programme (UNEP). There are already regional economic or trading blocs in many parts of the world, which are encouraging developments. This process should be used to advance the cause of landlocked states.

Indeed, the UN Convention on the Law of the Sea, which is the latest word on the right of free access to and from the sea of landlocked states, speaks of the need for regional and sub-regional cooperation agreements for the implementation of the rights secured under the convention. One cannot agree more with Professor Glassner when he states that economic cooperation 'short of complete economic and/or political integration' among landlocked and their transit states, 'is the only way that the handicap of landlockedness can be overcome'.[40] Indeed, the General Assembly of the UN has invited UNDP 'to promote, as appropriate, sub-regional,

regional, and inter-regional projects and programmes and to expand its support in the transport and communications sectors to the landlocked and transit developing countries and its technical cooperation for development geared towards promoting national and collective self-reliance among them'.[41]

Conclusion

Should there be an UNCLOS IV some time in the future, the landlocked states should endeavour to make their rights and freedoms self-executing, not dependent on the goodwill of transit states, and to have the term *legitimate interests* defined so that the latter cannot deny landlocked states their rights and freedoms under a variety of pretexts. Meanwhile, whatever the weaknesses of the 1982 Convention, it contains the best provisions possible at this point for landlocked states. That is why it is in their best interests to accede to or ratify the convention as soon as they can, for only then will they be able to claim their marine fishery rights, however weak and limited, in the EEZs of their coastal neighbours, participate in deep seabed mining activities through the International Seabed Authority, and benefit from the contributions to be made by coastal states from the exploitation of the natural resources in their continental shelves lying beyond 200 nautical miles.

The same can be said of international treaties dealing with transit transport of goods. As stated earlier, many such treaties have not yet been ratified by many developing landlocked and transit states. There are a number of reasons for such lack of participation. As pointed out in a report by the UNCTAD Secretariat, one of the principal reasons seems to be the absence of clear understanding on the part of such states of the content and implications of some of the conventions:

> The implicit obligations and prospective benefits after ratification are not necessarily obvious. This is a major challenge to the relevant international and intergovernmental organizations like UNCTAD, the regional economic commissions, Customs Cooperation Council, etc, to provide technical expertise to those member states that require it so as to clarify the implications and benefits of adhering to these Conventions.[42]

Indeed, UNCTAD and other UN agencies can do a great deal to help landlocked states not only to enable them to benefit from the existing international legal framework, but also to develop regional and sub-regional transit transport projects for the mutual benefit of both transit and landlocked states.[43]

This is because

> although the trade performance of landlocked developing countries depends critically on the nature of transit systems serving their overseas exports and imports, they, acting alone, cannot establish, manage and maintain such systems. Transit by road, rail or water necessarily implies the joint use by landlocked and coastal countries of the transport facilities of the latter, and also jointly agreed rules and procedures to facilitate speedy and efficient transit. Cooperation between landlocked countries and their transit neighbours is thus of critical importance.[44]

This recognition of the importance of cooperation between the landlocked and their transit neighbours seems to have influenced the entire agenda of the UN and its specialized agencies in the recent past. Accordingly, the entire emphasis has been on the promotion of cooperative projects in different parts of the world in various areas of economic activity. This process is very encouraging and should be accelerated by the various UN agencies, such as UNCTAD and UNDP. After a period of norm-setting, the UN should now concentrate on implementing the norms enshrined in various international instruments.

The UN has done a remarkable job in having the rights and freedoms of landlocked states firmly established in international law within the last five decades, but not enough in realizing these rights in practice. What are now needed are concrete supplementary and complementary measures based on regional and sub-regional cooperation between the landlocked and transit states to bring into effect the rights and freedoms of landlocked states, both for their benefit and that of their transit neighbours.

With regard to the implications of these efforts of the UN for Indo-Nepal relations, it can be said that with or without a bilateral transit treaty Nepal as a landlocked state is entitled to the rights embodied in the various international instruments, and whether or not Nepal or India become parties to the treaties discussed above, India is under an obligation to respect Nepal's rights under these treaties because most of their provisions have acquired the character of customary rules of international law.

Notes and References

1. An earlier version of this chapter was published in Martin Ira Glassner (ed.), *The United Nations at Work* (Westport, Connecticut: Praeger, 1998), pp. 134–60.

2. The geographical distribution of the 42 landlocked states is as follows: 15 in Africa (Botswana, Burkina Faso, Burundi, Central African Republic, Chad, Ethiopia, Lesotho, Malawi, Mali, Niger, Rwanda, Swaziland, Uganda, Zambia, and Zimbabwe); 12 in Asia (Afghanistan, Armenia, Azerbaijan, Bhutan, Kazakhstan, Kyrgyzstan, Laos, Mongolia, Nepal, Tajikistan, Turkmenistan and Uzbekistan); 13 in Europe (Andorra, Austria, Belarus, Czech Republic, the Holy See, Hungary, Liechtenstein, Luxembourg, Macedonia, Moldova, San Marino, Slovakia, and Switzerland); and two in South America (Bolivia and Paraguay).

3. There were only six independent developing landlocked states in 1957: Afghanistan, Bhutan, Bolivia, Laos, Nepal, and Paraguay; by 1992 the number had grown to 28. 47 states are currently classified as least developed, and 16 of these are landlocked. See, generally, a report by the UNCTAD secretariat, 'Transit Systems for Landlocked Developing Countries: Current Situation and Proposals for Future Action' of 26 March 1993: TD/B/LDC/AC.1/2.

4. A pioneering and widely read work on the problem of being landlocked is by Martin Ira Glassner, *Access to the Sea for Developing Land-locked States* (The Hague: Martinus Nijhoff, 1970).

5. General Framework Agreement for Peace in Bosnia and Herzegovina signed at Paris on 14 Dec. 1995 and Annexes with related Agreements and Conclusions of the Peace Implementation Conference held in London on 8–9 Dec. 1995 in Cm 3154, London: HMSO, Misce. no. 6 (1996).

6. TD/B/LDC/AC.1/2, p. 2.

7. A Mpazi Sinjela, *Land-locked States and the UNCLOS Regime* (London, Rome, New York: Oceana, 1983), p. 5.

8. TD/191, p. 200 (6 Jan. 1976), cited in Sinjela, ibid.

9. Martin Ira Glassner (ed.), *Bibliography on Land-Locked States: Fourth Revised and Enlarged Edition* (Dordrecht/Boston/London: Martinus Nijhoff, 1995), 'Introduction to the Second Edition', p. 3.

10. Hugo Grotius, *De Jure Belli ac Pacis,* bk II, ch. II, sec. iii; English trans. in Brown (ed.), *Classics of International Law*, 1925, pp. 196–7.

11. Emerich de Vattel, *Le Droit des Gens ou Principes de loi Naturelle Appliques a la Conduite aux Affaires des Nations et des Souverains,* English trans. in Brown, (ed.), *Classics of International Law* (1916), pp. 150–1.

12. League of Nations, *Treaty Series,* vol. 7, p. 11.

13. UN, Office of the Special Representative of the Secretary-General for

the Law of the Sea, *The Law of the Sea: Rights of Access of Land-locked States to and from the Sea and Freedom of Transit. Legislative History of Part X, Articles 124 to 132 of the United Nations Convention on the Law of the Sea* (hereinafter UN, *Rights of Access)* (New York: UN, 1987), p. 4.

14. See, generally, E. Lauterpacht, 'Freedom of Transit in International Law', *Grotius Society Transactions for the Year 1958 and 1959*, vol. 44, pp. 313–56; and for a very useful discussion of the developments within the UN and in international legal literature, see A/Conf 13/29 and Add 1 in *The First United Nations Conference on the Law of the Sea, Official Records*, vol. I.

15. GATT Secretariat, *The Results of the Uruguay Round of Multilateral Trade Negotiations: The Legal Texts* (Geneva, 1994), p. 492.

16. Quoted in UN, *Rights of Access,* p. 15.

17. Ibid.

18. E/CN.11/425, para. 103.

19. GA Resolution 1028 (XI) of 20 Feb. 1957.

20. Quoted in UN, *Rights of Access,* p. 9.

21. Ibid., p. 10.

22. Ibid., p. 11.

23. UN, *Treaty Series*, vol. 450, p. 11.

24. For a detailed account of such activities within and outside of the Conference, see UN, *Rights of Access.*

25. A/AC.138/93, *Official Records of the Third United Nations Conference on the Law of the Sea*, vol. III (Sales no E.75.V.5), A/Conf.62/C.2/L.29.

26. As quoted in UN, *Rights of Access*, p. 52.

27. See, generally, Surya P. Subedi, *Land-locked Nepal and International Law* (Kathmandu, 1989), ch. 5; and Government of Nepal, Ministry of Communications, *Nepal and India: Facts and Chronology of the Problem* (Kathmandu, 1989).

28. See, generally, Stephen C. Vasciannie, *Land-locked and Geographically Disadvantaged States in the International Law of the Sea* (New York: Oxford University Press, 1990), chs. 3, 4, and 6; and Lucius Caflisch, 'Land-locked States and Their Access to and from the Sea', *British Yearbook of International Law*, vol. 49, 1978, pp. 71–100.

29. UN, *The Law of the Sea: Official Text of the United Nations Convention of the Law of the Sea with Annexes and Index* (hereinafter UN, *Official Text of the Convention)* (New York: 1983), p. 29.

30. UN, *Official Text of the Convention,* p. 24.

31. For a detailed discussion of this point, see Surya P. Subedi, 'The Marine Fishery Rights of Landlocked States with Particular Reference to the EEZ', *International Journal of Estuarine and Coastal Law*, vol. 2, no. 4, pp. 227–39; and Farin Mirvahabi, 'The Rights of the Landlocked and Geographically Disadvantaged

States in Exploitation of Marine Fisheries', *Netherlands International Law Review*, vol. 26, no. 2, 1979, 130–62.

32. UN, *Official Text of the Convention*, p. 46.

33. The work of UNCTAD has been very carefully documented by Glassner in his *Bibliography on Land-locked States*, pp. 24–33.

34. See TD/B/42(1)/11-TD/B/LD/AC.1/7, 2 Aug. 1995.

35. Other noteworthy recent UNCTAD documents include 'Improvement of Transit Transport Systems in Land-locked and Transit Developing Countries: Issues for Consideration', (UNCTAD/LLDC/SYMP/3) and 'Sub-regional and Regional Synopsis of the Current Transit Transport Situation and Difficulties', (UNCTAD/LLDC/SYMP/4 of 16 Dec. 1994). While the first document focuses on sectoral problems related to various transit transport infrastructure facilities and services and highlights possible actions to overcome them, the second provides a very good account of the current transit transport situations in the different regions and sub-regions, as well as the constraints on improving them. See also TD/B/LDC/AC.1/8/Add.1 of 6 Sept. 1995; A/50/341 of 22 Sept. 1995; and UNCTAD/LDC/97 of 13 March 1995.

36. TD/B/LDC/AC.1/2 of 26 March 1993, pp. 27–8.

37. For more details on these and other projects, see UN Doc.A/50/341 of 22 Sept. 1995.

38. For a summary of the provisions of these treaties and the status of their implementation, see UNCTAD/LDC/92 of 5 Aug. 1994.

39. General Assembly Resolution 44/214 of 22 Dec. 1989.

40. Glassner, 'Introduction to the Fourth Edition', in his *Bibliography on Land-locked States,* p. 7.

41. General Assembly Resolution 50/97 of 20 Dec. 1995 on 'Specific Actions Related to the Particular Needs and Problems of Land-locked Developing Countries', operative para. 8.

42. UNCTAD/LDC/92, pp. 14–5.

43. See also the recommendations of the Second Meeting of Governmental Experts from Landlocked and Transit Developing Countries and Representatives of Donor Countries and Financial and Development Institutions held in New York in 1995, TD/B/42(1)/11-TD/B/LDC/AC.1/7, 2 Aug. 1995.

44. TD/B/LDC/AC.1/2, p. 3.

5

The Marine Fishery Rights of Landlocked States and Nepal's Rights in the EEZ of Neighbouring Countries

Introduction

The latter half of the last century became an era of great competition between coastal states to enclose as large areas as possible of the high seas within their zones of national jurisdiction.[1] Those areas of the high seas that continue to be 'open to all', have been radically reduced. With the introduction of the concept of the 200-miles Exclusive Economic Zone (EEZ) and the extensive claims to continental shelf areas, most of the economically valuable parts of the high seas are now subject to the jurisdiction of coastal states. The result is that often only the 'biological desert'[2] areas remain under the high seas regime.

In the sixteenth century, coastal states such as Spain and Portugal[3] divided the oceans between themselves, according to the current doctrine of *mare clausum*. However, the hard-won concept of *mare liberum* now seems to be reversing itself because of the jurisdictional extensions of the coastal states. In the twentieth century, 'the era of the re-colonization of the seas',[4] the 42 landlocked states (LLS) of the world have been struggling to obtain their fundamental rights of free access to and from the sea, and equal opportunities in the exploration and exploitation of the living and non-living resources they contain.

Between the Barcelona Convention and Statute on Freedom of Transit (1921)[5] and the 1982 Convention on the Law of the Sea (LOSC),[6] the LLS have sought to assert greater rights. The LLS gained a few rights in attempts made prior to the Third UN Convention on the Law of the Sea

(UNCLOS III). UNCLOS III provided them with an important opportunity, for it had been convened in order to seek to 'accommodate the interests and needs of all states, whether landlocked or coastal'[7] under international law of the sea, in accordance with the UN's purpose, inter alia, 'to achieve international cooperation in solving international problems', e.g. those having an economic or humanitarian character.[8]

Throughout the nine consecutive years of the conference period, the LLS strove to have their interests accommodated. Many coastal states, however, appeared to be against any significant concessions to the LLS, and finally a more or less coastal state oriented convention was adopted. The result is that the LLS have been described by writers such as Prescott,[9] Wijkman,[10] Sinjela,[11] and Larson[12] as the 'great losers' in UNCLOS III. However, some of the LLS' rights have been reaffirmed by the convention; some, although a limited number, have been introduced, and for some the prospects are good, so long as they are properly utilized. Among them, the marine fishery rights of the LLS, in general with reference to the high seas and in particular with reference to the EEZ, are of importance. During UNCLOS III, the LLS spent a considerable amount of energy in securing their rights under the new EEZ regime, and for many reasons this regime is significant for them.

This chapter aims at analysing the marine fishery rights of the LLS with particular reference to the EEZ. However, a discussion such as this must inevitably touch upon other issues concerning the entire body of problems faced by the LLS. That is why this chapter begins by an examination of the factual background of the LLS and their rights in general in relation to the law of the sea. It will then concentrate on the main issue, that of their fishery rights. Finally, an effort will be made to present some workable strategies for landlocked countries in general and Nepal in particular.

Landlocked States: Factual Background

Forty-two states of the world[13]—12 in Asia, 15 in Africa, two in Latin America, and 13 in Europe (although the status of five of the European states is described by some jurists as 'somewhat controversial')[14]—are landlocked, so defined by not having a sea coast.[15] All LLS are separated from the sea by coastal states and, apart from Bolivia, Lesotho, and Malawi, all lie far from the sea. In the past, the so-called transit states, through which traffic must pass from LLS to reach the sea, particularly of Asia,

Africa, and Latin America, have been inconsiderate with regard to significant concessions to their neighbouring LLS. On many occasions these transit states, in their own national interests, have unduly pressurized the LLS even to the extent of hindering the supply of commodities necessary for the survival of human life.[16]

The LLS belong to most economic and political groupings of the world, i.e., the European Union, the Organization of American States, the Non-Aligned Movement, and the Organization of African Unity, etc., but when the issue of facilities for the LLS is involved non-LLS often tend to ignore the interests of their economic and political allies. This was clearly seen during UNCLOS III. Although currently very few LLS have a fishing fleet or the capacity to fish, this does not mean that they are unlikely to exercise their rights. Most of the LLS are poor. Among the 31 least developed countries of the world, 16 are LLS,[17] and acutely in need of nutritious food for their increasing populations. According to Churchill and Lowe, not only do these LLS 'suffer from the lack of direct access to the sea and its resources but many of them are also deficient in natural land resources'.[18] That is why, rights to the living and non-living resources of the sea are vital to these states. Conscious of this, the LLS have been struggling to establish for themselves rights under general international law, for bilateral rights so often depend on the pleasure of the coastal states.

The Right of Free Access to the Sea

Until the 1960s, the LLS were primarily concerned with an assured right of free access to the sea. Without this right, no other rights, such as navigation, exploration, or exploitation of the living and non-living resources of the sea, can be exercised. That is why, before assessing marine fishery rights, a brief look at the other rights of LLS seems necessary. Sinjela suggests that the right of free access to the sea by the LLS was 'originally founded on principles of natural law'.[19] He adds that this is a 'necessary corollary to accepted notions of freedom of the high seas'. From the earlier writings of Grotius up to Lauterpacht, many jurists have maintained that LLS have the right of free access to and from the sea in international law.[20] Article 23(2) of the Covenant of the League of Nations,[21] the Barcelona Convention (1921),[22] Article V of GATT (1948),[23] Article 33 of the Havana Charter (1948),[24] and the UN General Assembly Resolutions 1028 (xi)[25] and 1105 (xi)[26] have recognized the rights of LLS to free access to the sea.

Similarly, Article 3 of the 1958 Geneva Convention on the High Seas firmly recognized such rights, but they were *pactum de contrahendo* because of the requirement of 'mutual consent'. The terminology of Article 3 of the 1958 High Seas Convention is as follows:

In order to enjoy the freedom of the seas on equal terms with Coastal States, States having no Sea-Coast should have free access to the sea ...[27]

Hence, the right of access under the HSC appears to be *lege ferenda* rather than *lex lata* because of the use of the word 'should' rather than 'shall'. As a result of further attempts by the LLS in the ECAFE Manila Conference (1963)[28] and the Tehran Conference (1964),[29] in 1964 UNCTAD prepared a Convention on the Transit Trade of Landlocked States which was adopted by a UN Conference in 1965.[30] Being the first convention solely relating to the rights of LLS, it provided wider rights because of free access to the sea for LLS, but its effect was considerably reduced by the insignificant number of ratifications: only 31 to date.[31]

After the efforts of LLS during UNCLOS III, Part X of LOSC does grant them clear rights of free access to the sea. These rights are more forcefully phrased (i.e. with the use of the word 'shall') and are independent of the requirement of 'mutual consent'.[32] Yet still the terms and modalities for exercising these rights reside in mutual consent.[33] However, the transit state can neither deny the LLS rights of free access nor avoid entering into mutual agreements for the terms and modalities. Lauterpacht argues that 'the legal right of freedom of transit arises independently of a treaty' and the coastal state, 'has a legal obligation to consent'.[34] This juristic view of the 'obligation to cooperate' resembles the purposes of the UN[35] and the UN General Assembly Resolution 2625 (XXV).[36] It should also be borne in mind that the LLS' right is not only based on treaty provisions, but is also founded in customary international law. For over a century the right of transit has been exercised by LLS, and other states have consented to it. The International Court of Justice (ICJ) in the *Right of Passage* case[37] lends some support to this view.

Other Rights

The LLS' rights of navigation, innocent passage, access to ports, and other facilities and immunities are also established as corollaries of the rights of free access to, and the freedom of, the high seas. The Treaty of Versailles (1919)[38] (Art. 273), and the various articles of HSC, TSC, and LOSC[39] have incorporated these rights: they are less controversial and are thus generally accorded to the LLS equally with other states. LLS have no rights to the sub-marine mineral resources of the rich continental shelves. Claims to the continental shelf, which began in 1945, were thought to be a derogation from the Grisbadarna Doctrine[40] and the high seas *res communis* character. Now, it has been considered to have entered into customary as well as conventional international law, mainly through the *North Sea Continental Shelf* cases,[41] the Continental Shelf Convention 1958,[42] and the LOSC.[43]

The LOSC contains a number of provisions relating to LLS' rights to share in the revenues from the exploitation of deep seabed resources. Yet, due to the lack of consensus in adopting the LOSC, some of the developed countries (which were expected to contribute financially and technologically to exploiting the deep seabed minerals) did not become a party to it right until 1994 when the Convention entered into force.[44] This was one of the principal obstacles to the functioning of the Deep Seabed Authority. The provisions of the Convention concerning the mining of the deep seabed were changed in 1994 through an agreement to satisfy the few developed countries, mainly the US. Even then the US has not ratified the Convention. The idea of mining the resources of the deep seabed for the benefit of mankind as a whole is now a far-fetched phenomenon and therefore the LLS are not likely to derive any benefit from these resources in the near future.

The Marine Fishery Rights of LLS

Fishery Resources

The sea has long been used primarily for navigation and fishing. Fisheries have provided a livelihood for a significant proportion of the world's population. For instance, the economy of Iceland is largely dependent on fish or fish products.[45] Along with the recognition of this fact in the *Fisheries Jurisdiction* case,[46] the ICJ accepted the Norwegian dependence on fisheries and supported its claim in the *Anglo-Norwegian Fisheries* case.[47] Fisheries, although finite in comparison with some other natural resources, are capable of perpetual renewal, and through proper management the fish population can be increased. Larson says that 80 per cent of the earth's animal life is found in the oceans.[48] In 1980, 64.6 million tonnes of fish were caught.[49] According to the most reliable estimates, the potential world catch of familiar types of marine fish is around 100 million tonnes per annum.[50] Its value is one of the major contributions to the total potential productivity of the world's oceans (which is worth at least 200 billion dollars).[51] The LLS are also among the claimants of this common, naturally endowed, wealth. Their rights will be examined by consideration of the high seas regime and the EEZ regime.

Access to the High Seas' Fisheries' Resources

Colombos writes: 'It follows from the doctrine of the freedom of the seas that fishing everywhere on the high seas is open to the subjects of all States'.[52] As we have seen, LLS have the right of free access to the sea for the purpose of enjoyment of the freedom of the high seas. Customary international law, Article 2 of the HSC and Article 87 of the LOSC stipulate that on the high seas all states (including LLS) should enjoy, inter alia, freedom of fishing.

However, for the LLS, exploiting fishery resources on the high seas is disadvantageous. The coastal states' jurisdictional expansion from the 'cannon-shot' rule to 200 miles of EEZ has pushed the LLS' high seas access too far from the shore. This will obviously result in more expensive fishing but, most importantly, the larger concentration of fish is in the EEZ; the high seas are not considered rich. Most of the familiar types of marine fishery stocks are under pressure from over-exploitation: the remaining ones are expensive to exploit, of low value, and difficult to process. Moreover, the technologically advanced states, which are able to fish at greater distances, will certainly harvest more in this free area. All these factors make the LLS unable to effectively utilize their rights.

Access to the EEZ Fisheries Resources

Factual Background

As far as marine resources are concerned, the EEZ is most important. It has embraced almost 36 per cent of the total area of the sea. Nearly 90 per cent of the world's fish catch is from the EEZ; 87 per cent of all hydrocarbon reserves, and most of the world's sea traffic and scientific research are also found in this area.[53]

Phytoplankton, consisting of microscopic plants, is the basic food source of fish. The richest phytoplankton pastures lie within 200 nautical miles of the continents. They need a supply of mineral salts, such as sodium chloride and calcium carbonate, as well as sunlight for their growth. These are commonly available in the upper layers of the seas around the world's coasts.[54] That is why the largest concentration of fish is within the EEZ, and now it has become the centre of attention for LLS as well as coastal states.

Legal Significance of the EEZ

The EEZ is an area beyond the 12-mile territorial sea not exceeding 188 miles (or 200 miles from the base-lines). The LOSC (while maintaining the freedom of the high seas, e.g., navigation, overflight, etc.), has given sovereign rights over this exclusive economic zone to the coastal state 'for the purpose of exploring, exploiting, conserving, and managing the natural resources'.[55] Akehurst argues that to some extent the word 'exclusive' is misleading because other states' economic interests are also included in this zone.[56] The EEZ is a specific legal regime, sui generis in character, which is the result of the compromise between the major maritime powers (i.e. the developed states) and the developing ones. Although the LOSC itself has come into force, the concept of the EEZ is also considered to have been entered into the international law of the sea, both through state practice and through international judicial decisions.[57]

When the coastal states began to claim an EEZ, no protests based on well-established rules were registered against such claims. In fact, some states, which had protested other states' earlier claims, began to claim theirs. Fishing zones' claims were motivated, as Harris states, *inter alia*, 'by a genuine concern for conservation' of fisheries.[58] As early as 1985, 104 out of 140 coastal states had claimed exclusive fishing rights within 200 miles.[59] The ICJ, in the *Fisheries Jurisdiction* case, while declining to answer the UK's general question as to whether Iceland's claim was valid *ergo omnes*, held that Iceland's claim was not opposable to the UK.[60] During UNCLOS III most of the states accepted the EEZ concept. Some states, such as the UK which did not initially claim an EEZ but an Exclusive Fishing Zone (EFZ), which is similar to the former but with particular respect to fishing rights, have not objected to the EEZ claims of other states. Churchill and Lowe consider this new fisheries regime 'to represent customary international law' because of the 'wealth of State practice'.[61]

The LLS, although initially opposed to this concept, later sought to accommodate their own rights within the EEZ regime rather than to continue to oppose it once its acceptance seemed certain. Through the Kampala Declaration (1974),[62] an alliance between the LLS and Geographically Disadvantaged States (GDS) (described by some writers as 'a private club'[63]), the Nandan Committee, the Group of 77, and the like, the LLS sought to incorporate their fishery rights into the LOSC. Most of the LLS voted in favour of the LOSC at its adoption. Within the LLS themselves, public opinion concerning the convention was enthusiastic. A notable example is landlocked Switzerland's leading paper's comment that the adoption of the LOSC is a success 'against the law of the jungle', which appeared under the heading 'Le "niet" de M. Reagan'.[64] With the exception of Andorra, Byelorussia, the Holy See, and San Marino, all the LLS are among the 159 signatories[65] to the LOSC; quite a few landlocked states, including Mali and Zambia, have also ratified it.[66]

Therefore, this new fishing regime (and both EEZ and Exclusive Fishing Zone (EFZ) are considered on a par for the purpose of this chapter), being a part of customary and conventional international law, may not be challenged by the LLS or any other states. This is the context within which the fishery rights of the LLS will be examined.

The LOSC Provisions

Article 69(1) of the LOSC provides that the LLS 'shall have the right to participate, on an equitable basis, in the exploitation of an appropriate part of the surplus of the living resources' of the neighbouring coastal states' EEZ, 'taking into account the relevant economic and geographical circumstances of all the States concerned' and in conformity with other provisions. This vague, elastic, and windy language imposes a lot of qualifications on the rights of the LLS and still leaves some crucial questions unanswered. First, while the coastal state has the right, inter alia, to *explore* and *exploit* in its EEZ (Art. 59(1)(a)), the LLS only have the right of *exploitation*. Second, while coastal states have rights over the living and non-living resources of its EEZ, the LLS have rights only over the living resources.

Third, the LLS only have rights over surplus resources and not over the entire surplus, but only to 'an appropriate part of the surplus'. Who will decide what is an appropriate part? Fourth, this participation must be 'on an equitable basis', but who is to decide how much is equitable? Between whom will this equitable basis apply? Is there no priority basis? Fifth, the relevant economic and geographical circumstances of all states concerned must be taken into account. Who is to take such account? What are relevant and irrelevant economic and geographical circumstances? Who is to decide this? Sixth, fishery rights will apply only in the same region or sub-region, but in the case of some states this may cause problems. Take, for example, the central African state of Chad which has as its immediate neighbours coastal states fronting the Mediterranean Sea, the Indian Ocean, and the Atlantic. Where is her region or sub-region for fishing? None of these questions are answered in this provision. Also, in section 2 of Article 69, still more qualifications are added, for the LLS' rights are made subject to agreement with other states.

Total Allowable Catch, Harvesting Capacity, and Surplus

The provisions of Article 69 are dependent on Articles 61 and 62. Article 61(1) requires the coastal state to determine the total allowable catch (TAC) of fisheries in its EEZ, and Article 62(2) requires the coastal state to determine its harvesting capacity. The difference between the TAC and the harvesting capacity is determined as surplus, over which the LLS, along with other states, have fishing rights.

Here the question arises whether the coastal state is under an obligation to determine the TAC. The word 'shall' in paragraph (1) of Article 61, and other provisions of paragraphs (2) and (5), appear to have made it obligatory. This is because the determination of the TAC is a technical task that is expected to be done on the 'best scientific evidence' available (para. (2)). Moreover, paragraph (5) gives LLS nationals access to the contribution and exchange of information such as 'catch ... statistics and other data'. However, if this data is simply not available, and in the absence of effective international organizations, the determination of the TAC, as Judge Oda says, would be 'extremely difficult'[67]—it could be set, according to Copes, 'possibly at zero'.[68] The same problems apply to the determination of harvesting capacity.

Hence, the very existence of LLS rights in the surplus is entirely dependent upon the coastal state determining that a surplus exists within its EEZ. This surplus is the difference between its declared TAC and its own harvesting capacity. In the absence of objective data on both issues it is a relatively simple matter for coastal states to determine that the TAC and harvesting capacity correspond and that there is therefore no surplus and LLS rights are effectively eliminated.

Even if such a surplus is declared, the LLS have no *automatic* access to the surplus, for Article 62(2) provides that such access is to be exercised only through 'agreements or other arrangements', and pursuant to the terms, conditions, laws and regulations of the coastal states relating to the, inter alia, conservation and management of the fisheries.

Coastal State Discretion

Thus, it can be seen that the coastal state has wide discretionary powers in permitting the access of other states to its surplus. Despite the US proposal during UNCLOS III to specify priorities, in particular for the LLS,[69] Article 62(3) leaves this matter to the discretion of the coastal states. Although this article *obliges* the coastal states by the use of the word 'shall' to take into account the rights of the LLS, it still permits coastal states to take into account 'all relevant factors' or even its own national interest. Therefore, the rights given to the LLS by the LOSC, are, as Prescott concludes, 'sufficiently ambiguous to allow any obdurate coastal state to stall applications from landlocked states indefinitely'.[70]

Other Provisions

Article 69(3) attempts to secure the rights of the LLS even if the coastal states' harvesting capacity approaches a point where there would be no surplus. In this situation, the states concerned 'shall cooperate in the establishment of equitable arrangements on a bilateral, sub-regional, or regional basis to allow for the participation of developing landlocked states' in that area. Thus, while Article 69(1) imposes legal obligations solely on a coastal state to give access to the LLS in the case of surplus, paragraph (3) widens this obligation from bilateral to multilateral regional or sub-regional cooperation. This provision again makes the rights of the LLS *pactum de contrahendo* among the states concerned. Whereas the rights of paragraph (1) are for all LLS, those of paragraph (3) are for *developing*

LLS only. Paragraph (4) further narrows the rights of *developed* LLS: it limits their rights in the EEZ to *developed* states which will rarely have a surplus because of their high capability.

If there is no surplus, there are no rights for *developed* LLS. O'Connell considers this as something of a concession to *developing* LLS, and as the effect of the New International Economic Order.[71] Article 71 eliminates the LLS' rights of fishing where a coastal state's economy is overwhelmingly dependent on the fisheries. Who is to decide this? Can it be challenged? Can coastal states act arbitrarily? These unanswered questions and the provision without qualification endanger the interests of the LLS.[72]

Article 72 restricts the LLS from transferring their rights to others. Prohibition also in joint ventures impedes the LLS' interests, not only in obtaining animal protein for their populations but also in employment opportunities and in developing their own fishing industries.

Legal Remedies

Legal rights without effective remedies are merely decorations. Disputes such as the refusal of coastal states to determine the TAC or harvesting capacity, or to allocate surplus, may arise. They may be settled, if not by negotiation, then by resource to any procedure agreed between themselves, or by submitting to a conciliation commission[73] (although its report is not binding). However, it is important to note that under Article 297(3), LOSC certain key disputes are excluded from compulsory adjudication. Article 297(3) provides:

> 'A State party which has made a declaration under paragraph 1 shall not be entitled to submit any dispute falling within the excepted category of disputes to any procedure in this Convention as against another State party without the consent of the party'.[74]

Thus, the coastal states with whom the LLS have to assert their rights are not subject to the *compulsory* dispute settlement procedure in relation to virtually all the issues on which disputes may arise. Disputes may only be settled by this procedure by mutual consent. Mutual consent raises reciprocity. According to Caflish, these small LLS 'have no reciprocity to offer'.[75] After surveying the national legislative trends of coastal states, Moore[76] finds that they have ignored any obligation to give access to any surplus to foreign vessels. Therefore, it appears that the LLS are unlikely to get justice from coastal states.

To summarize, the LLS, as Sinjela concludes, 'have almost lost everything in an area that has traditionally been part of the high seas'.[77] Copes adds that the provisions relating to the LLS 'appear to apply no more than moral pressure to the coastal state'.[78] However, there are many positive aspects of the new regime on which something can be built. For the LLS, being pessimistic would mean losing even more, while to be optimistic is to assert something. Basically, the LOSC looks like a 'framework treaty' or *loi-cadre*: it has stipulated basic rules and has left many of those questions apparently likely to arise in practice unanswered. Specifically in the case of some provisions relating to the LLS, it is obvious that they were left in abeyance in the hope that the aspirations of the LLS would be achieved by friendly and cooperative bilateral, regional or sub-regional, arrangements between states.

Conclusions and Suggestions

The concept of the EEZ is recent, and this maritime zone is the richest in resources. It has embraced that large proportion of the high seas which was open to all. The provisions of the LOSC have succeeded in giving some rights to the LLS, albeit few. In reality, however, the situation has been made difficult and ambiguous so that almost all the rights of the LLS are dependent on the good faith of the coastal states.

Article 300 of the LOSC obliges all states to act in good faith. Good faith is a well-established rule in international law.[79] The coastal states are expected to act in good faith in order to enable the LLS to have access to an equitable share of EEZ fishery resources. The latter are given the right of access to the surplus fishery yield, and most coastal states do generally have such a surplus. Even if the coastal states' harvesting capacity approaches the TAC, the LLS fishery rights are not extinguished.[80] Then coastal states are required to cooperate on a bilateral sub-regional or regional basis, with all the states concerned to give the LSS equitable rights.

It can be seen, therefore, that under the LOSC regime the rights of a coastal state in its EEZ are not absolute, but nor are the rights of the LLS automatic. The balance between the two is maintained by the requirement of mutual arrangements between the states concerned.[81] The coastal state is under a duty not to act arbitrarily, and is under an obligation to enter into such mutual arrangements.

Thus the LLS and the coastal states, through regional or sub-regional arrangements, can jointly exploit the living resources of the EEZ of the states concerned. The African LLS, Zambia and Uganda, proposed in UNCLOS III that regional economic zones, be established.[82] Paraguay and Bolivia made a similar proposal.[83] Although these proposals for regional economic zones were not taken up and included in the LOSC, nevertheless, regional arrangements could be made to exploit these areas. Alternatively, existing regional arrangements could be used to give LLS their maritime fishery rights on an equitable basis.

Arrangements could be made in Africa through the OAU, for example, by dividing the African LLS into an East African regional cooperative group, a West African group, etc. The two South American LLS could also be given a means to enforce their rights through sub-regional arrangements with their neighbours, who each have a very large EEZ. The Asian LLS also have good prospects for such regional cooperation; for instance, seven South Asian states (two landlocked States, Nepal and Bhutan, and five coastal states, Bangladesh, India, the Maldives, Pakistan, and Sri Lanka) established the South Asian Association for Regional Cooperation (SAARC) for regional economic cooperation in 1985.[84] Each of the five coastal states has a rich EEZ, but these states (such as the Maldives) are unable to exploit all the living resources of their respective EEZ. If all these states were to come to a regional arrangement, financial and technical assistance might be forthcoming from international agencies (such as the World Bank, the Asian Development Bank, and the UN). These agencies would undoubtedly prefer to assist with such regional arrangements aimed at developing the economies of the least-developed countries, particularly if this would assist in bringing the living standards of all these countries up to the basic level. Additionally, the rich area of the Indian Ocean could be exploited by means of joint ventures between such regional organizations and other technologically developed states, and the earnings shared on an equitable basis by all these poor countries.

The most abundant fishery resources of the sea lie within the EEZ. Through proper exploitation, conservation, and management, its maximum sustainable yield can be approached. In this event, the TAC will also go up. The coastal states' harvesting capacity will generally not approach the TAC, for most developing states do not have the capacity to harvest the entire allowable catch in their EEZ. If regional or sub-regional arrangements, similar to those proposed, are made, the productivity of EEZ would be increased; resources that at present are not optimally utilized will be directed to where they are most needed; and the aims of the provisions of the LOSC relating to the rights and opportunities of the LLS will truly have been achieved.

With regard to Nepal's rights in the fishery resources in the Indian and Bangladeshi EEZ in the Bay of Bengal, it is clear from the above discussion that Nepal is entitled to certain fishery rights in the EEZ of neighbouring countries under international law. However, Nepal does not seem to have explored this issue at all meaningfully. It may not be a practically attractive phenomenon at the moment for Nepal to aspire to exercise her limited fishing rights in the Bay of Bengal, but the country should register its interest in exercising her rights accorded by international law.

Notes and References

1. An earlier version of this chapter was published by me in the *International Journal of Estuarine and Coastal Law*, vol. 2, no. 4, Nov. 1987, pp. 227–39.

2. J.H. Ryther, as quoted in R.P. Anand, 'The Politics of a New Legal Order for Fisheries' (1982) II, *Ocean Development and International Law*, 265–9.

3. See T.W. Fulton, *The Sovereignty of the Sea* (1911), pp. 3–6.

4. See F. Mirvahabi, 'The Rights of the Landlocked and Geographically Disadvantaged States in Exploitation of Marine Fisheries' (1979) 26, *Netherlands International Law Review*, 130, 139.

5. Convention and Statute on Freedom of Transit, Barcelona, 20 April 1921, 7 LNTS 11.

6. Convention on the Law of the Sea, 1982, UN Doc. A/CONF. 62/122, 7 Oct. 1982.

7. UNCA Res. 2750 (XXV), *The Yearbook of the United Nations* (1970), pp. 81–2.

8. Art. 1(3) of the UN Charter: I Brownlie (ed.), *Basic Documents in International Law* (1984), p. 3.

9. J.R.V. Prescott, *The Maritime Political Boundaries of the World* (1985), p. XVI.

10. P.M., Wijkman 'The UNCLOS and the Redistribution of Ocean Wealth' (1982), 16, *Journal of World Trade Law* 27, 29.

11. A.M. Sinjela, *Land-Locked States and the UNCLOS Regime* (1983), p. 316.

12. D.L. Larson, 'Foreword' (1982), 11, *Ocean Development and International Law*, 1,5.

13. See, for the names of all 42 landlocked states in note number 2, Ch. IV.

14. R.R. Churchill and A.V. Lowe, *The Law of the Sea* (1985), p. 289. The following states are referred to: Andorra, Byelorussia, the Holy See Liechtenstein and San Marino.

15. Art. 3, HSC: UN Doc. A/CONF. 13/L.53.; Art 123(1)(a) LOSC: UN Doc. A/CONF. 62/122. 7 Oct. 1982.

16. A. Sarup, 'Transit Trade of Land-locked Nepal' (1972), 21, *International and Comparative Law Quarterly*, 287, 294.

17. L.C. Caflisch, 'Land-locked States and their Access to and from the Sea' (1978), 49, *British Yearbook of International Law*, 71, 74.

18. Churchill and Lowe, op. cit., n. 14, p. 278.

19. Sinjela, op. cit., n. 11, p. 40.

20. Grotius, Jefferson, Scelle, etc., as quoted in UN Doc. A/CONF. 13/26 and M. Dubey, 'International Law Relating to the Transit Trade of Land-locked Countries' (1965), XIV, *Indian Yearbook of International Affairs*, 22.

21. The Covenant of the League of Nations, UKTS 4 (1919).

22. Convention and Statute on Freedom of Transit, Barcelona, 20 April 1921, 7 LNTS 11.

23. General Agreement on Tariffs and Trade, 55 UNTS 187.

24. Havana Charter (adopted by the UN Conference on Trade and Employment), 1948, UN Doc. E/ CONF. 2/78.

25. GA Res. 1028, 11 UN GAOR, Supp. (No. 17) 12, UN Doc. A3572 (1957).

26. GA Res. 1105, 11 UN GAOR, Supp. (No. 17) 54, UN Doc. A/3572 (1957).

27. Convention on the High Seas, Geneva, 29 April 1958, UN Doc. A/CONF. 13/L.53.

28. See 1, UN ESCOR, UN Commn. On Trade and Development (35th Plenary Meeting), 3, UN Doc. E/CONF. 461, 141 (1964).

29. Ibid.

30. 597 UNTS 3.

31. M.J. Bowman and D.J. Harris, *Multilateral Treaties: Index and Current Status* (1984) (Suppl.: 1986), p. 295.

32. Art. 125(1) LOSC.

33. Art. 125(1) LOSC.

34. H. Lauterpacht, 'Freedom of Transit in International Law', 44, *Transactions of the Grotius Society*, 313, 349.

35. For instance, Arts. 1(3), 55 and 56 of the UN Charter.

36. Declaration on Principles of International Law Concerning Friendly Relations and Cooperation Among States in Accordance with the Charter of

the United Nations: *Yearbook of the United Nations*, vol. 24 (1970), pp. 784, 789.

37. [1960] ICJ Rep., 6.

38. Treaty of Peace between the Allied and Associated Powers and Germany, Versailles, 28 June 1919: 225 *Consolidated Treaty Series* 189, 279.

39. Art. 14 TSC; Art. 2 HSC; Arts. 17, 87, 90, and Arts. 124–32 LOSC.

40. The Doctrine, as propounded in the *Grisbadarna* case (between Norway and Sweden in 1909), states: '... in the law of the nations, it is a well-established principle that, it is necessary to refrain as far as possible from modifying the state of things existing in fact and for a long time'. See Wilson, *The Hague and Arbitral Cases* (1915), pp. 111, 129, and Sinjela, op. cit., n. 11, p. 234.

41. [1969] ICJ Rep. 3.

42. UN Doc. A/CONF. 13/L. 55.

43. UN Doc. A/CONF. 62/122, 7 Oct. 1982.

44. Bowman and Harris, op. cit., n. 31, pp. 476 (Suppl.) 99. See also LOSC (see Lagoni (1987) 2 IJECL 86).

45. Harris, *Cases and Materials on International Law* (1983), p. 348: his own findings.

46. [1974] ICJ Rep. 3.

47. [1951] ICJ Rep. 116.

48. Larson, loc cit., n. 12, p. 197.

49. Churchill and Lowe, op. cit., n. 14, p. 197.

50. P.A. Driver, 'International Fisheries', *in* R.P. Barston and P. Birnie (eds), *The Maritime Dimension* (1980), p. 30.

51. Wijkman, loc cit., n. 10, p. 27.

52. C.J. Colombos, *The International Law of the Sea* (1967), p. 367.

53. Churchill and Lowe, op. cit., n. 14, p. 126; Sinjela, op. cit., n. 11, p. 279.

54. P.A. Driver, op. cit., n. 50, p. 27.

55. Art. 56(a)(a) LOSC.

56. M.A. Akehurst, *Modern Introduction to International Law* (1984), p. 271. See also A.V. Lowe, 'Reflections on the Waters: Changing Conceptions of Property Rights in the Law of the Sea' (1986) 1 *IJECL* 1.

57. See, e.g. *Malta/Libya Continental Shelf* case [1982] ICJ Rep. 18.

58. Harris, op. cit., n. 45, p. 346.

59. 67 States, 200-mile Economic Zone; 22 States, 200-mile Exclusive Fishing Zone; 15 States, 200-mile Territorial Sea. See R.W. Smith, *Exclusive Economic Zone Claims: An Analysis and Primary Documents* (1986) Annex. I, pp. 13–6.

60. [1974] ICJ Rep. 3.

61. Churchill and Lowe, op. cit., n. 14, p. 206; R. Smith, op. cit., n. 59.

62. R. Platzoder, *Third United Nations Conference on the Law of the Sea: Caracas Session* (1974) (1985), p. I.

63. Mirvahabi, loc. cit., n. 4, p. 156.

64. *Journal de Genève*, 6 May 1982, as quoted in U. Wassermann, 'Law of the Sea Convention Adopted' (1982), 16, *Journal of World Trade Law*, 440, 443.

65. *Keesing's Archives of Contemporary World Events*, vol. XXXI, 33502–3 (1985).

66. Bowman and Harris, op. cit., n. 31, p. 99.

67. S. Oda 'Fisheries Under the United Nations Convention on the Law of the Sea' (1983), 77, *American Journal of International Law*, 739, 746.

68. P. Copes, 'The Impact of UNCLOS III on Management of the World's Fisheries' (1981), *Marine Policy*, 217, 218.

69. D.P. O'Connell, (I.A. Shearer, ed.), *The International Law of the Sea*, vol. I (1982), p. 567.

70. Prescott, op. cit., n. 9, p. 45.

71. O'Connell, op. cit., n. 69, pp. 570–81.

72. Oda, loc. cit., n. 67, p. 746.

73. Art. 297 and Annex. V, Art. 7(2) LOSC.

74. (1982) 21 ILM 1261, 1325.

75. Caflish, loc. cit., n. 17, p. 86.

76. G. Moore, 'National Legislation for the Management of Fisheries under Coastal State Jurisdiction' (1982) 11(2) *Journal of Maritime Law and Commerce*, 153, 160.

77. Sinjela, op. cit., n. 11, p. 316.

78. Copes, loc. cit., n. 68, p. 67.

79. The ICJ has also affirmed this principle in various cases, largely in the cases concerning *Conditions of Admissions to Membership in the United Nations* [1948] ICJ Rep. 63; *Rights of Nationals of the United States of America in Morocco* [1952] ICJ Rep. 212. See also H. Lauterpacht, *The Development of International Law by the International Court* (1958), p. 163.

80. Art. 69 (3) LOSC.

81. Arts. 62 (2) and 69 (2), (3) LOSC. See also A.V. Lowe, op. cit., pp. 8–12.

82. 28 UN GAOR. Supp. 21, vol. III, 89, UN Doc. A-9021, 1973, Art. 4, para. 1.

83. UN Doc. A/CONF. 62/C.2/L.65.

84. *Times*, 12 Nov. 1986, 14; *Keesing's*, XXXII, 34243 (1986).

6

Transit Arrangements between Nepal and India

Introduction

Nepal shares a 500-mile border with India which remains open.[1] Although Nepal borders on China to the north, it is extremely difficult for Nepal to gain access to the Chinese market and to the sea via Chinese territories as Nepal lies on the southern slopes of the Himalaya. Nepal is surrounded by India from all other sides, i.e. the east, west, and south. Although Nepal has trade relationships with nearly 70 states, the bulk of its trade is either with India or through India. The nearest seaport to Nepal is 1127 km away in Kolkata, India. Nepal could potentially use some of Bangladesh's ports, but Indian territory separates Nepal from Bangladesh. This makes Nepal virtually dependent on India for her access to the sea and international market. In other words, geography dictates the Nepal–India relationship.[2]

At the moment there is a transit treaty between Nepal and India, but what happens when difficulties arise between the two countries coinciding with the expiry of the treaty? Is the right of free access of landlocked countries established in general international law? If so, does this right operate even in the absence of a transit treaty with the transit state? If not, is this right conditional upon the conclusion of a transit treaty? Is Nepal entitled under international law to as many transit routes as are currently in use? If not, will Nepal's transit right be conditional upon its observance of the 'letter and spirit' of the 1950 treaty or upon Nepal's agreeing to a trade treaty favourable to India? Does international law oblige India to negotiate and conclude a new transit treaty with Nepal upon the expiry of the old one? These are the issues that this chapter aims to examine.

The Indo-Nepal Problem from a Legal Perspective

The principal international instruments concerning landlocked states are: the Barcelona Convention and Statute on Freedom of Transit of 1921;[3] the High Seas Convention (HSC) of 1958;[4] the Convention on Transit Trade of Landlocked Countries of 1965;[5] and the Convention on the Law of the Sea (LOSC) of 1982 (which is yet to come into force).[6] Both Nepal and India are party to the Barcelona Convention and Statute. Nepal is party also to the 1958 High Seas Convention and the 1965 Convention on landlocked states, but India is not party to these conventions. Although both countries are signatory to the 1982 Convention, neither has ratified it. Thus, so far as the governance of India-Nepal bilateral transit relations by multilateral treaties is concerned, only the Barcelona Convention and Statute seems relevant. This does not explicitly provide a right of free access for landlocked states but provides freedom of transit. While Article 1 of the statute defines the term 'traffic in transit', Article 2 lays down the principle that free transit should be facilitated by the states concerned. It reads as follows:

> Subject to the provisions of this Statute, the measures taken by the Contracting states for regulating and forwarding traffic across territory under their sovereignty or authority shall facilitate free transit by rail or waterway on routes in use convenient for international transit.

As both countries are signatory to the 1982 Convention, which inter alia, guarantees the right of free access for landlocked states,[7] it could be argued that the signatories are obliged, under Article 18 of the 1969 Vienna Convention on the Law of Treaties, to which both Nepal and India are party, 'to refrain from acts which would defeat the object and purpose' of the Convention.[8] Moreover, in view of the mandatory character of Article 125 (1) of the LOSC, and the approval of this provision by consensus during the UNCLOS III, the right of free access as embodied in the 1982 Convention could now be regarded as part of customary international law.[9]

A substantial weight of authority supports the view that the right of free access to and from the sea of landlocked states and the principle of freedom of transit are now a part of customary international law, binding on all states.[10] This was the view advanced by several landlocked states, including Nepal,[11] during UNCLOS III. Scholars too support this view: Fawcett writes that 'a duty to accord freedom of transit on reasonable conditions to another is now a customary rule'.[12] According to Lauterpacht, the right of transit exists in international law provided that the state claiming the right is able to justify it by reference to considerations of necessity or convenience and the exercise of the right does not cause harm or prejudice to the transit state.[13] He goes on to state that 'When circumstances warranting a claim to transit exist, the legal right to freedom of transit then arises. It exists independently of treaty.'[14]

The question as to whether the right of free transit is established in general international law has attracted considerable academic debate and a survey of all the arguments advanced for and against it is beyond the scope of this chapter. In so far as our discussion is concerned, India implicitly acknowledged during the 1989/90 crisis that the absence of an agreement did not excuse it from the obligation to provide access. Although P.V. Narasimha Rao, the then Indian minister of external affairs, speaking in the lower house of the Indian parliament on 26 April 1989, stated that as India was party neither to the 1965 Convention on landlocked states nor to the 1982 Convention on the Law of the Sea, 'in matters of transit, India has, strictly speaking, no obligation towards Nepal'. He, nevertheless, acknowledged during the same speech that 'In the field of transit, a *landlocked country has a **right*** only to one transit route to the sea under International Law' (emphasis added).[15] This was evidenced by the fact that even in the absence of a transit treaty India allowed, albeit under very restrictive conditions and only through two of the 15 transit routes that were in use prior to the expiry of the old treaty, Nepalese exports and imports to and from third countries. As Nepal had launched a publicity campaign to gain support and sympathy from the outside world in its problem with India, Indian officials were making strenuous efforts to convey the message that India did not intend to deny Nepal its right of transit even in the absence of a transit treaty.[16] However, what India was saying was that because of its 'special relationship' with Nepal it had been very 'generous' to its neighbour in extending transit facilities and now, as Nepal was intent on changing this special relationship, in the view of New Delhi, Nepal was merely another neighbour like Bangladesh and Pakistan, and, thus, not worthy of 'generous' treatment from India.

As quoted earlier, according to Indian officials, India was required by international law to provide only one transit route and not the 15 routes enjoyed by Nepal under the 1978 transit treaty.[17] This assertion on India's part has, however, no legal basis. No international legal rule states that only one route is sufficient. Although Vasciannie[18] writes that 'in strict terms, only one transit route is necessary for a landlocked state to reach the sea, and from this it may possibly be argued that additional routes are granted to the landlocked state for reasons other than those relating to its special geographical location', he fails to provide any clue on how he came to this conclusion. He seems to have left out of account the significance not only of Article V of the 1947 GATT (Article V of the GATT rules provides that the right of transit must be allowed 'via the routes [i.e. in plural] most convenient for international transit')[19] and Article 2 of the Barcelona Statute on Freedom of Transit (free transit shall be facilitated by states concerned 'on routes in *use* convenient for international transit').[20] Also, other relevant doctrines of international law such as the doctrine of prescription, according to Lauterpacht, 'may be of relevance in determining whether a state is entitled to the continued enjoyment of a means of transit of which the transit state seeks to deprive it either by outright prohibition or by the modification of the conditions of transit in a manner so unreasonable or onerous as to be tantamount to prohibition'.[21]

Nepal, for its part, argued that given its shape (Nepal is a narrow strip across India's northern frontier with a 500-mile border with India), geography (the terrain is mostly mountainous with several ranges running at different elevations from east to west and north to south), and the state of economic development (a large part of the country is still remote and not connected by modern means of transport to the capital and other industrial cities), Nepal needs several transit routes for its trade and communications. It is worth noting here that there remain some areas which cannot be reached by rail or road from other parts of the country without going via India. Nepal thus suffers from two geographical handicaps: one, that it is landlocked and the other that it is mountainous in nature without a proper network of modern transportation and communications. Because of this situation, there seems a clear need for several outlets not only for exports and imports, but also for the livelihood of some of the population. Although in ordinary circumstances a need might not justify a legal right, such a geographical need of a landlocked country justifies a legal right because the very source of the right of landlocked states is their special geographical situation. As 15 transit routes were in *use* under the 1978 transit treaty, India seems obliged under the Barcelona Statute to grant Nepal use of all the 15 routes even in the absence of a transit treaty. The words 'routes in use convenient for international transit' were inserted in Article 2 of the Barcelona Statute with a view to laying down that the right of free transit may not be exercised except over routes in existence. Hence, India is not obliged to construct new routes for Nepal but is obliged to allow Nepal's traffic transit through all routes in existence.

On the basis of the provisions of Article 2 of the Barcelona Statute on Freedom of Transit and the other principles of international law and the provisions of international instruments described above, it could be argued that Nepal's claim to several outlets is justified under international law. HSC Article 3(2) requires the transit state to take into account the 'special conditions' of the landlocked state in concluding transit agreements to give effect to the transit right of that state. It appears that if Nepal is able to justify its demand for several routes of transit by reference to considerations of necessity or convenience, India would be obliged to agree on the use of these routes.

Both HSC Articles 3 and LOSC 125 require the transit states to conclude appropriate agreements with landlocked states to give effect to the rights and freedoms they enshrine. However, one could argue that although Article 135 (1) provides for the right of free access for landlocked states, it does not provide independent measures for the implementation of this right as it is tied to freedom of transit. In other words, there is a right of free access for landlocked states but the exercise of this right will be governed by the rules of freedom of transit. Therefore, what seems more important here is the nature and scope of the institution of freedom of transit rather than the right of free access. Paragraph 2 of Article 125 makes this point clearer: the bilateral, sub-regional or regional agreements envisaged under this paragraph are for determining the terms and modalities *for exercising freedom of transit* but not for exercising the right of free access to and from the sea.

Nevertheless, as the legal effect of the notion of 'freedom of transit' can be equated to that of a 'right' of transit, the use of the term 'freedom of transit' in the second sentence of paragraph 1 and in paragraph 2 should not be regarded as undermining the legal position of the landlocked states. This is because the notion of freedom of transit also implies that the transit state concerned cannot interfere with lawful transit. As the transit state has a legal duty under the institution of freedom of transit to allow lawful passage to landlocked states, the use of the term 'freedom' is, as Vasciannie writes, 'sufficient to ensure that the latter will have an enforceable claim in instances where their access to the sea is barred'.[22] Therefore, 'In practical terms, this is equivalent to the result which would have been reached if free transit had been described as a 'right' in Part X.'[23]

It could therefore be contended that the transit state has a duty to negotiate and conclude a transit treaty with its landlocked neighbour, although this argument may sound quite absurd in view of the rule that states, as sovereigns, are free to enter or not to enter into such treaties as they wish. Yet, as Lauterpacht argues, 'practice and precedent have acknowledged that in a number of respects the freedom of a State *not* to conclude a treaty is not absolute. The *pactum de contrahendo* is a notion familiar to international lawyers as a binding arrangement between states on points to be incorporated in a future treaty.'[24]

LOSC Article 125(2) requires the conclusion of an agreement between the transit state and landlocked states concerned. After agreeing to the major principle in paragraph 1, the provision of paragraph 2, which contains subordinate procedural arrangements for the realization of the foregoing provision, may have been left open in the understanding that it will be properly implemented in each and every situation according to the principle of *pacta sunt servanda*. As the terms and modalities differ according to the location and situation of a landlocked state, it is not possible to incorporate all these practical issues in an 'umbrella' convention such as the LOSC. Nevertheless, the words in paragraph 2, 'shall be agreed', are of great significance. The transit state can neither simply delay the negotiations nor impose difficult conditions. The effective exercise of freedom of transit under this convention depends upon the conclusion of appropriate agreements between the landlocked state and transit state concerned providing for the terms and modalities for such exercise. Therefore, it can plausibly be argued that as Article 125(2) is a *pactum de contrahendo*, the transit state concerned would be legally obliged to reach an agreement with the landlocked one.

However, a transit state could argue that this provision only requires it to negotiate and not necessarily to come to an agreement if it is not satisfactory to it. As Article 125(2) does not envisage the possibility of the transit and the landlocked state failing to reach an agreement, it does not provide an alternative. A problem of this character does not fall under the competence of any tribunals established by the convention. Therefore, the refusal by a transit state to conclude an agreement could cause a serious problem for the landlocked state concerned. This is what actually happened between Nepal and India in 1989, and Nepal had no alternative but to change its policy and concede to the conditions put forward by India. Nevertheless, when a landlocked state's demands are based on past practice or multilateral treaties, the transit state concerned seems obliged to conclude a transit treaty. That appears to be precisely the case between Nepal and India. The latter had concluded a separate transit treaty with the former in 1978 providing for 15 transit routes for Nepal.[25]

Whether the past practice of these two countries amounts to a local custom[26] and whether Nepal is entitled under the concept of local custom to the same facilities as those enjoyed in the past may be a matter for argument, but what is clear is that if Nepal is asking for no more than what it enjoyed in the past under the old treaty, India seems bound not only to enter into negotiations in good faith with Nepal but also to conclude an agreement.[27] D.B.S. Thapa, a former law secretary in Nepal, maintains that the 1978 Transit Treaty 'had codified customary practices existing between the two countries from time immemorial'.[28] While examining the nature of Indo-Nepal trade and transit relations in the aftermath of the 1970/71 crisis between these countries, Sarup concluded that India was 'under a legal obligation to facilitate and conclude a transit treaty with Nepal'.[29]

One of the highly publicized issues in the 1989/90 crisis with India was that Nepal wanted to conclude a separate treaty on transit with India, whereas India wished to conclude a separate treaty dealing with all matters of bilateral trade and transit. Strictly speaking, India does not seem obliged to conclude a separate treaty dealing only with transit, provided that it accords Nepal all the transit facilities that she is entitled to under international law and bilateral practice. It is however quite logical to argue that while trade is a periodic arrangement, transit is a necessary permanent condition for international trade for landlocked states and should be treated as such under a separate treaty.[30] Then one might ask, should the transit treaty be of permanent character? The answer can be both yes and no.

'Yes', in the sense that as the freedom of transit is recognized in international law, that freedom should be incorporated in a permanent treaty whereby a change of mind of the transit state or the change of the government in the transit state would not affect the transit facilities of the landlocked country. As being landlocked is a permanent condition a treaty dealing with this condition, should also be of permanent character. 'No', however, in the sense that neither the population nor the economic activities of the landlocked states are static, and their requirements of transit facilities tend to expand. The legal provisions have to keep pace with the changes in technology and science. From a purely legal point of view too, a permanent transit treaty is not necessary if we accept that freedom of transit is established in international law. A freedom already firmly established does not need new documents to establish it. As I stated earlier, as India recognizes Nepal's right of free access and freedom of transit under international law, there is no need to seek India's commitment through a permanent transit treaty.

Although it may be helpful to insert a clause on freedom of transit in a bilateral treaty of permanent character spelling out the basic nature of the overall relationship between the two countries, a transit treaty that also deals with the terms and modalities of transit cannot be of permanent character. Alternatively, the transit right may be incorporated in a permanent transit treaty, provided that the treaty contains only the basic principles of transit and the details on the terms and modalities of the exercise of this right are incorporated in the protocols attached to it which could be reviewed periodically without affecting the main treaty.

Nepal's Transit Arrangements with India

Background

After India gained independence, a Treaty of Trade and Commerce was concluded by Nepal with India in 1950. Under this treaty India recognized in favour of Nepal 'full and unrestricted right of *commercial transit*'.[31] Although this right was restricted to commercial transit, the facilities provided for such transit were generally favourable to Nepal. The Trade and Transit Treaty of 1960[32] between the two countries replaced the 1950 Treaty of Trade and Commerce. Although the 1960 treaty also granted Nepal fairly liberal transit facilities, it made Nepal's transit right reciprocal[33] and no reference was made to its landlocked character.

When this treaty expired on 31 October 1970, Nepal wished to conclude two treaties, one governing the right of transit and the other dealing with bilateral trade. This was after the adoption of the 1965 New York

Convention on Trade and Transit of Landlocked States, which recognizes in its preamble transit as a right of landlocked states.[34] India, however, wanted both these subjects to be dealt with within a single treaty, maintaining that both were interrelated. As the differences could not be sorted out, Nepal proposed that the status quo of the expired treaty be maintained for another year to enable both sides to hold more talks towards concluding a new treaty. India declined this plea too and, according to Nepalese officials, resorted to pressure tactics by imposing restrictions on the export–import trade with Nepal and even stopped the supply of essential commodities to her. This action on India's part was characterized in Nepal as 'economic blockade'.[35]

The political background leading up to this crisis seems to have been Nepal's unilateral denunciation in 1969 of a secret arms agreement signed in 1965 with India and Nepal's assertion that the 1950 Treaty of Peace and Friendship had fallen into disuse as India had not consulted Nepal either at the time of the 1962 Sino–Indian armed conflict or during the 1965 Indo–Pakistan war. Nepal had also demanded the immediate withdrawal of the Indian military personnel deployed along Nepal's border with China as well as the Indian Military Liaison Group which had supposedly entered Nepal under the 1950 Peace and Friendship Treaty. Although this uneasy chapter in Indo-Nepal relations ended in the conclusion of a mutual trade and transit treaty on 13 August 1971, Nepal emerged as a clear loser as there was neither a separate treaty on transit nor a recognition by India of Nepal's demand for an overland transit route to Bangladesh (formerly East Pakistan). Nepal lost on other fronts too. For instance, the term 'freedom of transit' was given a narrower meaning than under the previous treaty. India would have the right to take all indispensable measures to ensure that the freedom of transit, accorded by it on its territory did not in any way infringe on its legitimate interests of any kind.[36] According to a former foreign minister of Nepal, India, under this treaty, could legally stop transit to Nepal if in its opinion Nepal was importing more than its requirement or exporting more than its available surplus because the freedom of transit was restricted to 'goods required by each contracting party and goods available for export from that party'.[37]

After the expiry of the 1971 treaty of trade and transit, India and Nepal concluded on 17 March 1978 two separate treaties, one governing transit facilities and the other governing trade. This time Nepal had some reasons to celebrate the conclusion of the treaties. First, Nepal had secured a separate treaty on transit, its long-standing demand. Second, the new transit treaty recognized that 'Nepal as a landlocked country needs access to and from the sea to promote its international trade'.[38] Third, India agreed to provide Nepal necessary overland transit facilities through Indian territory (known as the Radhikapur route) to Bangladesh. Fourth, while the trade treaty was concluded for five years, the transit treaty was for seven years. This was done with the understanding that both treaties would not expire at the same time and separate negotiations could be conducted for separate treaties. It was hoped that this arrangement would make future negotiations easier and matters of bilateral trade would not creep in during negotiations for a transit treaty.

Nevertheless, India was able to tailor things[39] in such a way that not only both trade and transit treaties but also the agreements relating to petroleum products and some other essential commodities expired in March 1989.[40] For some weeks chaos reigned in Nepal; the government claimed that no goods were entering Nepal from India;[41] all exports and imports were suspended; long queues for essential commodities, including cooking fuel, sugar, salt, and other petroleum products, in cities like Kathmandu brought life virtually to a standstill. Although India stated that two transit routes would be kept open for Nepal's international trade in keeping with international law even in the absence of a transit treaty, owing to administrative confusion and chaos in the aftermath of the expiry of the trade and transit treaties, Nepal's international trade to and from the Indian port of Kolkata was hampered and essential commodities had to be flown in from other countries. Most industries were shut down due to the lack of raw materials and oil. Nepal's GDP, which was growing at 5.7 per cent annually before the crisis was reported to have contracted by 2 per cent in the financial year ending July 1990.

These activities on India's part were described by Nepal as economic blockade, allegations denied by India.[42] However, after some weeks, Nepal's transit trade began to flow through the two transit points designated unilaterally for Nepal by India. This no-treaty regime continued for over a year and ended when both sides decided to revert to the status quo ante under a joint communiqué issued at the conclusion of the new Nepalese prime minister's visit to India in June 1990, and this unpleasant chapter was finally closed on 6 December 1991 when the two parties signed two new treaties, one on trade and the other on transit.

Principal Provisions of the 1991 Transit Treaty[43]

The Treaty of Transit signed on 6 December 1991 was the second separate transit treaty concluded by Nepal with India and the first one concluded after the overthrow of the panchayat system. The 1978 transit treaty was the first treaty between these two countries solely concerned with transit. Prior to that, transit matters used to be incorporated in single treaties dealing with both trade and transit.

It should be stated at the outset that the 1991 transit treaty repeated, with minor alterations, the provisions of that of 1978.[44] The preamble to the treaty recognized that 'Nepal as a landlocked country needs access to and from the sea to promote its international trade'. However, this recognition is diluted by the inclusion in the treaty of the principle of reciprocity. Moreover, the treaty fails to specify that as a landlocked country Nepal has the right to free access to and from the sea or needs access to and from the sea in order to enjoy the freedom of the high seas. Under Article I the contracting parties agreed that:

> The Contracting Parties shall accord to 'traffic in transit' freedom of transit across their respective territories through routes mutually agreed upon. No distinction shall be made which is based on flag of vessels, the places of origin, departure, entry, exit, destination, ownership of goods or vessels.

This article makes the transit right of Nepal subject to reciprocity, which is not consistent with the very concept of a right of free access of landlocked states. According to Article 125 of the LOSC, the right of free access to and from the sea is not subject to reciprocity but is unilaterally and solely available to landlocked states.

Article III defines the term 'traffic in transit', but the definition is narrower even than that provided for in the Barcelona Statute on Freedom of Transit, let alone the LOSC. Among other things, the definition excludes persons, accompanied baggage, and most importantly, the means of transport. Article IV exempts traffic in transit 'from customs duties or other charges except reasonable charges for transportation and such other charges as are commensurate with the costs of services rendered in respect of such transit'. Article VII accords, subject to Indian laws and regulations, only to *merchant ships* sailing under the flag of Nepal treatment no less favourable than accorded to ships of any other foreign country. Although Nepal does not at present have any warship, this article should have extended this facility to all ships flying the Nepal flag as Nepal may in the future need warships to protect its commerce and fishing vessels in the high seas and the Indian and, arguably, Bangladesh's EEZ under Article 69 of the LOSC when it enters into force.[45]

Articles II, VIII and IX of the transit treaty impose several types of limitations on the freedom of transit accorded to traffic in transit. While the limitations of Articles VIII and IX seem justifiable as being broadly in line with international practice, the limitations imposed under Article II raise some questions. This article reads as follows:

(a) Each Contracting Party shall have the right to take all indispensable measures to ensure that such freedom, accorded by it on its territory does not in any way infringe its legitimate interests of any kind.

(b) Nothing in this treaty shall prevent either Contracting Party from taking any measures which may be necessary for the protection of its essential security interests.

The vague words 'all indispensable measures' and 'legitimate interests of any kind' might allow an obdurate government, and especially during friction between two countries, to impose unnecessary limitations on Nepal's transit rights: they should be more specific on 'measures'.[46] In the absence of any indication of what may be regarded as 'indispensable measures'[47] and 'legitimate interests', India may consider itself free to impose any restrictions deemed 'necessary'[48] by it to protect its 'legitimate interests'. In fact, the limitation imposed under Article II (b) suffices to encompass the main purpose of limitations. The limitation imposed under Article II (a) is arbitrary, undesirable, and ambiguous. As the restrictions imposed under Articles VIII and IX of the transit treaty are designed to protect those interests of India which could appropriately be called 'legitimate interests', it is not clear what other interests are intended to be protected under Article II (a).[49]

Details of port facilities and transit routes are incorporated in a protocol to the Treaty of Transit and exports and imports procedures applicable to Nepal's traffic in transit are outlined in a memorandum attached to the treaty. The protocol designates 15 routes for Nepal's traffic in transit. It allows Nepal to use both Indian rail and road facilities for her convenience. However, in contrast to the 1978 treaty, the 1991 treaty does not provide Nepal any facilities in Haldia. The 1978 treaty had stated that India would arrange with the trustees for the port of Kolkata to make suitable land in Haldia available for the construction of facilities for the storage of Nepalese cargo.

Evaluation of the Treaty

On the surface, Nepal seems to have achieved a satisfactory transit treaty with India as the latter conceded to the Nepalese demand for a separate treaty on transit and for 15 transit routes, in contrast to the stance taken by New Delhi during the Indo-Nepal stalemate that under international law Nepal was entitled to only one transit route. India agreed to continue to provide overland transit facilities through Radhikapur for Nepal's trade with or via Bangladesh. This could well be hailed as a success. However, the reality is that the entire exercise on the right of landlocked states during UNCLOS III and the incorporation in the resulting 1982 Law of the Sea Convention of the right of free access of landlocked states does not seem to have influenced the latest treaty. Nor, apparently, has account been taken of other provisions of the LOSC on landlocked states. For instance, the transit treaty disregards not only Article 125(1), but also Article 126 of the LOSC. Nepal has secured neither simplified exports and imports procedures[50] nor India's recognition of Nepal's 'right' of free access to and from the sea. No new facility has been added and no new concession secured. Rather, Nepal appears to have lost the facilities available to it in Haldia under the 1978 treaty. Most striking of all is the incorporation in the treaty of the principle of reciprocity. The elimination of the requirement of reciprocity in Part X of the LOSC represented a major breakthrough for the landlocked states, but if a bilateral transit treaty concluded nearly ten years after the conclusion of the LOSC still embodies the principle of reciprocity it could be regarded, from the international law point of view, as disastrous.[51]

At first glance, Kathmandu's granting of reciprocal transit facilities to India does not sound disastrous so long as India is interested merely in securing general transit facilities in the event of need. In fact, India too is entitled to certain transit facilities under the general principle of the freedom of transit.[52] The reality however is that Nepal's exercise of the right of free access to and from the sea should not be made dependent on Nepal's granting similar facilities to India which is not landlocked. It is hardly justifiable to ask Nepal to offer similar facilities in return for something that is available to Nepal by virtue of its being landlocked. As the 1991 treaty is intended to provide transit facilities to Nepal for her access to the sea, the reciprocity requirement seems, in practical terms, meaningless, as landlocked Nepal, by definition, lacks the means to reciprocate.[53] In fact, India's transit trade through Nepal is nil; it does not actually need to use Nepalese territories for its international trade. India seems to have employed this reciprocity clause merely as political leverage. Moreover, the requirement of reciprocity incorporated in Article 1 of the transit treaty is in conflict with India's own admission in the preamble to the treaty that 'Nepal as a landlocked country needs access to and from the sea to promote its international trade'.

So far as the Indo-Nepal relationship is concerned, the concept of reciprocity raises numerous issues. As stated earlier, India wishes to tie Nepal's transit right to other issues like bilateral trade, treatment of Indians living in Nepal, India's strategic interests. This is because Nepal and India have a very complex bilateral relationship governed by a number of treaties, some of which are quite ambiguous and outmoded.

Nevertheless, the new transit treaty represents some success for Nepal in the sense that India, a regional superpower and a conservative transit state, agreed after all this legal wrangling to conclude a separate treaty on transit and conceded to the Nepalese demand to have 15 transit routes reinstated by the new treaty. The separation of transit matters from other bilateral issues is vital to Nepal and the new transit treaty has achieved this objective. From this, Nepal can hope that India will not try again in the future to exert pressure on Nepal by mixing the question of transit facilities with other bilateral matters. In that case Nepal's right of access will have been strengthened as a legal right rather than as facilities dependent on the transit state's goodwill.

Notes and References

1. An earlier version of this chapter was published by me in *Geopolitics and International Boundaries*, Summer 1997, vol. 2, no. 1, 175–96 by Frank Cass publishers, London. I am grateful to Frank Cass for granting permission to reproduce this chapter in this book.

2. See K. Natwar Singh, 'An Agenda for Talks with Mr Bhattarai', *Times of India* (7 June 1990), 8.

3. 7 *League of Nations Treaty Series*, nos. 1–3, pp. 11ff.

4. 450 *United Nations Treaty Series*, pp. 11–113.

5. 597 *United Nations Treaty Series*, pp. 42–63.

6. UN Doc. A/CONF. 62122, 7 Oct. 1982.

7. Art. 125(1) of the 1982 Convention on the Law of the Sea.

8. The Vienna Convention entered into force on 27 Jan. 1980. See text of the Convention UKTS no. 58 (1980), Cmnd.7964; 8 ILM 679 (1969).

9. Cf. The preamble to the HSC which states that its provisions are 'generally declaratory of established principles of international law' and its Art. 3.

10. See generally, UN, UNCLOS I, *Official Records*, I, UN DOC. A/CONF.13/29 and Add. 1, 311ff; M.I. Glassner, *Access to the Sea for Developing Land-Locked States* (1970); V.C. Govindraj, 'Landlocked States and their right of access to the sea', *Indian Journal of International Law* (1974), 190; A.M. Sinjela, *Land-Locked States and UNCLOS Regime* (1983).

11. UNCLOS III, *Official Records*, 2, p. 238. See also Czechoslovakia, in the Seabed Committee, A/AC. 138/SC. II/SR. p. 56.

12. J. Fawcett, 'Trade and Finance in International Law', *Hague Recueil Des Cours*, 1 (1968), pp. 215–310, at p. 267.

13. E. Lauterpacht, 'Freedom of Transit in International Law', *Grotius Society Transactions, 1958 & 1959*, pp. 313–56, at p. 332. See generally, Reid, *International Servitude in Law and Practice* (1932), p. 168; Caflisch, 'Land-locked States and their Access to and from the Sea', *British Yearbook of International Law* (1978), pp. 71–100. Vasciannie, *Land-Locked and Geographically Disadvantaged States in International Law of the Sea* (Oxford: Clarendon Press 1990), Chapter 8.

14. Lauterpacht, ibid., p. 349.

15. *Foreign Affairs Record*, 35/5 (New Delhi: May 1989), pp. 131–3. Here it should be noted that at the UNCLOS III, proposals were put forward by the Group of Landlocked and Geographically Disadvantaged States maintaining that the absence of a bilateral transit treaty could not be invoked by transit states to deny the right of free access to landlocked states. Proposals dated 28 April 1976 (in R. Platzoder *Third United Nations Conference on the Law of the Sea: Documents* 4 [Oceana Publications 1984], p. 332) and ibid. (28 June 1977), 381 at p. 387. As none of these proposals was incorporated in the LOSC, India could have argued that it is not obliged to grant transit facilities to Nepal in the absence of a transit treaty with India but it did not adopt this approach. This may be due to her conviction that transit is a right of a landlocked Nepal as well as the principle, as Freid writes, that 'international law does not permit, except for reasons recognized by it, to harm or, in the extreme case, as it were, to blockade another country by cutting off its transit trade'. John H.E. Fried, 'The 1965 Convention on Transit Trade of Land-Locked States', *Indian Journal of International Law* 6 (1966) 9–30 at 16.

16. See *Times of India* (17 April 1989). A similar problem had occurred in

1970 after the expiry of the 1960 trade and transit treaty with India. At that time too India had unilaterally issued a notification providing for continued trade between the two countries. Notification no. 192-ITC(PN) p. 70 of 31 Dec. 1970, *The Gazette*, Govt. of India, New Delhi. See in A. Sarup, 'Transit trade of land-locked Nepal', *International and Comparative Law Quarterly* 21 (1972), 287–306 at 294.

17. See supra note 34. See also Dilip Mukerjee, 'Himalayan Stalemate: Indian Stake in Nepali Goodwill', *Times of India* (4 April 1989) 4; 'India Rejects Nepal Plea on Treaties', ibid. (27 March 1989), 1.

18. Vasciannie, op. cit., p. 193.

19. 55 *United Nations Treaty Series*, 187; 210 (1950).

20. Supra.

21. Lauterpacht, op. cit., n. 13, p. 333.

22. Vasciannie, op. cit., n. 13, p. 190.

23. Ibid.

24. Lauterpacht, op. cit., n. 13, p. 347.

25. See also Art. 43 of the Vienna Convention on the Law of Treaties of 1969 (to which both India and Nepal are party). It states that the invalidity, termination, or denunciation of a treaty does not 'impair the duty of any state to fulfil any obligation embodied in the treaty to which it would be subject under international law independently of the treaty'. 8 *International Legal Materials* 679 (1969); *United Kingdom Treaty Series*, no. 58 (1980).

26. See the *Case Concerning Right of Passage Over Indian Territory* (Merits) I.C.J. Reports, (1960), p. 6. At p. 39 the judgement stated that 'the Court sees no reason why long continued practice between two States accepted by them as regulating their relations should not form the basis of mutual rights and obligations between the two States'. The court then decided that Portugal enjoyed a right of transit for private persons, civil officials, and goods between two of its territories enclaved within India and the coastal district of Daman by virtue of a local custom to this effect.

27. See the judgement of the International Court of Justice in the *North Sea Continental Shelf Cases*, I.C.J. Reports (1969), p. 47, for the court's opinion on the nature of obligations of states to enter into negotiations with a view to arriving at an agreement.

28. Dhruba B.S. Thapa, 'India-Nepal Relations, Perspectives on Present Problem: A Legal Approach', paper presented at a seminar on 'Transit' organized by the Nepal University Teachers Association, Kathmandu, May 1989, 2. Making a statement on the topic of public importance at a meeting of the National Assembly (Rastriya Panchayat), the then Nepalese foreign minister also asserted that the 15 transit points designated by the 1978 treaty were customary transit

points. See *Nepal and India: Facts and Chronology of the Problem* (HMG/Nepal: Department of Printing and Publications, 1989), pp. 88–9.

29. Sarup, op. cit., p. 302.

30. See for a similar argument by the then Nepalese Foreign Minister, S.K. Upadhyay, in 'Nepal Suffers But is Standing Firm', *Independent*, London, 11 April 1989.

31. Art. I of the treaty. See Bhasin, p. 124.

32. Ibid., p. 125.

33. Art. VII of the 1960 trade and transit treaty provides that 'Goods intended for import into or export from the territories of either Contracting Party from or to a third country shall be accorded freedom of transit through the territories of the other party'. Bhasin, op. cit., p. 127.

34. Principle I of the Preamble of the Convention.

35. Editorial in *Rising Nepal*, 6 Jan. 1971.

36. Art. VIII of the Treaty of Trade and Transit of 1971. See for text of the treaty (1971), 257 *Indian Trade Journal* 2132 (380.5 GOV), B-890–9.

37. Shaha, op. cit., p. 132.

38. Preamble to the treaty of transit. See, for text of the treaty, Surya P. Subedi, *Land-Locked Nepal and International Law* (Kathmandu: 1989), pp. 85–112.

39. See Thapa, supra and 'India Rejects Nepal Plea on Treaties', *Times of India* (27 March 1989), 1.

40. Until this date the trade and transit treaties were being renewed for differing periods after they had expired.

41. 'No Goods From India Enter Nepal for 15th Day' was a front page headline in the government-owned national daily English newspaper *Rising Nepal* (4 April 1989); Tony Allen-Mills, 'Nepal Suffers But is Standing Firm', *Independent* (London: 11 April 1989) and the editorial of the same date: 'Coming of Age in India'.

42. The Nepalese ambassador to India said in a press conference in New Delhi on 7 April 1989 that as India was not allowing even essential commodities to enter Nepal this action on her part was economic blockade. However, an Indian external affairs ministry spokesman stated on the same date that 'An economic blockade of Nepal is the furthest from our intentions'. The spokesman claimed that two transit points were being kept open for Nepal's trade. *Times of India* (7 April 1989), 7.

43. See for text of the *Treaty of Transit, Treaty of Trade and Agreement of Co-operation to Control Unauthorised Trade between His Majesty's Government of Nepal and the Government of India* (Kathmandu, Nepal: Nepal Transit and Warehousing Co. Ltd., 1991).

44. See, for an assessment of the 1978 Transit Treaty, Subedi, op. cit., ch. 3.

45. See Surya P. Subedi, 'The Marine Fishery Rights of Land-locked States with Particular Reference to the EEZ', *International Journal of Estuarine and Coastal Law* 2/4 (1987), 227–39.

46. For instance, under Article XXI(b) of the GATT the 'essential security interests' which may be protected, must be of very specific character: they must either be '(i) relating to *fissionable* materials ...' or '(ii) to the traffic in *arms*, ammunition and implements of war and to such traffic in other goods ... as is supplying the *military* establishment;' or '(iii) taken in time of war or other emergency in *international* relations'. Cited in John H.E. Fried, 'The 1965 Convention on Transit Trade of Land-locked States', *Indian Journal of International Law* 6 (1966), 9–30, at 26. As Fried writes, it is difficult to conceive how it could become 'necessary' for 'essential' security reasons to suspend any of the basic rules of transit. A clause like this does not give a carte blanche to disregard the essentials of the right of transit. Ibid., 26–7.

47. It should, however, be noted that the term 'indispensable measures' used in the transit treaty is much more restrictive than the word 'necessary measures' used in Article 125(3) of the LOSC. Therefore, it can be viewed as a positive indicator from Nepal's perspective.

48. However, as Caflisch writes, 'the reference to "necessary" measures suggests, *a contrario* that the transit State has no power to take measures which are objectively unnecessary'. Caflisch, op. cit., n. 13, p. 96.

49. Art. 11 of the 1965 Convention on Transit Trade of Landlocked States.

50. See, for a discussion on cumbersome customs and transit procedure, Subedi, op. cit., ch.3. Pilferage of Nepalese goods on Indian railways increases Nepalese export costs. According to a survey, transit costs consume 8 per cent of Nepal's GDP. See *Far Eastern Economic Review* (8 March 1990), 24.

51. Among other deficiencies of the 1991 transit treaty is the absence of a dispute resolution provision. As the transit dispute has often soured the entire Indo-Nepal relationship as a whole, it was high time to provide for a dispute resolution mechanism in the treaty. As both Nepal and India are party to the Barcelona Convention and the Statute on Freedom of Transit, any dispute arising from matters covered by the statute could be taken for adjudication before the International Court of Justice (ICJ) in accordance with Art. 13 of the statute, which provides that disputes relating to the interpretation or application of the statute could be brought before the former Permanent Court of International Justice (PCIJ), and Art. 37 of the Statute of the International Court of Justice, to which both Nepal and India are party, which states that whenever a treaty or convention in force provides for reference of a matter to the PCIJ, the matter shall, as between the parties to the present statute, be referred by the ICJ. However, there are many matters in the transit treaty which are not covered by the Barcelona Convention and the Statute, and for such matters no international tribunal has

jurisdiction, unless both states, by special agreement, consent to take the case to an international tribunal or to the ICJ.

52. Art. 2 of the Barcelona Statute on Freedom of Transit provides a general freedom of transit for all states party to it. This general freedom of transit is however limited to transit by rail or waterway.

53. Caflisch, writes that 'The natural and ordinary meaning of the term "reciprocity" in matters of transit would seem to be that if a coastal transit State gives a landlocked country *access to and from the sea* by granting it rights of transit, that country has to concede the *same right* to the coastal transit State. This is absurd, for by definition a land-locked State lacks a sea-coast and hence is incapable of giving anyone access to the sea.' Caflisch, op. cit., n. 13, p. 89.

7

Hydro-diplomacy between Nepal and India, and the Mahakali River Treaty

Introduction

A number of rivers originate in the Nepal Himalaya and flow through the valleys and plains of Nepal to India and ultimately to the Bay of Bengal. They can provide a great deal of hydroelectric power, a cheap and durable form of energy, much needed by populous nations such as India and Bangladesh. It is estimated that these Nepalese rivers could generate up to 83,000 MW of hydroelectric power,[1] which is more than the combined total hydroelectric power produced by USA, Canada, and Mexico. For instance, the Karnali Project, a single hydroelectric power project, will have an installed capacity of 10,800 MW, the second largest in the world.[2] These rivers have also been very useful in irrigating the low-lying parts of Nepal as well as the fertile Indo-Gangetic plains in India. This is one of the reasons why India became interested from as early as the 1950s in utilizing the Nepalese rivers in the interests of both India and Nepal.

However, many Nepalese took the view that India was keen to exploit Nepal's hydropower potential to its advantage. This opinion was based on Nepal's experience with the Koshi and Gandak agreements in the 1950s under which India secured disproportionate benefits to Nepal's detriment.[3] The public opinion in Nepal has always been critical of these two agreements. As the barrages were constructed quite close to the Indian border, Nepal was unable to benefit from them. Had the projects been located further up in Nepal, it could have received a fair share of waters for irrigation from them. What is more, a large area of Nepal bordering

India was submerged by the execution of these projects meant to benefit India, with Nepal on the receiving end of the negative impact of the projects.[4] Addressing the Nepal Council of World Affairs in August 1996, the then minister for water resources called these agreements 'unequal agreements'.[5] He said that the Koshi and Gandak Projects, though built on Nepalese territory, 'gave Nepal few palpable benefits. Nepal had entered into these project arrangements at a time when it was extremely ill-equipped in terms of its administrative set up, technical expertise, international exposure, negotiating experience, and above all, awareness of the country's resources and their utility'.[6] A former Indian foreign secretary acknowledges that the benefits of the Koshi and Gandak agreements to Nepal 'proved marginal and negative'.[7]

It was this hang-up of the past that led to the insertion of a clause, at the insistence of all major political parties within Nepal, in the new Constitution of Nepal of 1990[8] to ensure that no government in Nepal, whether under Indian pressure or otherwise, could conclude a treaty to utilize and share the water resources of Nepal without securing a two-thirds majority in parliament. It is against this background that it is proposed to analyse in this chapter the provisions of the principal water resources-related treaties concluded between Nepal and India.

During the British Raj

Water cooperation between India and Nepal began in 1920 during the British Raj in India. Earlier however, during the rapid expansion of the Raj in South Asia, Kathmandu with its temperate climate was perhaps eyed by the British as a probable summer capital for the Indian Dominion. As a result, Britain and Nepal went to war in 1815. There were two legendary and equally patriotic leaders in Nepal, Amarsingh Thapa and Bhimsen Thapa, who held diametrically opposed views about the idea of going to war with the then expanding and mighty British empire. Bhimsen Thapa won the argument and, with the support of Amarsingh Thapa, Nepal, a tiny Himalayan kingdom, went to a two-year war with Britain. Although the war ended with the conclusion of a peace treaty between Nepal and Britain in 1817, known as the Treaty of Sugauli, Nepal came out a clear loser. Nepal ceded nearly one-third of its territory—the low lying and most fertile territory bordering India—to Britain. From then on Nepal followed a policy of withdrawal and isolation while the argument on the wisdom and farsightedness on the part of the political and army leaders to go to war with Britain kept on rumbling within the country.

However, after some time, when the consolidation of the Raj was clearly in sight, the Nepalese rulers adopted a policy of cooperation with the British. It was at this juncture of history that Nepal started supplying its own troops, known as the Gurkhas, for the services of the Raj and permitted the recruitment for the British army of young people from the hills and mountains of Nepal with inborn resilience and tough physical character, qualities greatly in need in the armed forces created for the sustenance of the Raj. It was this spirit of cooperation demonstrated by the rulers of Nepal that led Britain to voluntarily return to Nepal part of the territory ceded by the latter during the 1815–16 war. It was in this climate of cooperation that Nepal concluded a first ever water cooperation treaty with Britain in 1920 designed to facilitate the construction of a canal for irrigation purposes by Britain on the Mahakali River, known in India as the Sharada River.

Under the 1920 agreement, Nepal agreed to provide some 4,000 acres of land to the British government for the Sharada Canal Project. In return, the British government was to give Nepal land equal in area that is adjacent to the Indian territory. In addition, Nepal was to receive from the British government free of charge a supply of 460 cusecs of water. Provided that there was a surplus available, Nepal would also receive a further supply of up to 1,000 cusecs of water for cultivation from the Sharada canal's headworks during the *kharif* season (rice plantation time), i.e., from 15 May to 15 October; and 150 cusecs during *rabi* (dry season), i.e., from 15 October to 15 May. Nepal was not required to make any contribution towards the costs of construction of the canal. Thus, it was basically a land exchange (in equal amount) agreement concluded between the two governments under which Nepal stood to gain some additional benefits from the project (in terms of the supply of water free of charge) in return for its decision to cooperate with the British government.

After Indian Independence

(i) The Koshi Agreement

The second example of water cooperation between India and Nepal is the Koshi Agreement, concluded between the two countries in 1954 to utilize the waters of the River Koshi, Nepal's third biggest river, for the generation of hydroelectric power and irrigation. The agreement provides for the construction by and at India's cost a barrage, headworks, and other appurtenant work(s) inside Nepal about five miles up-stream of a Nepalese town, Hanuman Nagar, on the Koshi River with afflux bond and flood banks, and canals and protective works, on land lying within the territories of Nepal, for the purpose of flood control, irrigation, generation of hydroelectric power, and prevention of erosion of areas in Nepal on the right side of the river, upstream of the barrage. The agreement envisaged that a large land area within Nepal would be submerged once the project was completed. Nepal also agreed to authorize and give necessary facilities for investigations of storage or detention dams on the Koshi or its tributaries, soil conservation measures such as check dams, afforestation, etc., required for a complete solution of the Koshi problem in the future. Nepal permitted the Indian government to quarry the construction materials required for the project within Nepal.

Article 4 of the agreement gave complete freedom to India 'to regulate all the supplies in the Koshi River at the barrage site and to generate power at the same time for the purposes of the project'. This was without prejudice to Nepal's right to withdraw for irrigation or any other purpose in Nepal such supplies of water as may be required from time to time. India would be the owner of all land acquired for the project, albeit Nepal retained sovereignty rights and territorial jurisdiction over such land. Nepal would also permit India to quarry the construction material required for the project within Nepal. The agreement gave India a free hand to construct and maintain roads, tramways, ropeways, etc., required for the project in Nepal and vested in India the ownership and the control of the metalled roads, tramways, and railway.

What is more, it required Nepal to grant its consent and provide land for these purposes or for the future construction of storage or detention dams and other soil conservation measures not only on the main Koshi River but also on its tributaries on payment of compensation. Although Nepal retained the navigational rights on the Koshi River, the use of any water-craft like launches and timber rafts within two miles of the barrage and headworks was to be controlled by the Indian authorities. Likewise, fishing, even by Nepalese people, within two miles of the barrage and headworks was prohibited.

In return for all this, Nepal would be entitled to use up to 50 per cent of the hydroelectric power generated at the barrage site power house on payment of such tariff rates as may be fixed for the scale of power by the Indian government in consultation with the government in Nepal. It was also to receive royalty in respect of power generated and utilized in India as well as of stone, gravel, and ballast obtained from Nepali territory for the construction and the future maintenance of the barrage at rates to be settled by agreement. The land required for the purposes of the project was to be acquired by Nepal, and India was to provide compensation for such land.

As is evident from the above summary of the principal provisions of the 1954 Koshi Agreement, it was an agreement concluded to generate electricity and provide for irrigation mainly for India. The project was to be constructed within Nepal using a major Nepalese river and flooding Nepalese territory but Nepal was to receive little in return from it the bulk of the benefits going to India. Ironically, this agreement concluded by a newly independent Asian brother with its small neighbour proved to be a lopsided one and a great deal worse for Nepal than that one concluded with British–Indian government in 1920. While the agreement with Britain provided for some additional benefits such as a supply of certain amount of water and electricity free of charge to Nepal for its willingness to cooperate in a land exchange agreement for a similar project on the River Mahakali, the agreement with India provided no such benefits for Nepal. Nepalese territory and a Nepalese river were to be used by India for its own irrigation and electricity needs without offering Nepal any substantial benefits in return.

This inequality in the agreement and the absence of mutuality created resentment within Nepal and the agreement was branded as a 'sell-out' to India in certain quarters. In the face of such public criticism of the agreement, India and Nepal decided to amend it in 1966. However, Nepal still holds the view that even the revised agreement did not go far enough to remedy the inequality in the 1954 agreement. As the project envisaged by the 1954 agreement was already in place, there was not much left to negotiate. The revised agreement was partly to legitimize the deviation from the original agreement that had occurred during the construction of the project and partly to insert new provisions to strengthen Nepal's position vis-à-vis certain matters relating to it.

While the original agreement did not state anything about its duration, which perhaps implied that it was for an indefinite period, the revised agreement said that it would remain valid for a period of 199 years. Another significant change to the agreement was that the land that Nepal had made available to India for the project was on lease and the duration of the lease was 199 years. Unlike the previous agreement, the new one did not transfer to India the ownership of the land allocated for the project, but only leased it, and in return Nepal was to receive an annual rent from India in lieu of the use of the land for the project. Under a separate letter exchanged between the two governments, after the conclusion of the new agreement, it was envisaged that Nepal would be able to take over the project properties at the end of the lease. In that case Nepal would compensate India to 'cover borne the cost born to date and such other cost as may be incurred in future by the Government of India with the agreement of His Majesty's Government [of Nepal]'.

The revised agreement required India to seek prior approval before carrying out any construction or other work relating to the project. The wording regarding the utilization of the waters of the Koshi River was changed to make it clear that Nepal would have every right to withdraw for irrigation and for any other purpose in Nepal, water from the river and from the Soon–Koshi River or within the Koshi basin from any other tributaries of the Koshi River as may be required from time to time and that India would have the right to regulate only the balance of supplies in the river at the barrage site thus available from time to time and to generate power at the Eastern Canal. The agreement also expanded the scope of Nepal's entitlement to the hydroelectric power generated by any power house constructed under the agreement to include in Nepal's 50 per cent share of the power generated, not only the power generated at the barrage site as envisaged in the old agreement but also that generated by any power house situated within a 10-mile radius from the barrage site.

The revised agreement also made it clear that all navigation rights in the Koshi River in Nepal shall rest with Nepal. Nepal reserved the right to issue permits for the use of any water-craft like boats, launches, and timber rafts even within the two miles of the barrage and headworks. Under the old agreement this right belonged to the Indian executive engineer of the barrage. Similar changes were made with regard to the fishing rights. The new agreement also provided for the establishment of an Indo-Nepal Koshi Project Commission. Both the old and new agreements contained a provision for arbitration for the settlement of disputes arising out of the operation and implementation of the project or the application or interpretation of the agreement. Under a separate letter exchanged between the two governments after the conclusion of the new agreement, India agreed to surrender to Nepal part of the land obtained by India under the old agreement on which the Nepal Link Bund was situated. All in all, the new agreement seems to have been concluded by the new panchayat government to minimize the damage done to the interests of Nepal under the old agreement concluded by a Nepali Congress government.

(ii) The Gandak Agreement

Soon after the conclusion of the Koshi Agreement, India and Nepal concluded another agreement in 1959 relating to the Gandak Irrigation and Power Project, to utilize the waters of the River Gandaki, the second largest river in Nepal, for the generation of hydroelectric power and irrigation. The agreement provided for the construction within the territory of Nepal of a barrage, canal head regulators, and other appurtenant works for purposes of irrigation and development of power for Nepal and India. The nature and scope of this agreement is very similar to the original Koshi Agreement concluded in 1954. Nepal was required to acquire or requisition, as the case may be, all such lands as are required by India for the project and transfer such lands to the latter on payment of reasonable compensation by India.

All works connected with the project in the territory of Nepal was to become the property of and be operated and maintained by India. The government of India was to construct at their own cost for the benefit of Nepal the Western Nepal Canal, including the distributory system for it, down to a minimum discharge of 20 cusecs of water to provide flow irrigation in the gross command area estimated to be about 40,000 acres, and the Eastern Nepal Canal up to the River Bagmati, including the distributary system, down to a minimum discharge of 20 cusecs of water to provide flow irrigation in Nepal for the gross command area estimated to be 103,500 acres.

As was the case in the Koshi agreement, the principal purpose of the Gandak agreement was to generate hydroelectric power and irrigation mainly for India. Nepal was to receive only a small amount of power, i.e. 15,000 KW, generated by the project on payment of a charge based on the actual cost of production plus the cost of transmission. The rest of the electric power was to go to India. Although Nepal would continue to have the right to withdraw for irrigation or any other purpose from the river or its tributaries in Nepal such supplies of water as required from time to time, this right was restricted by the requirement that such exercise of its rights by Nepal was not to affect the water requirements of the project as set out in the schedule annexed to the agreement. The schedule gives the minimum quantities of water required for the project after making the allowance for the withdrawal of water from the upper reaches of the Gandak River and its tributaries sufficient for the irrigation of 200,000 acres which was the maximum area estimated to be available for the purpose at the time of the conclusion of the agreement.

A letter exchanged between Nepal and India on the day this agreement was signed, states that if at any time, due to natural causes, the supplies in the river are insufficient for all the purposes, Nepal would be entitled to continue to withdraw water sufficient for the irrigation of an area up to 200,000 acres. However, the principal agreement further provided in Article 10 that whenever the supply of water available for irrigation falls short of the requirements of the total area under the project for which irrigation has to be provided, the shortage would be shared on pro rata basis between Nepal and India. Like the Koshi Agreement, this one also included a provision for arbitration of any dispute arising out of the application and implementation of the agreement. However, unlike the revised Koshi agreement, the Gandak agreement appears to remain valid for an indefinite period and no amendment was made to this when the Koshi agreement was revised.

(iii) The Tanakpur Agreement

A newly elected government of the Nepali Congress Party concluded in 1991 an agreement with immediate effect with India to allow it to build a 577-metre long afflux bond on Nepalese territory to ensure the success of an Indian hydroelectric power project being built at Tanakpur, located on the Indian side of the Indo-Nepal border river (i.e. the Mahakali), using the waters of this river.

An Indo-Nepal Joint Commission had been established by the governments of the two countries in order to help identify areas for mutual economic cooperation between the two governments and advise them on the feasibility and modalities of such cooperation. This joint commission had been asked, inter alia, to examine the possibilities of cooperation in harnessing Nepal's water resources in the interests of both India and Nepal and to make appropriate recommendations to the governments. In order to facilitate its work on cooperation in matters relating to water resources the commission had set up a sub-commission on water resources. On the basis of the recommendation's of the sub-commission, the joint commission took certain decisions in the form of Agreed Minutes on 5 December 1991 which included the following decision on the Tanakpur barrage project:

(i) The site at Mahendranagar municipal area in the Jimuwa village will be made available for tying up of the Left Afflux Bund, about 577 metres length (with an area of about 2.9 hectares) to the high ground on the Nepalese side ... The availability of land for construction of Bund will be effected in such a way by HMG/N [Nepal] that the work could start by 15th of December 1991.

(ii) India will construct a head regulator of 1, 000 cusecs capacity near the left under-sluice of the Tanakpur Barrage, as also the portion of canal up to Nepal–India border for supply of up to 150 cusecs of water to irrigate between 4,000 to 5,000 hectares of land on Nepalese side ...

(iii) In response to a request from Nepalese side, as a goodwill gesture the Indian side agreed to provide initially 10 MW of energy annually free of cost to Nepal in spite of the fact that this will add to further loss in the availability of power to India from Tanakpur Power Station ...[9]

This decision of the Joint Commission was endorsed by the prime ministers of India and Nepal through a joint press communiqué issued during the Nepalese prime minister's visit to India between 5–10 December 1991. The site on which the main project is located is the land ceded to British India by Nepal after the two-year (1813–15) war between them. The land on which Nepal permitted India under the Tanakpur Agreement to build the 577-metre long afflux bund is the land returned to Nepal by British India in 1860 in return for Nepal's assistance in crushing the Indian sepoy rebellion against the British Raj.

India appeared to have started construction work on its soil in 1983 on the Tanakpur barrage project to harness the water of the Mahakali river, an Indo-Nepal border river, without consulting Nepal. Only when the Indian side realized that without constructing an afflux bund on the Nepalese side of the border, the project would be unable to deliver the desired amount of electricity or water for India, the government of India seems to have approached its Nepal counterpart in order to secure Nepal's prompt approval for the construction of an afflux bund on Nepalese soil to make the project being built on Indian soil a success. As the then political party in power in Nepal was often characterized by critics as a party supported and favoured by India, it was perhaps the best time for India to secure Nepal's approval. It was against this background that the prime ministers of India and Nepal decided to conclude an agreement, without calling it an agreement, with immediate effect through an informal document entitled 'Agreed Minutes' in order to avoid parliamentary procedure of ratification of treaties and agreements.

Though many observers believed that the agreement itself was not entirely a bad deal for Nepal, the manner in which the agreement was concluded aroused nationalist sentiment within Nepal. If the prime minster of Nepal had come clean and tabled the agreement before parliament for approval as a normal bilateral transaction, the agreement could perhaps have been easily endorsed as the government had a majority in parliament. However, when he tried to avoid parliamentary scrutiny, he was forced to submit to the scrutiny of the judiciary. It was in this context that the Supreme Court of Nepal held that the so-called 'Agreed Minutes' was an agreement in law and it had to be approved by parliament under Nepal's constitutional provisions.

The 1996 Mahakali River Treaty between Nepal and India

The most recent treaty dealing with water resources cooperation between Nepal and India, is the 1996 Mahakali River Treaty. It is a major water cooperation treaty concerning the integrated development of the Mahakali river including Sharada Barrage, Tanakpur Barrage, and Pancheshwar Project (hereafter referred to as the 'Mahakali Treaty').[10] This is perhaps the most ambitious and comprehensive water cooperation treaty concluded in the troubled history of Indo-Nepal relations. The Pancheswar Project is basically an undertaking to construct a reservoir type project on the Mahakali river, a boundary river, designed primarily to generate huge amounts of hydroelectricity and to trap the monsoon runoff for irrigation during dry season and flood control.

(i) The Principal Provisions of the Treaty

The Mahakali river is a boundary river between Nepal and India. It originates in the southern flanks of the Himalaya in the north-western part of Indo-

Nepal border. Under a treaty concluded by Nepal with British India in 1815[11] and subsequent changes made to the provisions of the treaty in later years with British India, this river constitutes a boundary between Nepal and India on the western border of Nepal. After leaving the Indo-Nepal border in the south-western part of the border the river flows through Indian territory and empties into the river Ganges in India. The river has a tendency to change its course, especially in the north-western part, and appears to be moving eastwards (i.e. towards the area of Nepal). Nepal swapped some land with the British Indian government under a 1920 treaty[12] to allow the Raj to construct an irrigation project known as the Sharada Barrage in the south-western part of the border. That is why the river does not necessarily constitutes a boundary all along the Indo-Nepal border in the west.

After pondering for decades about the pros and cons of several schemes of cooperation in the field of water utilization for irrigation and the generation of hydropower in the best mutual interests of both countries, India and Nepal decided to conclude a treaty concerning the Mahakali river. The treaty was designed to prescribe a formula for the sharing of the waters of this boundary river and to utilize these for irrigation and for the construction of a hydropower project on the basis of a 50:50 share in the cost and benefit. This treaty was expected to be a catalyst for the conclusion of other treaties designed to harness Nepal's immense water potential for the benefit of both countries. However, the implementation of this treaty itself has hit the buffers by delaying the whole process of future cooperation between the two countries. The treaty has the following principal objectives:

(i) To legitimize the previous arrangement[13] made with regard to the construction of the Tanakpur Barrage with some 'enhanced benefits' for Nepal.

(ii) To agree on the construction of a major multipurpose project known as the Pancheswar Multipurpose Project.

(iii) To lay down the principles governing the rights and duties of the two parties vis-à-vis the waters of this boundary river and the basic principles of cooperation between the parties for the preparation and implementation regarding the Pancheswar Multipurpose Project.

(iv) To establish a joint river commission entrusted with the task of assessing and overseeing the implementation of the treaty and making appropriate recommendations to the parties on measures to be taken to ensure compliance with its provisions.

(v) To provide for a dispute settlement mechanism in the event of a dispute arising out of the interpretation and implementation of the treaty between the parties.

The Arrangement Relating to the Tanakpur Barrage

As stated earlier, the Mahakali river forms Nepal's western border with India. It was in the early 1980s that India had constructed a barrage (the Tanakpur Barrage) in a course of the river with a part of the eastern afflux bund at Jimuwa and the adjoining pondage area of the barrage lying in the Nepalese territory. India undertook the construction of the barrage without any agreement with Nepal. Only when it became necessary to construct the eastern afflux bund in the Nepalese territory for the success of the project, did India approach Nepal, and the Tanakpur agreement was concluded in 1991 in the form of a Memorandum of Understanding (MoU). However, when the Supreme Court of Nepal stated in a judgement[14] that the 1991 MoU was a treaty in law and had to be ratified by parliament, the MoU was thrown into disarray. Thus, the two governments agreed to incorporate the provisions of the Tanakpur agreement into the Mahakali Treaty with slightly enhanced benefits for Nepal.

Under Article 1 of the treaty, Nepal has the right to a supply of 1,000 cusecs of water from the Sharada Barrage in the wet season (i.e. from 15 May to 15 October) and 150 cusecs in the dry season (i.e. from 16 October to 14 May). This was a recognition by India of Nepal's right to the waters of this border river as the Sharada Barrage had been constructed on the Indian side of the river to use the waters of the river without seeking Nepal's agreement. India also undertook to maintain a flow of not less than 350 cusecs downstream of the Sharada Barrage in the Mahakali river to maintain and preserve the river's ecosystem.

Under Article 2, Nepal gave its consent to the use of a piece of land of about 577 metres in length (an area of about 2.9 hectares) of Nepalese territory and a certain portion of the no-man's land on either side of the border for the construction of the eastern afflux bund of the Tanakpur Barrage by India. However, Nepal retained her sovereign rights over the territory to be used for the barrage and the land lying on the west of the said land (about 9 hectares) up to the Indo-Nepal border which forms a part of the pondage area. It should be noted here that the construction of the barrage had already gone ahead and this provision of the treaty was included merely to grant Nepal's retroactive consent to the construction.

In lieu of the eastern afflux bund of the Tanakpur Barrage, Nepal had the right to a supply of 1000 cusecs of water in the wet season (i.e. from 15 May to 15 October) and 300 cusecs in the dry season (i.e. from 16 October to 14 May) as well as a supply of 70 millions kilowatt-hour (unit) of energy on a continuing basis annually and free of cost from the date of the entry into force of the treaty. For the purpose of providing the amount of water to Nepal under Articles 1 and 2, India undertook to construct the head regulator(s) near the left under-sluice of the Tanakpur Barrage and also the waterways of the required capacity up to the Indo-Nepal border and such head regulator(s) were to be operated jointly. India also undertook to construct a 132 KV transmission line up to the Nepal-India border from the Tanakpur Power Station for the purpose of supplying the stated amount of energy to Nepal.

Thus, Nepal appears to have come out much better under the new Mahakali Treaty, than under the 1991 Tanakpur MoU, with regard to the benefits to be received from the Tanakpur Barrage. This was one reason why the opposition political parties in Nepal, which had opposed the previous Tanakpur MoU, came round to support the Mahakali Treaty in parliament when the treaty was tabled for parliamentary approval for ratification (discussed below).

The Agreement on the Pancheswar Multipurpose Project

Under Article 3 of the Mahakali Treaty, the contracting parties agreed to construct a major multipurpose project known as the Pancheswar Multipurpose Project on a stretch of the Mahakali river where it forms the boundary between the two countries. It will be a massive 315 metre high dam designed to generate energy. With an installed capacity of 6480 MW.[15] Thus, it is a treaty designed to implement a future project on the river in accordance with a detailed project report (DPR) being jointly prepared by the parties rather than a treaty endorsing a project proposal already prepared and awaiting endorsement for implementation. The project will be a multipurpose project meant primarily for hydroelectric power generation, irrigation, and flood control. The nature and scope of cooperation on this ambitious project is outlined in paragraphs 1 to 4 of Article 3 in the following terms:

1. The Project shall, as would be agreed between the Parties, be designed to produce the maximum total net benefit. All benefits accruing to the both the Parties with the development of the Project in the forms of power, irrigation, flood control etc. shall be assessed.

2. The Project shall be implemented or caused to be implemented as an integrated project including power stations of equal capacity on each side of the Mahakali River. The two power stations shall be operated in an integrated manner and the total energy generated shall be shared equally between the Parties.

3. The cost of the Project shall be borne by the Parties in proportion to the benefits accruing to them. Both the Parties shall jointly endeavour to mobilize the finance required for the implementation of the Project.

4. A portion of Nepal's share of energy shall be sold to India. The quantum of such energy and its price shall be mutually agreed upon between the Parties.

Through a letter exchanged between the prime ministers of India and Nepal on the day the treaty was concluded, the two states agreed to finalize the detailed project report (DPR) within six months from the date the treaty came into force. They agreed that 'For this purpose, necessary data and reports shall be exchanged expeditiously. While assessing the benefits from the Project during the preparation of the DPR, net power benefit shall be assessed on the basis of, *inter alia*, saving in costs to the beneficiaries as compared with the relevant alternatives available. Irrigation benefits shall be assessed on the basis of incremental and additional benefits due to augmentation of river flow and flood control benefit shall be assessed on the basis of the value of works saved and damages avoided.'[16] The project was aimed to be completed within eight years from the date of the agreement for its implementation, subject to the provisions of the DPR.

The Principles Governing the Rights and Duties of the Parties

Various articles of the treaty lay down the principles governing the rights and duties of the two parties vis-à-vis the waters of this border river and the basic principles of cooperation between the parties for the preparation and implementation regarding the Pancheswar Multipurpose Project. Article 3 incorporates the principle of equal rights over the waters of the river. India and Nepal agreed that 'they have equal entitlement in the utilization of the waters of the Mahakali River'. However, there is a qualification attached to this principle which states that the principle of equal entitlement is applicable 'without prejudice to their respective existing consumptive uses of the waters of the Mahakali River'.

It is this qualification that has become a matter of acute controversy in Nepal and has delayed the whole process of preparing and finalizing the DPR since people in certain quarters in Nepal point out that first, there is no definition of the term 'consumptive use' in the treaty, second, there is no indication of the amount of water being used by India for its so-called 'consumptive use', and third, the treaty does not affect or take into account the disproportionate amount of water already being used by India for various purposes. They maintain that this qualification seriously undermines the principle of equal rights enunciated in the treaty. They argue that both Nepal and India should have equal entitlement to the waters of this border river regardless of the existing consumptive uses of the parties.[17] There is a further explanation attached to the nature and scope of Article 3; Section 3 (b) of the Side Letter exchanged between the two parties together with the treaty provides that:

> It is understood that Paragraph 3 of Article 3 of the Treaty precludes the claim, in any form, by either party on the unutilized portion of the shares of the waters of the Mahakali River of that Party without affecting the provision of the withdrawal of the respective shares of the water of the Mahakali River by each Party under this Treaty.

Article 5 of the treaty provides that 'Water requirements of Nepal shall be given prime consideration in the utilization of the waters of the Mahakali River'. However, this provision is subject to the principle of equal entitlement in the water less the amount being used by the parties under Article 3 as well as to the provision of paragraph 2 of Article 4 which states that: 'Both the Parties shall be entitled to draw their share of waters of the Mahakali River from the Tanakpur Barrage and/or other mutually agreed points as provided for in this Treaty and any subsequent agreement between the Parties.' Therefore, the provision of Article 5 appears to be no more than a hollow statement. As India has been diverting a hugely disproportionate quantity of water from the river for various projects, there is hardly enough water left to give 'prime consideration' to the water requirements of Nepal. Thus, from a critical point of view, one way or the other, under the treaty

Nepal appears to have lost not only in fact but also in law its rights over a significant quantity of water of this boundary river.

Article 6 provides that 'Any project, other than those mentioned herein, to be developed in the Mahakali River, where it is a boundary river, shall be designed and implemented by an agreement between the Parties on the principles established by this Treaty.' Article 7 is also of significance:

> In order to maintain the flow and level of the waters of the Mahakali River, each party undertakes not to use or obstruct or divert the waters of the Mahakali River adversely affecting its natural flow and level except by an agreement between the Parties. Provided, however, this shall not preclude the use of the waters of the Mahakali River by the local communities living along both sides of the Mahakali River, not exceeding five (5) per cent of the average annual flow at Pancheswar.

Article 8 provides that 'This Treaty shall not preclude planning, survey, development and operation of any work on the tributaries of the Mahakali River, to be carried out independently by each Party in its own territory without adversely affecting the provision of Article 7 of this Treaty.' The provisions of Article 9 are of great significance. This article lays down the basic principles governing the activities of a joint river commission established under the treaty which is entrusted with a wide-ranging powers of assessing and overseeing its implementation and making appropriate recommendations to the parties on measures to be taken to ensure compliance with its provisions. This article provides that 'The Commission shall be guided by the principles of equality, mutual benefit and no harm to either Party.' As we shall see later, this language is very similar to that of the 1996 Ganges Treaty concluded between India and Bangladesh. As the Mahakali is a boundary river the application of these principles seem to be perfectly reasonable to the sharing of its waters.

However, if the same principles were to be adopted in future agreements between India and Nepal with regard to other successive rivers that flow from Nepal into India, these principles would be more beneficial to India than to Nepal. This is because, in such a water thirsty region with fully utilized rivers, any use of its waters by Nepal upstream is likely to be claimed as harmful to it by India. This is one reason why Nepal, an upper riparian state, is likely to benefit more if it were to adopt the international law principle of equitable and reasonable utilization rather than the principle embodied in the Mahakali Treaty.

The Principal Point of Disagreement: The Concept of Existing Consumptive Use

The main controversy surrounding the ratification of the Mahakali Treaty, and the subsequent controversy surrounding the finalization of the DPR was the nature and scope of the term 'existing consumptive use', and the exclusion of the amount of water already in use by the parties from the definition of the equal entitlement of the parties in the utilization of the waters of the Mahakali River. It has been the perception in Nepal that India's existing consumptive use is much higher than Nepal's, and if this is excluded from the new definition of equal entitlement Nepal emerges the loser. The dispute was made worse when India came up with the interpretation that the term 'existing consumptive use' also included the waters being used by India for the Second Auxiliary Sharada Canal.[18]

The lower or Second Auxiliary Sharada canal is located about 170 km downstream from the main Sharada (Banbasa) project. Although the lower or auxiliary Sharada canal appears to be part of the main Sharada canal, the auxiliary canal is located far inside the Indian territory. What India seems to have maintained is that the term 'consumptive use' in the treaty recognizes the water being used by India for both the main and the second auxiliary Sharada canals. However, Nepal's position is that the term covers only the waters being used for the main Sharada canal on the river and not the second or lower canal located inside the Indian territory. The difference between these two claims is about 201 cusecs. From the Nepalese view of point, under the term existing consumptive use, India is entitled to no more than 248 cusecs on average needed for the main canal.

Nepalese officials have maintained that the Indian position is against the principle of equal sharing of water of the river enunciated in the treaty.[19] As explained by a columnist of a Nepalese English daily newspaper, 'The reason this issue is important is because sharing of the regulated waters after Pancheswar, which along with its power and flood control components are termed "benefits", is tied with the sharing of the costs of building the joint-Pancheswar project. As envisioned in the treaty, both the countries are to share the costs and benefits of the project equally'.[20] As both the cost of constructing the Pancheswar Project and the benefits from it are to be shared equally, the recognition of the right of prior use, that includes the lower or secondary Sharada barrage, would result in disproportionate benefit for India. This is because India would benefit more from the regulated flow of water after the construction of the Pancheswar Project on the basis of its claim of existing consumptive use for both the main and the auxiliary Sharada canals. The Side Letter to the treaty provides that 'Irrigation benefits shall be assessed on the basis of incremental and additional benefits due to augmentation of river flow and flood control benefit shall be assessed on the basis of the value of works saved and damages avoided'.[21] India seem to have asked for a supply of 449 cusecs at the main canal to ensure the supply of enough water even for the lower or second canal. The Indian position is that the lower Sharada canal has been around since 1974, long before the conclusion of the Mahakali Treaty in 1996 and should thus come under the definition of the term existing consumptive use.[22]

It is as a result of this controversy that it is necessary to examine the following questions: What is meant by the 'existing consumptive use' in the treaty? Is it permissible under international watercourse law to qualify the principle of equitable utilization by one criterion, i.e. the existing consumptive use alone, in defining the entitlement of the states in the waters of a border river such as the Mahakali river? Is the 'existing consumptive use' an absolute right of a riparian state to be taken into account when allocating the waters of a river? or is this a qualified right subject to other relevant factors to be taken into account in achieving 'equitable utilization' of the waters of the river between the co-riparian states?

States make use of the waters of any given river for a variety of purposes. The main types of uses are: (i) for domestic and sanitary purposes; (ii) for navigation; (iii) for power generation; and (iv) for irrigation purposes. As stated by Fuentes, 'there is no pre-established hierarchy between the various factors that may be considered in the establishment of an equitable regime for the utilization of international rivers'.[23] Indeed, Article VI of the 1966 Helsinki Rules on the Uses of the Waters of International Rivers states that 'A use or category of uses is not entitled to any inherent preference over any other use or category of uses'.[24] A similar provision can be found in Article 10(1) of the 1997 UN Convention on the Law of the Non-Navigational Uses of International Watercourses:

1. In the absence of agreement or custom to the contrary, no use of an international watercourse enjoys inherent priority over other uses.

2. In the event of a conflict between uses of an international watercourse, it shall be resolved with reference to articles 5 to 7, with special regard being given to the requirements of vital human needs.[25]

The reference to Articles 5 to 7 is to the principle of equitable and reasonable utilization (Article 5), the factors relevant to equitable and reasonable utilization (Article 6), and the obligation not to cause significant harm (Article 7). In the Statement of Understanding Pertaining to Certain Articles of the Convention, issued by the chairman of Working Group of the Whole, some clarification was offered as regards the term 'vital human needs': 'In determining "vital human needs", special attention is to be paid to providing sufficient water to sustain human life, including both drinking water and water required for production of food in order to prevent starvation.'[26]

Having said that international watercourses law provides for no clear hierarchy between different uses of water of an international watercourse, it is now proposed to examine the concept of existing consumptive use. Neither the Mahakali Treaty nor any of the ILA or ILI instruments or the 1997 UN Convention provides a definition of the term 'consumptive use'. However, there is some indication in the practice of states as well as in some legal writing with regard to the meaning of the term 'consumptive use'. For instance, after analysing the provisions of the Colorado River Compact of 1922 concluded between various federal states of the US, Meyers states that the term 'consumptive use' in the compact was probably going to be interpreted to mean an existing use of water which was 'to be measured by diversions less return flows' into the river.[27] Just as in the Mahakali Treaty, the term 'consumptive use' was mentioned but not defined in the 1922 Compact and was the subject of dispute between various federal states within the US. However, when the US and the Republic of Mexico concluded a water treaty in 1944 concerning the Rio Grande and Colorado Rivers, Article 1(j) of the treaty stated that 'in general' consumptive use 'is measured by the amount of water diverted less the part thereof which returns to the stream'.[28]

Even then it is not clear whether it means net depletion of the virgin flow, as argued by the upper basin states of the Colorado River, or whether it means consumptive use at the site of use, that is, the net loss to the stream at the place of use, as argued by the lower basin states.[29] Generally speaking, an existing consumptive use includes existing uses for domestic, sanitary, and irrigation purposes but not the uses for power generation. However, it is debatable whether the water used by India for the Second Auxiliary Sharada Canal falls under the definition of the term 'existing consumptive use' of the Mahakali Treaty since Nepal has maintained that the understanding reached between the parties as to the meaning of this term during the negotiations of this treaty did not intend to include the waters used by India for the second canal located far inside the Indian territory, long after the river ceases to be a boundary river. Nepal also argues that this is a new demand on India's part and cannot thus be recognized as 'an existing consumptive use'. If that is the case, this 'new' demand on India's part does not probably fall under the 'existing consumptive use' of the treaty for, as stated earlier, international law of watercourses does not accept any hierarchy when it comes to different competing uses nor does it give any preference for any existing consumptive uses at the expense of other relevant factors in ensuring equitable utilization of the water resources of a river.

However, India's position is that all consumptive uses in existence at the time of the conclusion of the treaty, including the water for the Second Auxiliary Sharada Canal, are India's consumptive uses for the purposes of the treaty. From Nepal's point of view, the term 'existing consumptive use' was intended to include the waters being used by India under the 1920 Sharada Canal Treaty[30] concluded by Nepal with British India, but not the waters for the Second Auxiliary Sharada Canal. However, from the Indian point of view, India's entitlement to use the waters of the Mahakali River for all the projects that were in existence at the time of the conclusion of the treaty remain unaffected by the sharing formulae of the Mahakali Treaty. That was one of the reasons why the treaty included provisions to recognize the existing consumptive uses of the parties. Questions such as this could perhaps be decided on the basis of the understanding of the parties at the time of the conclusion of the treaty or the legislative history of the treaty. Unfortunately, no official publications of either government shed any light on these issues.[31]

With regard to the question of accommodation of an existing use in the equitable sharing of water, Article VII of the Helsinki Rules provides that 'A basin State may not be denied the present reasonable use of the waters of an international drainage basin to reserve for a co-basin State a future use of such waters'. Article VIII goes on to elaborate on the situation of existing reasonable uses:

> 1. An existing reasonable use may continue in operation unless the factors justifying its continuance are outweighed by other factors leading to the conclusion that it be modified or terminated so as to accommodate a competing incompatible use.
>
> 2. (a) A use that is in fact operational is deemed to have been an existing use from the time of the initiation of construction directly related to the use or, where

such construction is not required, the undertaking of comparable acts of actual implementation.

(b) Such a use continues to be in existing use until such time as it is discontinued with the intention that it be abandoned.

3. A use will not be deemed an existing use if at the time of becoming operational it is incompatible with an already existing reasonable use.

However, no such provision in favour of giving some preference to existing uses is included in the 1997 UN Convention on International Watercourses. The Helsinki Rules of the ILA are not binding ones; they are rules compiled and agreed upon by an international professional body, the ILA, consisting of a group of experts on the subject. Of course, they carry a considerable legal weight and have actually influenced a great deal of the outcome of the ILC's work on the Draft UN Convention. Some of the rules do even represent rules of customary international law in existence at the time of the adoption of the Helsinki Rules.[32]

However, under the 1997 UN Convention on International Watercourses, the sole objective seems to have been to achieve equitable and reasonable utilization. Nevertheless, Article 6 of the convention requires states to take into account 'existing and potential uses of the watercourse' in agreeing on equitable and reasonable utilization. This does not however mean that when sharing the waters of an international watercourse on an equitable basis only the amount of water less the amount already in use have to be shared equally by the parties. The 'existing use' factor is neutralized by other factors mentioned in this article of the convention. Nevertheless, what is true is that existing consumptive uses for drinking and other domestic uses can always enjoy the highest priority in allocating the waters of a river. Therefore, it is perfectly legitimate to make special allowance for those existing consumptive uses of India or Nepal for drinking and other domestic uses.

However, an existing use, other than those for drinking and other domestic uses, is one factor and certainly not a decisive one in determining the amount of water to be shared by the parties concerned in an equitable and reasonable manner. Unlike the 1966 Helsinki Rules, the 1997 UN Convention requires that 'existing use' however historic or however reasonable be reconciled with other factors, and the Mahakali Treaty does not do this. From this point of view, the provisions of the Mahakali Treaty, defining the equal rights of Nepal and India only on the water less the amount already in use does not in principle seem to be compatible with the principle of equality or equitable utilization with regard to the waters of the Mahakali River. The 'existing consumptive use' is not an absolute right, but a qualified right subject to other considerations.

Yet, neither India nor Nepal are party to the UN Convention, nor has the Convention itself entered into force. Of course, it can be argued that most of the provisions of the convention in question are based on customary rules of international law[33] and the convention as a whole is the last word of the international community on the law of the non-navigational uses of international watercourses. However, the convention itself states that 'In the absence of an agreement to the contrary, nothing in the present Convention shall affect the rights or obligations of a watercourse State arising from agreements in force for it on the date on which it became a party to the present Convention.'[34] Moreover, the Mahakali Treaty is a treaty concluded in the spirit of mutual cooperation between two sovereign and democratic states and it is not unusual to find in a treaty of this nature that allows for preferential treatment for the 'existing consumptive uses' of the parties. After all, the main principle enunciated in the UN Convention not only calls for an 'equitable' utilization but also for a 'reasonable' utilization of the waters of an international watercourse. However, that does not mean that all existing uses even within Indian territory, i.e. even after the river ceases to be a boundary river, can be included in the definition of the term 'existing consumptive uses'.

The concern expressed in parliament by Nepalese lawmakers from the United Marxist and Leninist (UML) opposition political party during the debate on the Treaty was with respect to the absence of any statement regarding the actual amount of water currently used by India for its 'consumptive use'. In their opinion, it was necessary to have a statement or an indication from India about the amount of water actually being used by India in order to avoid any future disputes between the two countries. However, the statement was not forthcoming from India and the Nepalese minister for water resources maintained that it was difficult for India to give a precise figure as the level of water used by India for consumptive use varied in different months and was somewhere between 126 and 326 cusecs, depending on the actual flow of water in the river in any given month. The minister added that the actual amount of water being used by India would be specified only after the detailed project report of the Pancheswar project was completed. When requested for India's understanding of this provision of the treaty, the Indian ambassador to Nepal stated in his reply that the government of India 'would be happy to discuss these and other relevant matters and reach mutually satisfactory understandings on them *after ratification of the Treaty*, at the time of finalizing the Detailed Project Report' (emphasis added).[35] In conclusion, it is doubtful whether the term 'existing consumptive use' in the treaty also includes the uses inside the Indian territory when the river is no longer a boundary river. To recognize all such uses as existing consumptive uses may very well be against the principle of equality enshrined in the treaty or the principle of equitable utilization under international watercourses law, including the provisions of the 1997 UN Convention. Accepting India's position on the 'existing consumptive use' would mean strengthening the no-harm principle rather than applying the principle of equitable and reasonable use. The thrust of the compromise reached in adopting the 1997 UN Convention was to give precedence to the equitable and reasonable use over the no-harm principle.

Evaluation of the Mahakali Treaty

Nepal appears to have lost not only in fact but also in law its rights over a significant quantity of water of this boundary river under the treaty, which sets a bad precedent for future dealings with India with regard to other rivers. For instance, Article 9 provides that the Indo-Nepal joint commission 'shall be guided by the principles of equality, mutual benefit and no harm to either Party'. Since the Mahakali is a boundary river, the application of these principles seem to be perfectly reasonable to the sharing its waters. However, if the same principles were to be adopted in future agreements between India and Nepal with regard to other successive rivers that flow from Nepal into India, these principles would be more beneficial to India than to Nepal. This is because in such a water thirsty region with fully utilized rivers any use of its waters by Nepal upstream is likely to be claimed as harmful to it by India. This is one reason why Nepal, an upper riparian state, is likely to benefit more if it were to adopt the international law principle of equitable and reasonable utilization rather than the principle embodied in the Mahakali Treaty.

Similarly, Article 5 of the treaty (which provides that 'Water requirements of Nepal shall be given prime consideration in the utilization of the waters of the Mahakali River') is no more than a hollow statement if this provision is read together with other provisions of the treaty, especially the provision concerning the 'existing consumptive use'. This is because, international watercourses law provides no clear hierarchy between different uses of water of an international watercourse. No provision in favour of giving some preference to existing uses is included in the 1997 UN Convention on International Watercourses. The sole objective seems to be to achieve equitable and reasonable utilization. An existing use, other than those for drinking and other domestic uses, is one one and certainly not a decisive one in determining the amount of water to be shared by the parties concerned in an equitable and reasonable manner. From this point of view, the provisions of the Mahakali Treaty defining the equal rights of Nepal and India only on the water less the amount already in use does not seem to be compatible with the principle of equality or equitable utilization with regard to the waters of the Mahakali river. The 'existing consumptive use' is not an absolute right, but a qualified one subject to other considerations.

The Mahakali Treaty is based on the principle of equal entitlement of Nepal and India to the waters of the Mahakali River rather than on the principle of equitable and reasonable utilization to be found in the 1966 Helsinki Rules of the ILA or the 1997 UN Convention on the Law of the Non-Navigational Uses of International Watercourses. The Nepalese official publications claimed that it was the skilful negotiating ability of the Nepalese negotiators that persuaded India to accept the principle of equal entitlement rather than an equitable entitlement in the waters of the Mahakali River. Nepal claimed this as a significant achievement. However, when examined closely, the provisions of the Mahakali Treaty appear to be more harmful to Nepal than would have been the case if the principle of equitable utilization had been embodied in the treaty.

The application of the principle of equal entitlement is perhaps better with regard to a boundary river since this principle will result in a clear and equal allocation of the waters of the river between the co-riparian states. However, this principle cannot be applied to the so-called successive rivers that flow from one state into another. That is why the claim by Nepal that the incorporation of the principle of equality in the Mahakali Treaty is a significant achievement for Nepal and it might set a nice precedent favourable to Nepal is not a justifiable one. This is especially true of the Mahakali Treaty, as it takes into account only one relevant factor, i.e. the existing consumptive use of the parties (which is more favourable to India as India's existing consumptive use is much higher than Nepal's), rather than all other relevant factors enumerated in international instruments in allocating the waters of the Mahakali River.

A more satisfactory formulae for Nepal for this particular boundary river would have been the application of either a straightforward equal allocation formulae without attaching any qualifications, as applied in the 1909 Boundary Waters Treaty between Canada and the US, or the principle of equitable utilization which would take into account not only the existing consumptive use but also all other relevant factors to arrive at a satisfactory method of allocation. The principle applied in the Mahakali Treaty is neither the US–Canada formulae nor the equitable utilization principle; it is a hybrid formula that appears to favour India as the quantity of its existing consumptive use is way above the existing use of Nepal.

India has an irrigation system developed from the time of the Raj; it started investing heavily in irrigation and the generation of power quite early, and the consumption of water by Indian industries is much higher than Nepal's. Therefore, the acceptance by Nepal of the principle of equality based on taking into account only one factor, i.e. the existing consumptive use, is likely to be harmful to Nepal both in the short and long term. It is a small and weak country virtually surrounded by a powerful neighbour. That is why it should have adhered to the principles of international watercourses law rather to the deceptively attractive propositions such as the principle of equality that is conditioned to one factor, and one that is beneficial to India. As stated earlier, under international law no existing use has any preference over other uses, both actual and potential. The other relevant factors outlined both in the Helsinki Rules and the 1997 UN Convention are capable of neutralizing any claim based on existing consumptive and non-consumptive uses of a riparian state.

The Indian argument is that the river is a boundary river only on major stretches of the border and it is quite reasonable to recognize India's existing consumptive uses even below the point from where the river crosses the Indo-Nepal border and becomes an Indian river. In fact, the treaty seems to have incorporated the Indian argument by stating in paragraph 3 of the preamble that 'the Mahakali River is a boundary river *on major stretches* between the two countries' (emphasis added). Article 3 reiterates the spirit of the preamble in slightly different words and in a different context. Speaking to the press after initialling the treaty in January 1996, the Indian Foreign

Minister, Pranab Mukherjee, made it clear that 'India had not conceded to the Nepalese demand to define the Mahakali as a '"border river" which would have entitled Nepal to half of all the benefits from all projects on the river. The Mahakali is a border river *only for a short stretch*' (emphasis added).

Although the last sentence of this statement does not quite appear to follow the paragraph in the preamble of the treaty mentioned above, the intended outcome, from the Indian point of view, of the formulation of this provision of the treaty and the Indian foreign minister's assertion would be the same: the river is a boundary river on major stretches between the two countries but those major stretches constitute only a short stretch when the whole length of the river (i.e. from its origin to the point where it enters the Ganges), is considered. This Indian interpretation and its implicit recognition in the treaty by not simply calling this river a boundary river but only 'a boundary river *on major stretches* between the two countries' is prone to raise controversy and perhaps give India more rights with regard to the utilization of the waters of or at least legitimize India's existing consumptive use for various projects, including those unilaterally built by India.

In international law, the Mahakali River is a boundary river as it forms a boundary between the two countries on major stretches of the western border of Nepal with India. To qualify as a boundary river a river does not necessarily have to constitute a boundary along its entire course or all along the border between the two countries. Insofar as the law of international watercourses is concerned, whether a river constitutes a boundary only on major stretches of the border or all along the border does not necessarily make much difference as it is the principle of equitable and reasonable utilization that applies to all international rivers, whether successive or contiguous or boundary rivers. The issue that the length of a river within one state is greater than the length within another state per se is also immaterial as this is not a decisive criterion recognized in international law to be applied in apportioning the waters of the river between the co-riparian states. As stated above, in international law the sole objective is to achieve equitable and reasonable utilization on the basis of the relevant factors agreed upon by the states parties concerned. Of course, the co-riparian states may decide to take into account the length of the river within one state as a relevant factor together with all other relevant factors in sharing or utilizing the waters of the international or boundary river in question, but in the absence of such an agreement the mere fact that the length of a river within one state is longer than that within another cannot alone, define the corresponding rights of the co-riparian states.

Therefore, India's argument—i.e., since the Mahakali river is a boundary river only on major stretches of the river India has more rights over the waters of the river—is not supported by international law. Of course, when it comes to sharing or utilizing the waters of the river in accordance with the principle of equitable and reasonable utilization the two states may take into account the fact that the length of the river in India is longer than the length where it constitutes a boundary between the two states as a relevant factor on the basis of India's greater need. When this factor is weighed against other competing relevant factors, India may legitimately end up acquiring larger share of the waters of the river. That however is not to say that because the Mahakali River is a boundary river only on major stretches of the Indo-Nepal boundary, India has more rights over the waters of the river or can unilaterally divert waters of such a boundary for its various projects on its side of the border. Unilateral apportionment or diversion of waters of a boundary river by a riparian state even on its side of the border, which affects the rights of the other state, is not justifiable in international law.

From this point of view, neither the argument advanced by the Indian foreign minister nor the projects carried out unilaterally by India even on its side of the border to utilize the waters of the river to the detriment of Nepal is supported by international law of watercourses. However, Nepal seems to have, once again, succumbed to the Indian argument and concluded the Mahakali Treaty legitimizing the situation that is not quite consistent with the prevailing rules of international law.

The Mahakali Treaty is in essence a framework treaty, requiring the conclusion and ratification of a number of other treaties in the future to bring the main treaty into full and effective operation. Therefore, it could perhaps be said that it was unwise on the part of both Nepal and India to conclude a framework treaty such as the Mahakali Treaty on a complex issue such as the utilization of the water resources between the two countries without doing enough groundwork to make it a success. Even in a skeleton or framework form, the DPR should have been prepared and appended to the treaty and the term 'consumptive use' defined. This is what Canada did before ratifying the Columbia River Treaty of 1961 with the US. In other words, Canada did not ratify the treaty until its manner of implementation was further defined through a protocol and until arrangements were made to sell the first 30 years of Canada's entitlement to the power deriving from each storage project. The treaty was concluded on 17 January 1961 but the ratification process was completed only on 16 September 1964 when a Protocol which amplifies and clarifies the treaty was appended to it. Perhaps, Nepal and India hurried to ratify the Mahakali Treaty without appending a protocol to it outlining the items of basic understanding between the two countries concerning its implementation.

Conclusion

It will be unfortunate if the spirit of cooperation for mutual benefit between India and Nepal in the field of the development and utilization of the water resources of the international rivers of the region were to be thwarted by the events such as the ones surrounding the Mahakali Treaty. For Nepal, one of the poorest countries in the world, with no other known significant natural resources, development of its water resources seems to be a way out towards raising the living standards of its people in close cooperation with India. On the other hand, India is a country with a vast population concentrated along the Indo-Gangetic plains. Not only do these plains need more water for irrigation, but also the rapidly growing industries all over northern India need more energy. Yet, the ability to produce more and an inexpensive form of energy lies in cooperation with Nepal. There is a community of interests or mutuality of interests between the two countries to develop the water resources of the rivers of this region of the world.

As stated in the preceding pages, most of the water cooperation agreements concluded by Nepal with India in the past have been in the interests of India. India ignored Nepal's rights when unilaterally constructing the Tanakpur barrage in the first place. The unilateral construction of the barrage on a border river by India was against the principles of international law. But this time, this treaty aims to meet the interests of both sides on an equal footing in most of cases. Modern-day diplomacy is always about 'give and take'. No nation can move forward if it expects only gains without being prepared to allow for gains to the other side too. There appear to be significant benefits to be gained by Nepal from the implementation of the Pancheswar Project, which will at the same time give huge benefits to India because it is a lower riparian state, because Nepal has limited ability to utilize her water resources on her own, because Nepal's is predominantly a mountain terrain, and because India-locked Nepal has only one ready buyer of its surplus energy, India. Strictly speaking, in the absence of meaningful cooperation based on equal benefit to Nepal and India, Nepal could possibly invoke the principle of permanent sovereignty of states over their natural resources to unilaterally terminate the lopsided Koshi and Gandak Agreements.

Notes and References

1. 'Only 0.64 per cent of that potential is now harnessed. Foreign consultants say 25,000 MW are easily exploitable if and when India and Nepal reach some agreement on pricing.' *Far Eastern Economic Review*, 8 March 1990, 26.

2. *The Foreign Affairs Record*, vol. XXXVII, no. 3 (March 1991), p. 35 (Delhi: Ministry of Foreign Affairs, Government of India).

3. The Koshi Agreement concluded between the two countries in 1954 to utilize the waters of the river Koshi, Nepal's third largest river, was for the generation of hydroelectric power, irrigation, and flood control mainly for India. It is a multipurpose project designed to construct a barrage over the river Koshi for the diversion of the waters of the river to feed two canal systems—the western and eastern canals. See for the text of the Koshi agreement, FAO Development Law Service, *Treaties Concerning the Non-Navigational Uses of International Watercourses: Asia* (FAO Legislative Study, no. 55, FAO, 1995), pp. 60–3; United Nations Legislative Series, *Legislative Texts and Treaty Provisions Concerning the Utilization of International Rivers for Other Purposes than Navigation* (1963) (ST/LEG/SER.B/12, United Nations Sales no. 63.V.4), pp. 290–4; A.S. Bhasin (ed.), *Documents on Nepal's Relations with India and China 1949–66* (Bombay/New Delhi: Academic Books Ltd., 1970), pp. 152–65. India and Nepal concluded another agreement in 1959 relating to the Gandak Irrigation and Power Project to utilize the waters of the river Gandaki, the second largest river in Nepal, for the generation of hydroelectric power, irrigation, and flood control again mainly for India. Like the Koshi Agreement, the Gandak Agreement too was a multi-purpose project designed to construct a barrage on the Nepalese territory near the Indo-Nepal border. See text of the agreement, United Nations Legislative Series, ibid., pp. 295–300; Bhasin, ibid., pp. 166–72.

4. A senior Nepalese water resources engineer and executive director of the Water and Energy Commission and another official working at the Ministry of Water Resources state in relation to the Koshi agreement that 'Ignoring the very appropriate site at Chatra gorge, the Koshi barrage was constructed on the alluvial plain on the Nepalese side of the border, which ensured that almost all the diverted

water would be used in India. This created large-scale submergence of the limited plain land of Nepal, where, with the passage of time, the accumulation of silt caused by the barrage in the stretch between the barrage and Chatra resulted in the danger of the Koshi breaking its banks even under normal flood conditions.'

With regard to the Gandak agreement they say the following: 'if the barrage had been constructed near Deoghat, upstream of the Chitwan Valley in Nepal, some more land in Nepal could have been supplied with irrigation water; but the barrage was constructed at the Nepal–India border, with India withdrawing water up to 29,000 cusecs and leaving Nepal with the provision of withdrawing only up to 850 cusecs'. They then go on to conclude that 'in the country where almost all the waters originate [Nepal], and a project (with its inevitable submergence of land) is fully or partially located, there is, apparently, no possibility of water diversion for the much needed irrigation. As a result, even the limited land available on one side of the border is mostly barren in the non-monsoon period, while the other side of the border has been able to utilize these river waters to the maximum because of the disproportionately advantageous location of the project or other related structures.' Hari Man Shrestha and Lekh Man Singh, 'The Ganges Brahmaputra System: A Nepalese Perspective in the Context of Regional Co-operation', *in* Asit K. Biswas and Tsuyoshi Hasimoto (eds), *Asian International Waters: From Ganges—Brahmaputra to Mekong* (Oxford University Press, Bombay, 1996), pp. 81–94, at 85–7.

5. Pasupati S.J.B. Rana, 'The Prospect of Water Resources of Nepal and the Mahakali River Integrated Development Treaty', Nepal Council of World Affairs, 16 August 1996 (a copy of this paper is on file with me).

6. Ibid.

7. Jagat S. Mehta, 'Opportunity Costs of Delay in Water Resource Management between Nepal, India, and Bangladesh', *in* David J. Eaton (ed.), *The Ganges–Brahmaputra Basin: Water Resource Co-operation between Nepal, India and Bangladesh* (Austin, Texas: Lyndon B. Johnson School of Public Affairs, University of Texas at Austin, 1992), pp. 1–13, at 5.

8. The 1990 Constitution of Nepal provides in Article 126 that the ratification, accession, acceptance or approval of treaties or agreements on the following matters will have to be done by a majority of two-thirds of the Members present in the joint session of both Houses of Parliament: (a) Peace and Friendship; (b) Defence and strategic alliance; (c) Boundaries of the Kingdom of Nepal; (d) Natural resources and distribution in the utilization thereof. Pursuant to this provision of the Constitution, the Nepal Treaty Act, 1990 was enacted. My own translation from the Nepali text of the 1990 *Constitution of the Kingdom of Nepal* (Kathmandu: Ministry of Law and Justice, 2047 Kartik 23 (Oct. 1990), p. 73. See also Albert P. Blaustein and Gisbert H. Flanz (eds), *Constitutions of the Countries of the World: Nepal* (Release 94–4, June 1994), Oceana, New York. See, for the text of the

Nepal Treaty Act, 2047, Dhruba Bar Singh Thapa (ed.), *Recent Laws of Nepal*, vol. 3 (3), May–June 1991 (Kathmandu: Legal Research Associates), pp. 6–8.

9. See *Nepal Gazette* of 8 Poush of B.S. 2049 (corresponding to Dec. 1991), pt. VI, sect. 41, no. 36, pp. 9–10.

10. The text of the treaty has been reproduced in 36 ILM 531 (1997). See a report to this effect, 'India, Nepal Sign Pact on River Water', *Times of India*, 13 Feb. 1996.

11. See in C.U. Aitchison, *Treaties and Engagements Relating to Nepal*, pt. II (Calcutta: Government of India Printing Department, 1909), pp. 110–12; see also the Treaty of 1 Nov. 1860, ibid., pp. 122–3.

12. The text of the treaty is on file with me.

13. See the Memorandum of Understanding between the Governments of Nepal and India concerning the Tanakpur Project in *Nepal Gazette* of 8 Poush of BS 2049 (corresponding to Dec. 1991), pt. VI, sect. 41, no. 36, pp. 9–10. The Memorandum has been reproduced in Dhruba Bar Singh Thapa (ed.), *Recent Laws of Nepal*, vol. 4 (1), March–April 1992 (Legal Research Associates, Kathmandu), pp. 46–8.

14. *B.K. Neupane* v *the Prime Minister, G.P. Koirala et al.* Decision of the Special Bench of the Supreme Court of Nepal of 30 Marga, 2049 (corresponding to AD 1992). My own translation from the Nepali text of the judgement reproduced in Deshbhakta Baral (ed.), *Tanakpur: From the Beginning to the End* (Kathmandu: Pairavi Publications, 1993), pp. 87–97. See, for a detailed analysis of this judgement, Surya P. Subedi, 'When is a Treaty a Treaty in Law? An Analysis of the Views of the Supreme Court of Nepal on a Bilateral Agreement between Nepal and India', 5 *Asian Yearbook of International Law* (1997), pp. 201–10.

15. 'A Watershed on the Mahakali', *HIMAL South Asia*, March 1996, pp. 11–2.

16. Para. 3 (a) of the Side Letter.

17. See, for a summary of different viewpoints of various political parties, Ministry of Water Resources, *Treaty concerning the Sharada Barrage, Tanakpur Barrage, and the Integrated Development of the Mahakali River including the Pancheswar Project and the Exchange of Letters Thereof and the Views of Different Individuals, Articles and Letters Relating to the Ratification Process of the Treaty* (29 Kartik 2053, corresponding to Nov. 1997, (Kathmandu: HMG/Nepal) (this publication is mostly in Nepali, but it includes the English text of the Treaty and a few other articles and letters in English) (hereafter referred to as the 'Ministry of Water Resources Documents').

18. It was reported that during the negotiations for the preparation of the DPR India said that it needed an additional flow of 201 cusecs on the Mahakali River to maintain her Second Auxiliary Sharada Project. It is this 'new' development

that seems to have delayed the whole process of finalizing the DPR. See 'Nepal Negates Prior Consumptive Rights on Mahakali', *Kathmandu Post*, 1 Dec. 1997.

19. See the views of the Nepalese Water Resources Minister, Pashupati S.J.B. Rana, in *Kathmandu Post*, 7 Nov. 1997. See also the views of a Nepalese lawmaker, Khanal, ibid., 30 Dec. 1997, p. 1.

20. See 'Nepal, India Fail to Find Common Ground as DPR Talks End', *Kathmandu Post*, 10 Nov. 1997, pp. 2–4.

21. Para. 3 (a) of the Side Letter.

22. *Kathmandu Post*, 10 Nov. 1997, pp. 2–4.

23. Ximena Fuentes, 'The Criteria for the Equitable Utilization of International Rivers', 69 BYIL 1998, pp. 337–412, at 351.

24. The International Law Association, *Report of the Fifty-Second Conference*, Helsinki, 14–20 Aug. 1966 (London, 1967), pp. 484–532.

25. 36 ILM 700 (1997), at 707.

26. 36 ILM 719 (1997).

27. Charles J. Meyers, 'The Colorado Basin', *in* A.H. Garreston et al. (eds), *The Law of International Drainage Basins* (Dobbs Ferry, New York: Oceana, 1967; published for the Institute of International Law, New York University School of Law), pp. 486–607, at 508.

28. As quoted, ibid., p. 560.

29. See Meyers, op. cit., n. 27 at 530.

30. Nepal had concluded a first ever water cooperation treaty with British India in 1920 designed to facilitate the construction of a canal for irrigation purposes by Britain on the Mahakali River, known as the Sharada River in India. Under the 1920 agreement Nepal agreed to provide some 4,000 acres land to the British government for the Sharada Canal Project. In return, the British government was to give Nepal land equal in area from adjacent Indian territory. In addition, Nepal was to receive from the British government free of any charge a supply of 460 cusecs of water and, provided the surplus was available, a supply of up to 1,000 cusecs when cultivation grew at any future time from the Sharada canal head work during the Kharif (rice plantation time), i.e. from 15 May to 15 October; and of 150 cusecs during *rabi* (dry season), i.e. from 15 October to 15 May. Nepal was not required to make any contribution towards the cost of construction of the canal. Thus, it was basically a land exchange (in equal amount) agreement concluded between the two governments under which Nepal stood to gain some additional benefits from the project (in terms of the supply of water free of charge) in return for its decision to cooperate with the British government. The text of the agreement is on file with me.

31. The publication that the government of Nepal brought out to inform the public about the whole range of documents, articles, and speeches concerning

the Mahakali Treaty contains no reference to negotiation or legislative history or to any points of understanding reached bilaterally with regard to particular terms or principles embodied in the treaty. This collection of documents, articles, and speeches published by the Ministry of Water Resources on 29 *Kartik* 2053 is mostly in Nepali and is on file with me. See the *Ministry of Water Resources Documents, supra.*

32. See generally, Lucius Caflisch, 'The Law of International Waterways and Its Sources', *in* Ronald St. John Macdonald (ed.), *Essays in Honour of Wang Tieya* (Dordrecht: Martinus Nijhoff, 1994), pp. 115–29; Patricia K. Wouters, 'Allocation of the Non-Navigational Uses of International Watercourses: Efforts at Codification and the Experience of Canada and the United States', *Canadian Yearbook of International Law* (1992), 43–88.

33. For instance, see Caflisch and Wouters, ibid.

34. Art. 3 of the 1997 UN Convention.

35. See a letter of 19 Sept. 1996 from the ambassador of India to Nepal to the Nepalese foreign minister in the *Ministry of Water Resources Documents*, supra.

8

The Supreme Court of Nepal and the Tanakpur Agreement between India and Nepal

Introduction

For a small country, Nepal has produced more than its share of political oddities. It has a constitutional monarch, worshipped by many as an incarnate deity. It is also one of the few countries to have freely voted communists into power ... On August 28th Nepal discovered it also had a Supreme Court prepared to overrule both king and party. The Court decided that King Birendra's decision in June to dissolve parliament and call an election was unconstitutional.[1]

These lines were written in *The Economist* after the Supreme Court of Nepal had delivered an extraordinary decision stating that the decision of the King of Nepal of June 1995 to dissolve parliament and call an election on the recommendation of the prime minister was unconstitutional.[2] In 1992 this court also delivered a very interesting decision, touching upon the law of treaties and affecting Nepal's relations with India. The latter judgement is the subject of analysis in this chapter.

A newly elected government of the Nepali Congress Party in 1991, led by G.P. Koirala, had concluded an agreement with immediate effect with India (hereafter the 'Tanakpur Agreement'), allowing it to build a 577-metre long afflux bund[3] on Nepalese territory to ensure the success of an Indian hydroelectric power project being built at Tanakpur, located on the Indian side of the Indo-Nepal border river, Mahakali, using the water of this river. The agreement was to enter into force without awaiting or requiring the approval of the Nepali parliament. A case was brought before the Supreme Court of Nepal challenging the validity of the agreement.[4] The prime minister, who endorsed the 'Agreed Minutes' through a joint communiqué, contested the case stating that the these did not constitute an agreement in law but were a mere understanding reached between the two countries to allow India to build the afflux bund on Nepalese territory for the Tanakpur project in return for certain concessions. Hence, in his opinion, it was not necessary to table this understanding before parliament since the Constitution of Nepal and the Nepal Treaty Act required the government to table only treaties and agreements and not understandings.

It is interesting that the government of the day did not try to argue that the deal was an executive agreement and therefore not subject to the requirement of being tabled before parliament. What the prime minister was in fact saying was that the documents exchanged between Nepal and India were of a technical and administrative nature and related to matters for the regulation of which the executive was competent. The government of Nepal focused all its efforts on denying that the instruments concluded between the two countries constituted a treaty.

In a very interesting judgement of far-reaching implications, the Supreme Court of Nepal held that the understanding reached between India and Nepal was a treaty for all purposes and that the government of Nepal was under an obligation to table it before parliament for its approval for ratification.

Provisions of the Constitution of Nepal and the Treaty Act

The 1990 Constitution of Nepal provides in Article 126 that:

(1) The ratification of, accession to, acceptance of or approval of treaties or agreements to which the Kingdom of Nepal or His Majesty's Government is to become a party shall be as determined by law.

(2) The laws to be made pursuant to clause (1) shall, *inter alia,* require that the ratification of, accession to, acceptance of or approval of treaties or agreements on the following matters be approved by a majority of two-thirds of the Members present at a joint session of both Houses of Parliament:

(a) Peace and Friendship;

(b) Defence and strategic alliance;
(c) Boundaries of the Kingdom of Nepal;
(d) Natural resources and the distribution of their uses.

Provided that out of the treaties and agreements referred to in sub-clauses (a) and (d), if any treaty or agreement is of an ordinary nature, which does not affect the nation in a pervasively grave manner or on a long-term basis, such treaty or agreement may be approved for ratification, accession, acceptance or approval by the House of Representatives by a simple majority of the Members present.

(3) A treaty or agreement not ratified, acceded to, accepted or approved as the case may be pursuant to this Article shall not bind the Kingdom of Nepal or His Majesty's Government after the commencement of this Constitution.

(4) Notwithstanding anything mentioned in clause (1) and (2), no treaty or agreement shall be concluded which compromises the territorial integrity of the Kingdom of Nepal.[5]

Pursuant to clause (1) of this Article, the 1990 Nepal Treaty Act was enacted.[6] Article 4 of the act requires the government of Nepal to table before the House of Representatives all treaties and agreements (other than those referred to in Article 126 paragraph 2 of the constitution) that need to be ratified, acceded, accepted, or approved by Nepal. Such treaties may be ratified, acceded, accepted, or approved with the consent of the House of Representatives by a simple majority of the members present and voting. The Treaty Act also provides that once ratified, acceded, accepted or approved, the provisions of such treaties and agreements will be applicable as the law of Nepal and will prevail over other laws in the event of inconsistency with those laws.

Given these provisions of the constitution and the Treaty Act, the issues before the Supreme Court were whether the Indo-Nepal agreement on Tanakpur constituted an Agreement for the purposes of the constitution and the Nepal Treaty Act and, if so, whether it affected Nepal 'in a pervasively grave manner or on a long-term basis' and was not 'of an ordinary nature'. The definition of a treaty provided in the Nepal Treaty Act is identical to that of the 1969 Vienna Convention on the Law of Treaties: '"Treaty" means an agreement concluded between two or more States or between a State and an international organization in written form and this word encompasses any document of this nature whatever its particular designation.'

The Nature of the Document

An Indo-Nepal Joint Commission had been established in order to help identify areas for mutual economic cooperation between the two governments and advise them on the feasibility and modalities of such cooperation. This Joint Commission had been asked, inter alia, to examine the possibilities of cooperation in harnessing Nepal's water resources in the interests of both India and Nepal and to make appropriate recommendations to the governments. In order to facilitate its work on cooperation in matters relating to water resources, the commission had set up a sub-commission on water resources. On the recommendation of the sub-commission, the joint commission took certain decisions in the form of Agreed Minutes on 5 December 1991 which included the following provisions on the Tanakpur barrage project:

> (i) The site at Mahendranagar municipal area in the Jimuwa village will be made available for tying up of the Left Afflux Bund, about 577 meters in length (with an area of about 2.9 hectares) to the high ground on the Nepalese side ... The availability of land for construction of the Bund will be effected in such a way by HMG/N that the work could start by the 15th of December 1991.
>
> (ii) India will construct a head regulator of 1,000 cusecs capacity near the left under-sluice of the Tanakpur Barrage, as also the portion of the canal up to the Nepal–India border for supply of up to 150 cusecs of water to irrigate between 4,000 to 5,000 hectares of land on the Nepalese side ...
>
> (iii) In response to a request from the Nepalese side, as a goodwill gesture the Indian side agreed to provide initially 10 MW of energy annually free of cost to Nepal in spite of the fact that this will add to further loss in the availability of power to India from the Tanakpur Power Station ....[7]

The decision of the joint commission was endorsed by the prime ministers of India and Nepal in a joint press communiqué issued during the Nepalese prime minister's visit to India between 5–10 December 1991. The Supreme Court of Nepal had to decide whether the two instruments formed a treaty for the purposes of the Constitution of Nepal and the Nepal Treaty Act.

Factual Background

The site on which the main project is located is the land ceded to British India by Nepal after the two-year (1813–15) war between the two countries.[8] The land on which Nepal permitted India under the Tanakpur Agreement to build the 577-metre long afflux bund is the land returned to Nepal by British India in 1860 in return for Nepal's assistance in crushing the Indian Sepoy Rebellion against the British Raj.[9] It appears that as early as 1983 India had already started construction work of the Tanakpur Barrage project on its soil to harness the water of the Mahakali River without consulting Nepal.[10] It seems that only when the Indian side realized that without constructing an afflux bund on the Nepalese side of the border the project would not be able to deliver the desired amount of electricity or water for India, the government of India approached the government of Nepal with a view to securing Nepal's prompt approval for the construction of the bund. The political party that was in power in Nepal at the time was often characterized by critics as a party supported and favoured by India. It was against this background that the prime ministers of India and Nepal decided to conclude an agreement (without calling it an agreement) with immediate effect through an informal document entitled 'Agreed Minutes' in order to avoid the parliamentary procedure of ratification of treaties and agreements.

The Decision of the Supreme Court

Delivering its judgement on the case on 15 December 1992, the Supreme Court stated, inter alia that the documents in question concluded between Nepal and India

> do not appear to have been concluded in any formal and traditional form. However, the joint press statement and the Joint Press Communiqué issued at the end of bilateral talks between the two Prime Ministers as well as the notice published to this effect in the Nepal Gazette on behalf of the Ministry of Water Resources and Energy of His Majesty's Government demonstrate that the recommendations of the Joint Commission were endorsed by the two Prime Ministers and the Governments of the two countries. Thus, there is no logical reason to believe that the decisions included in the Agreed Minutes concerning water resources and endorsed by the two Prime Ministers and the Governments of the two countries did not amount to an agreement or a treaty and were mere recommendations or understandings.

The argument of the attorney-general was that as there was no treaty or agreement of any formal or customary form concluded between the two countries the agreed minutes or understandings cannot be regarded as a treaty or an agreement. The Court however, went on to say that this argument was not consistent with the definition of a treaty or an agreement provided in section (a) of Article 2 of the Nepal Treaty Act, 1990. According to this definition, whatever its particular designation may be, if an agreement has been concluded between the two countries in written form that agreement has to be regarded as a treaty. After all, a treaty is a mutual agreement between the two parties to create legal rights and obligations.

The court held that neither the Vienna Convention on the Law of Treaties of 1969 nor the opinion of publicists or the decisions of international courts and tribunals require that a treaty be concluded in any particular form. In international practice, in addition to formal treaties, all other instruments known as memorandum, protocol, exchange of notes, declaration, convention, charter, covenant, final act, statute, modus vivendi, agreed minutes, etc., have been regarded as treaties and agreements. Depending on the situation, even a joint press statement or a joint press communiqué can constitute a treaty. The court added:

> It happens every now and then that States enter into transactions akin to treaties but having no legally binding force because they create moral or political obligations rather than legal obligations and rights between States and are often known as political or moral understandings. But the decisions in question in this case were made through Agreed Minutes between Nepal and India which included provisions designed to create mutual rights and obligations between the two countries. For instance, the Agreed minutes provide that Nepal will make its land available to India for the project but will not give up its right to exercise its continuous control and sovereign rights over such land and the natural resources therein. In return, Nepal will receive electricity and water for irrigation from India.

The Court went on to conclude that

> The Agreed Minutes also provide that India will be allowed to build a canal up to the Nepalese border and to carry out a survey with a view to constructing a road, etc. These decisions were included in the joint press statement and press communiqué issued after bilateral talks between the Prime Ministers of the two countries and published by the Ministry of Water Resources and Energy of His Majesty's Government in the Nepal Gazette. Thus, these decisions cannot be regarded as mere non-binding instruments of political and moral character; they appear to be the type of treaties which create mutual rights and obligations.[11]

Thus, the Supreme Court of Nepal seems to have subscribed to the view that the agreed minutes and the joint communiqué do not merely give an account of discussions and summarize points of agreement. They enumerate the commitments to which both India and Nepal have consented and thus create rights and obligations in international law for these two countries. That is how the public and the official and semi-official media understood the texts when they described the deal between India and Nepal as 'a breakthrough on the vexed issue of water resources development' between the two countries.[12] Consequently, the agreement written in the form of agreed minutes and included in the joint press communiqué should be submitted to parliament for approval in accordance with the Constitution of Nepal before the agreement could legally enter into force.

Concluding Observations

Although it is rare to find a municipal law court in a developing country that challenges the power of the executive branch of the state with regard to its conduct of foreign policy affairs, the above-mentioned views of the Supreme Court of Nepal are consistent with the views of international courts and tribunals. For instance, the International Court of Justice stated in 1978 in the *Aegean Sea Continental Shelf* case that the Court 'knows of no rule of international law which might preclude a joint communiqué from constituting an international agreement'.[13] Similarly, in 1994 the ICJ, in the case between Qatar and Bahrain concerning a maritime delimitation and a territorial dispute, held that the Agreed Minutes of 1990 between these two countries constituted an international agreement since they created rights and obligations in international law for the parties by enumerating the commitments to which the parties had consented.[14]

Indeed, in its commentary on the definition of 'treaty' which was incorporated without change in the final text of the 1969 Vienna Convention on the Law of Treaties, the International Law Commission of the UN stated that '[t]he term 'treaty' is used throughout the draft articles as a generic term covering all forms of international agreement in writing concluded between States'. The ILC went on to remark that 'very many single instruments in daily use, such as an 'agreed minute' or a 'memorandum of understanding', could not appropriately be called *formal instruments,* but they are undoubtedly international agreements subject to the law of treaties'.[15]

There are a number of instruments concluded between two or more states and termed 'agreed minutes' which have been recognized by the international community as legally binding international agreements. For instance, the 1963 boundary agreement between Iraq and Kuwait was concluded in the form of 'agreed minutes'. During and after the Gulf War in the wake of the Iraqi invasion of Kuwait, the UN and the international community treated this instrument as a legally binding international agreement. In its resolution 687 (1991) the Security Council of the UN demanded that

> Iraq and Kuwait respect the inviolability of the international boundary and the allocation of islands set out in the 'Agreed Minutes between the State of Kuwait and the Republic of Iraq regarding the restoration of friendly relations, recognition, and related matters', signed by them in the exercise of their sovereignty at Baghdad on 4th October 1963 and registered with the United Nations ...[16]

The decision of the Supreme Court of Nepal can be regarded as a bold decision which acts as a check against any excesses by the executive in foreign policy matters. Such decisions of municipal courts are quite helpful in ensuring that relations between states are based on transparency and democracy and that the government of the day does not conclude an agreement with a foreign power under a different name and as an informal instrument in order to avoid parliamentary and constitutional scrutiny. This is particularly so in a country such as Nepal whose leaders have in the past concluded certain lopsided treaties with India without properly weighing their long-term pros and cons for the future of the country. Therefore, this decision is likely to strengthen not only the constitutional system of parliamentary scrutiny of executive acts in foreign policy matters but also the democratic process in the country.

Notes and References

1. 'The Monarch and the Marxists', *Economist,* 2 Sept. 1995, 53.

2. An earlier version of this chapter was published by me in the *Asian Yearbook of International Law*, vol. 5, 1995, Kluwer Law International, pp. 201–10.

3. See D.B.S, Thapa (ed.), *Recent Laws of Nepal,* Jan.–Feb. 1992, vol. 4, no. 2 (March–April 1992), p. 46.

4. The case was brought before the Supreme Court under writ jurisdiction as a public interest litigation by B.K. Neupane, an advocate of the Supreme Court of Nepal, asking the court to review the decisions of the government to go ahead with the Tanakpur Project without seeking parliamentary approval. The reason for bringing the case directly to the Supreme Court was to seek under certiorari jurisdiction judicial review of the agreement with India, in accordance with the rights granted to the citizens of Nepal to go directly to the Supreme Court to have any decision of the government quashed if the decision was unconstitutional or if the fundamental rights of individuals had been violated.

5. Trans. by me from the Nepali text of the 1990 *Constitution of the Kingdom of Nepal,* (Kathmandu: Ministry of Law and Justice), 2047 Kartik 23 [Oct. 1990], p. 73.

6. *Nepal Gazette*, 8 Poush 2047 (Dec. 1990), pp. 77–9.

7. See *Nepal Gazette*, 8 Poush of BS 2049 (Dec. 1991), pt. VI, sec. 41, no. 36, 9–10.

8. D.B. Baral, *Tanakpur: From the Beginning to the End* (Kathmandu: Pairavi Publications, 1993) p. 4.

9. Ibid.

10. As mentioned in the written pleadings (Memorial) submitted to the Supreme Court on behalf of the government. See ibid., pp. 39–57.

11. My own translation from the Nepali text of the judgement as published in D.B. Baral, op. cit., p. 91.

12. See, for instance, the front page coverage of the deal in the *Times of India*, 12 Dec. 1991, 1, under the heading: 'Indo-Nepal Talks: Water Resources Issue Resolved'.

13. ICJ Rep. (1978) p. 39. 96.

14. ICJ Judgement of 1 July 1994, General List no. 87, p. 13.25.

15. II Yearbook of the International Law Commission (1966), p. 188.

16. See, generally, M.H. Mendelson and S.C. Hulton, 'The Iraq-Kuwait Boundary', 64 BYIL (1993) p. 135 et seq.

Conclusions

Democratization, transparency, and co-operation rather than confrontation are the elements needed if Indo-Nepal relations are to be made to work to the mutual advantage of the two countries. Nepal needs to nurture the goodwill it enjoys among the Indian people and the Indian political leaders should understand that India has an invaluable asset in the goodwill of the Nepalese people. Unless India acknowledges, as Mukerjee has argued, that 'a strong and vibrant Nepalese nationalism is the best possible guarantee that the people will not permit anyone within and outside the country to use Nepal as a cat's paw against India',[1] bilateral matters surrounding Indo-Nepal relations will remain difficult to resolve. India should stop looking at Nepal as India's own backyard. The tendency on the part of both the mandarins of the South Block and the Indian political leadership to regard Nepal as requiring some sort of a tutelage is responsible for generating resentment in Nepal. Therefore, South Block has to realize that the policies it has thus far adopted in relation to Nepal have not had the anticipated favourable results.

Nepal, in turn, should do its utmost to engage in a constructive dialogue with India in order to resolve the outstanding problems. The tendency to denigrate her larger neighbour for any perceived ills is not healthy. Blaming India for Nepal's problems achieves little that is positive. The majority of the Nepalese have grown to be apprehensive of India; such apprehension may ultimately block any major effort on the part of the two countries to work together to address the issues facing them. The range and speed of changes in international relations demand a change in approach. India and Nepal, too, have now to adopt a modern approach and regulate their relations in a democratic, modern, and transparent form. The leaders have to take the people into confidence and demonstrate that whatever moves are being made derive from the assumption of sovereign equality and mutual benefit. They have to set aside some of the old treaties and replace them with new ones based on modern principles of international law.

Both India and Nepal have carry forward their relations into the new phase, prepared for and capable of facing the challenges of the twenty-first century. They have to move away from the old dogmas and embrace transparency and democratic norms in the conduct of their relations. Should the governments fail to do so, the imperfect state of Indo-Nepal relations will continue to be exploited by both Indian and Nepalese politicians as they try to win votes in their respective election campaigns. For this, the immediate task at hand is to:

1. Regulate the Indo-Nepal border and require an ID card in some form when nationals of either of the countries cross the border;
2. Resolve the border disputes such as those relating to Kalapani;
3. Implement the Mahakali River Treaty in a manner that is satisfactory to both parties;
4. Ratify the Power Trade Agreement to enable the two countries to engage in programmes of meaningful economic cooperation; and
5. Conclude a new friendship treaty to replace the 1950 Treaty of Peace and Friendship and formally cancel the 1965 Arms Agreement and any other 'secret' agreements.

Against this background, I have proposed a comprehensive draft treaty of peace and friendship covering all aspects of bilateral relations between Nepal and India which is annexed to this book. The draft treaty, which should replace the 1950 treaty, is based on internationally accepted norms, yet at the same time takes into account the distinct characteristics of Indo-Nepal relations.

Normally, a peace and friendship treaty is supposed to function as a framework or 'umbrella' treaty outlining all the basic norms of bilateral relations. Other protocols and agreements should thus expand upon it to flesh out the skeleton designed in the main framework treaty. A peace and friendship treaty is incomplete if it fails to deal with the fundamentals of bilateral relations between the two countries. For instance, because Nepal is a landlocked country, one of the first and foremost provisions in a peace and friendship treaty with India should be to guarantee Nepal's freedom of transit and right of free access to and from the sea. However, the 1950 treaty contains no such provisions. As freedom of transit is recognized in international law, that freedom should also be incorporated into a peace and friendship treaty of a more permanent character and thus independent of any change of government or policy in either New Delhi or Kathmandu. Furthermore, when the issues surrounding the troubled 1950 Treaty have been discussed and agreed upon once and for all, these two countries should be able to conclude meaningful, mutually beneficial water cooperation, and other economic agreements.

The speed of changes in international relations is accelerating, yet India and Nepal appear to be making too little effort and have been slow in hammering out a sensible deal to resolve their outstanding issues. None of the issues between Nepal and India are as complex as those that exist between India and China or between India and Pakistan. Even so, China was able to conclude an economic cooperation agreement to supply enriched uranium to India on commercial terms.[2] There is no reason why Nepal should not be able to conclude and implement a number of water cooperation agreements with India, designed to generate hydropower. Significantly, India has concluded an agreement to buy spare electricity from Pakistan.[3] It therefore appears illogical that India will not need or will not buy hydropower from Nepal. There has to be a desire to work together in harnessing the resources available in Nepal for the benefit of both countries. Diplomacy assumes negotiation and compromise. Both Nepal and India should be able to translate into action the tremendous goodwill they have towards each other, and to reach an equitable compromise for the achievement of the higher goals of economic development and prosperity, especially for the poor of their respective countries.

References

1. Dilip Mukerjee, 'Himalayan Stalemate: Indian Stake in Nepali Goodwill', *Times of India*, 4 April 1989.

2. 'Nuclear Pay-Off', the *Far Eastern Economic Review*, 19 Jan. 1995, 22.

3. 'India to Buy Spare Pakistani Power', *Guardian* (London), 20 May 1997, 14.

Appendices

Treaties Relating to Indo-Nepal Relations

Appendix I

Treaty of Commerce with Nepaul, 1 March 1792

Treaty authenticated under the seal of Maha Rajah Run Behauder Shah Behauder Shumshere Jung; being according to the Treaty transmitted by Mr Jonathan Duncan, the Resident at Benares, on the part of Right Honourable Charles, Earl Cornwallis, K.G., Governor-General in Council, and empowered by the said authority to conclude a Treaty of Commerce with the said Maha Rajah, and to settle and fix the duties payable by the subjects of the respective States of the Honourable English Company and those of Nepaul, the said gentleman charging himself with whatever relates to the duties thus to be payable by the subjects of the Nepaul Government to that of the Company; in like manner as hath the aforesaid Maha Rajah, with whatever regards the duties thus to be payable by the subjects of the Company's Government to that of Nepaul; and the said Treaty having been delivered to me (the said Maha Rjah) by Mowlavy Abdul Kadir Khan, the aforesaid gentleman's vakeel, or agent; this counterpart thereof having been by the Nepaul Government, hath been committed to the said Khan, as hereunder detailed:

Article 1

Inasmuch as an attention to the general welfare, and to the ease and satisfaction of the merchants and traders, tends equally to the reputation of the administrators of both Governments of the Company and of Nepaul; it is therefore agreed and stipulated, that $2^1/_2$ per cent shall reciprocally be taken, as duty, on the imports from both countries; such duties to be levied on the amount of the invoices of the goods which the merchants shall have along with them; and to deter the said traders from exhibiting false invoices, the seal of the customs houses of both countries shall be impressed on the back of the said invoices, and copy thereof being kept, the original shall be restored to the merchants; and in cases where the merchant shall not have along with him his original invoice, the custom house officers shall, in such instance, lay down the duty of $2^1/_2$ per cent on a valuation according to the market price.

Article 2

The opposite stations hereunder specified, within the frontiers of each country, are fixed for the duties to be levied, at which place the traders are to pay the same; and after having once paid duties and receiving a rowannah thereon, no other or further duty shall be payable throughout each country or dominion respectively.

Article 3

Whoever among the officers on either side shall exceed in his demands for, or exaction of duty, the rate here specified, shall be exemplarily punished by the government to which he belongs, so as effectually to deter others from like offences.

Article 4

In the case of theft or robberies happening on the goods of the merchants, the Foujedar, or officer of the place, shall advising his superiors or Government thereof speedily cause the zamindars and proprietors of the spot to make good the value, which is in all cases, without fail, to be so made good to the merchants.

Article 5

In cases where in either country any oppression or violence be committed on any merchant, the officers of country wherein this may happen shall, without delay, hear and inquire into the complaints of the persons thus aggrieved, and doing them justice, bring the offenders to punishment.

Article 6

When the merchants of either country, having paid the established duty, shall have transported their goods into the dominions of one or the other State if such goods be sold within such State, it is well; but if such goods not meeting with sale, and that the said merchants be desirous to transport their said goods to any other country beyond the limits of either of the respective States included in the Treaty, the subjects and officers of these latter shall not take thereon any other of further duty than the fixed one levied at the first entry; and are not to exact double duties, but are to allow such goods to depart in all safety without opposition.

Article 7

This Treaty shall be of full force and validity in respect to the present and future rulers of both Governments, and, being considered on both sides as a Commercial Treaty and a basis of concord between the two States, is to be, at all times, observed and acted upon in times to come, for the public advantage and the increase of friendship.

On the 5th of Rejeb, 1205 of the Hegira, and 1199 of the Fussellee style, agreeing with the 1st of March 1792 of the Christian, and with the 22nd of Phagun 1848 of the Sunbut AEra, two Treaties, to one tenor, were written for both the contracting parties, who have mutually engaged that from the 3rd Bysack 1849 of the Sunbut AEra, the officers of both States shall, in pursuance of the strictest orders of both Governments, immediately carry into effect and observe the stipulations aforesaid, and not wait for any further or new direction.

(True copy and translation)
(Sd.) J. DUNCAN
Resident
Revenue Department.
(A true copy)
(Sd.) G.H. BARLOW
Sub-Secretary

Appendix II
Treaty with the Raja of Nepaul, 1801

Whereas it is evident as the noonday sun to enlightened understanding of exalted nobles and of powerful Chiefs and Rulers, that Almighty God has entrusted the protection and government of the universe to the authority of Princes, who make justice their principle, and that by the establishment of a friendly connection between them universal happiness and prosperity is secured, and that the more intimate the relation of amity and union the greater is the general tranquillity; in consideration of these circumstances, His Excellency the Most Noble the Governor-General, Marquis Wellesley, etc., etc., and the Maharaja have established a system of friendship between the respective Governments of the company and the Raja of Nepaul, and have agreed to the following Articles:

Article 1

It is necessary and incumbent upon the principals and officers of the two Governments constantly to exert themselves to improve the friendship subsisting between the two States, and to be zealously and sincerely desirous of the prosperity and success of the Government and subjects of both.

Article 2

The incendiary and turbulent representations of the disaffected, who are the disturbers of our mutual friendship, shall not be attended to without investigation and proof.

Article 3

The principals and officers of both Governments will cordially consider the friends and enemies of either State to be the friends and enemies of the other; and this consideration must ever remain permanent and in force from generation to generation.

Article 4

If any one of the neighbouring powers of either State should commence any altercation or dispute, and design, without provocation, unjustly to possess himself of the territories of either country, and should entertain hostile intentions with the view of taking that country, the vakeels on the part of our respective Governments at either Court will fully report all particulars to the head of the State, who, according to the obligations of friendship subsisting between the two States, after having heard the said particulars, will give whatever answer and advice may be proper.

Article 5

Whenever any dispute of boundary and territory between the two countries may arise, such dispute shall be decided, through our respective vakeels or our officers, according to the principles of justice and right; and a landmark shall be placed upon the said boundary, and which shall constantly remain, that the officers both now and hereafter may consider it as a guide, and not make any encroachment.

Article 6

Such places as are upon the Frontiers of the dominions of the Nabob Vizier and of Nepaul, and respecting which any dispute may arise, such dispute shall be settled by the mediation of the vakeel on the part of the Company, in the presence of one from the Nepaul Government, and one from His Excellency the Vizier.

Article 7

So many elephants, on account of Muckanacinpoor, are annually sent to the Company by the Raja of Nepaul, and therefore the Governor-General with a view of promoting the satisfaction of the Raja of Nepaul, and in consideration of the improved friendly connection, and of this new Treaty, relinquishes and foregoes the tribute above-mentioned, and directs that the officers of the Company, both now and hereafter, from generation to generation, shall never, during the continuance of the engagement contracted by this Treaty (so long as the conditions of this treaty shall be in force), exact the elephants from the Raja.

Article 8

If any of the dependents of inhabitants of either country should fly and take refuge in the other, and a requisition should be made for such persons on the part of the Nepaul Government by its constituted vakeel in attendance on the Governor-General, or on the part of the Company's Government by its representative residing at Nepaul, it is in this case mutually agreed that if such person should have fled transgressing the laws of his Government, it is incumbent upon the principals of both Governments immediately to deliver him up to the vakeel at their respective courts, that he may be sent in perfect security to the frontier of their respective territories.

Article 9

The Maha Raja of Nepaul agrees, that a pergunnah, with all the lands attached to it, excepting privileged lands and those appropriated to religious purposes, and to jaghires, &c., which are specified separately in the account of collections, shall be given up to Samee Jeo for his expenses, as a present. The conditions with respect to Samee Jeo are, that if he should remain at Benares, or at any other place within the Company's provinces, and should spontaneously farm his jaghire to the officers of Nepaul, in that event the amount of collections shall be punctually paid to him, agreeably to certain kists which may be hereafter settled; that he may appropriate the same to his necessary expenses, and that he may continue in religious abstraction, according to his agreement, which he had engraved on brass, at the time of his abdication of the Roy, and of his resigning it in my favour. Again, in the event of his establishing his residence in his jaghire, and of his realizing the collections through his own officers, it is proper that he should not keep such a one and other disaffected persons in his service, and besides one hundred men and maid servants, &c., he must not entertain any persons as soldiers, with a view to the collection of the revenue of the pergunnah; and to the protection of his person he may take two hundred soldiers of the forces of the Nepaul Government, the allowances of whom shall be paid by the Raja of Nepaul. He must be cautious, also of commencing altercation, either by speech or writing; neither must be give protection to the rebellious and fugitives of the Nepaul country, nor must he commit plunder and devastation upon the subjects of Nepaul. In the event of such delinquency being proved to the satisfaction of the two Governments, the aid and protection of the Company shall be withdrawn from him; and in that event, also, it shall be at the option of the Raja of Nepaul whether or not he will confiscate his jaghire.

The Maha Raja also agrees, on his part, that if Samee Jeo should take up his residence within the Company's provinces, and should farm out his land to the officers of Nepaul, and that the kists should not be paid according to agreement, or that he should fix his residence on his jaghire, and any of the inhabitants of Nepaul should give him or the ryots of his pergunnah any molestation, a requisition shall be made by the Governor-General of the Company, on this subject, to the Raja. The Governor-General is security for the Raja's performance of this condition, and the Maha Raja will immediately acquit himself of the requisition of the Governor-General, agreeably to what is above written. If any profits should arise in the collection of the said pergunnah, in consequence of the activity of the officers, or any defalcation occurs from their inattention, in either case the Raja of Nepaul will be totally unconcerned.

Article 10

With the view of carrying into effect the different objects contained in this Treaty, and of promoting other verbal negociation, the Governor-General and the Raja of Nepaul, under the impulse of their will and pleasure, depute a confidential person to each other as vakeel, that remaining in attendance upon their respective Governments, they may effect the objects above specified, and promote whatever may tend to the daily improvement of the friendship subsisting between the States.

Article 11

It is incumbent upon the principals and officers of the two States that they should manifest the regard and respect to the vakeel of each other's Government which is due to their rank, and is prescribed by the laws of nations; and that they should endeavour, to the utmost of their power, to advance any object which they may propose, and to promote their ease, comfort, and satisfaction, by extending protection to them, which circumstances are calculated to improve the friendship subsisting between the two Governments, and to illustrate the good name of both States throughout the universe.

Article 12

It is incumbent upon the vakeels of both States that they should hold no intercourse whatever with any of the subjects or inhabitants of the country, excepting with the officers of Government, without the permission of those officers; neither should they carry on any correspondence with any of them; and if they should receive any letter or writing from any such people, they should not answer it, without the knowledge of the head of the State, and acquainting him of the particulars, which will dispel all apprehension or doubt between us, and manifest the sincerity of our friendship.

Article 13

It is incumbent upon the principals and officers mutually to abide by the spirit of this Treaty, which is now drawn out according to their faith and religion, and deeming it in force from generation to generation that they should not deviate from it; and any person who may transgress against it will be punished by Almighty God, both in this world and in a future state.

(A true translation)
C. RUSSELL
Assistant Persian Translator

Ratified by the Governor-General and Council, on the 30th of October 1801, and by the Nepaul Darbar on the 28th of October 1802.

Separate Article of a Treaty with the Rajah of Nepaul concluded at Dinapore, 26th of October 1801.

The Engagement contracted by Maha Rajah, &c., &c., with His Excellency the Most Noble the Governor-General, &c., &c., respecting the settlement of a provision for the maintenance of Purncahir Goonanund Swammee Jee, the illustrious father of the said Maha Rajah, is to the following effect:

That an annual income, amounting to Patna Sicca Rupees eighty-two thousand, of which seventy-two thousand shall be paid in cash and ten thousand, in elephants, half male and half female, to be valued at the rate of one hundred and twenty-five rupees per cubit, shall be settled on the said Swammee Jee, commencing from the month of Aughun 1858, as an humble offering to assist in the maintenance of his household; and for the purpose of supplying the said income, that the Purgunnah of Beejapoor, with all the lands thereunto attached (excepting rent-free lands, religious or charitable endowments, jaghires, and such like as specified separately in the account of collections) be settled on the said Swammee Jee, under the following conditions: That, in the event of his residing at Benares of other place within the territories of the Honourable Company, and of his voluntarily committing the collections of the said jaghire to the servants of the Nepaul Government, in such case seventy-two thousand rupees in cash, and elephants to the value of ten thousand rupees, shall be punctually remitted year after year, by established kists, to the said Swammee Jee, without fail or delay, so that, appropriating the same to his necessary expenses, he may devote himself to the worship of the Supreme being in conformity to his own declaration, engraved on copper at the time of his abdicating the Raje and of his bestowing it on the said Maha Rajah; and further, in the event of his establishing his residence upon his jaghire and of his realizing the collections through his own officers, it is requisite that he should not keep in his service fomenters of sedition and disturbance, that he shall retain no more than one hundred male and female attendants, and that he shall not retain about his person soldiers of any description. That for the purpose of collecting the revenues of the aforesaid pergunnahs and for his personal protection, he may have from the Rajah of Nepaul as far as two hundred men of the troops of that country, and the allowance of such men shall be defrayed by the Maha Rajah himself. He must not attempt, either by speech or writing, to excite commotion nor harbour about his person rebels and fugitives from the territories of Nepaul, neither must he commit any depredations upon the subjects of that country. And in the event of such delinquency being established to the satisfaction of both parties, that the aid and protection of the Honourable Company shall be withdrawn from the said Swammee Jee, in which case it shall be at the option of the Maha Rajah to confiscate his jaghire. It is also agreed by Maha Rajah that, provided Swammee Jee should fix his residence within the Honourable Company's territories, and should commit the collections of his jaghire to the officers of the Nepaul Government, in that case, should the kists not be paid according to the conditions above specified, or in the event of his residing upon his jaghire, provided any of the subjects of Nepaul give him or ryots of his pergunnah any molestation, in either case the Governor-General and the Honourable Company have a right to demand reparation from the Rajah of Nepaul. The Governor-General is guarantee that the Rajah of Nepaul performs this condition, and the Maha Rajah, on the requisition of the Governor-General, will instantly fulfil his engagements as above specified. In any augmentation of the collections from the judicious management of the officers of Swammee Jee, or in any diminution from a contrary cause, the Maha Rajah is to be equally unconcerned, the Maha Rajah engaging that, on delivering over the Pergunnah of Beejapoor to the officers of Swammee Jee, the amount of the annual revenue shall be Patna Sicca Rupees 72,000; that should it be less he will make good the deficiency, and in case of excess, that Swammee Jee be entitled thereto.

(A true translation)
W.D. Knox

Ratified by the Governor-General and Council on the 30th of October 1801, and by the Nepaul Durbar on the 28th of October 1802.

Appendix III
Treaty of Peace (the Sugauli Treaty) between Nepal and the British East India Company and Related Instruments, 1815–16

TREATY OF PEACE between the HONOURABLE EAST INDIA COMPANY and MAHA RAJAH BIKRAM SAH, Rajah of Nipal, settled between LIEUTENANT-COLONEL BRADSHAW on the part of the HONOURABLE COMPANY, in virtue of the full powers vested in him by HIS EXCELLENCE the RIGHT HONOURABLE FRANCIS, EARL OF MOIRA KNIGHT of the MOST NOBLE ORDER of the GARTER, one of HIS MAJESTY'S MOST HONOURABLE PRIVY COUNCIL, appointed by the Court of Directors of the said Honourable Company to direct and control all the affairs in the East Indies, and by SREE GOOROO GUJRAJ MISSER and CHUNDER SEEKER OPEDEEA on the part of MAHA RAJAH GIRMAUN JODE BIKRAN SAH BAHADUR, SHUMSHEER JUNG, in virtue of the powers to that effect vested in them by the said Rajah of Nipal, *2nd December 1815.*

Whereas war has arisen between the Honourable East India Company and the Rajah of Nipal, and whereas the parties are mutually disposed to restore the relations of peace and amity which, previously to the occurrence of the late differences, had long subsisted between the two States, the following terms of peace have been agreed upon:

Article 1

There shall be perpetual peace and friendship between the Honourable East India Company and the Rajah of Nipal.

Article 2

The Rajah of Nipal renounces all claim to the lands which were the subject of discussion between the two States before the war; and acknowledges the right of the Honourable Company to the sovereignty of those lands.

Article 3

The Rajah of Nipal hereby cedes to the Honourable the East India Company in perpetuity all the undermentioned territories, *viz.*—

First.—The whole of the low lands between the Rivers Kali and Rapti.

Secondly.—The whole of the low lands (with the exception of Bootwul Khass) lying between the Rapti and the Gunduck.

Thirdly.—The whole of the low lands between the Gunduck and Coosah, in which the authority of the British Government has been introduced, or is in actual course of introduction.

Fourthly.—All the low lands between the Rivers Mitchee and the Teestah.

Fifthly.—All the territories within the hills eastward of the River Mitchee, including the fort and lands of Nagree and the Pass of Nagarcote, leading from Morung into the hills, together with the territory lying between that Pass and Nagree. The aforesaid territory shall be evacuated by the Gurkha troops within forty days from this date.

Article 4

With a view to indemnify the Chiefs and Barahdars of the State of Nipal, whose interests will suffer by the alienation of the lands ceded by the foregoing Article, the British Government agrees to settle pensions to the aggregate amount to two lakhs of rupees per annum on such Chiefs as may be selected by the Rajah of Nipal, and in the proportions which the Rajah may fix. As soon as the selection is made, Sunnuds shall be granted under the seal and signature of the Governor-General for the pensions respectively.

Article 5

The Rajah of Nipal renounces for himself, his heirs, and successors, all claim to or connexion with the countries lying to the west of the River Kali, and engages never to have any concern with those countries or the inhabitants thereof.

Article 6

The Rajah of Nipal engages never to molest or disturb the Rajah of Sikkim in the possession of his territories; but agrees, if any differences shall arise between the State of Nipal and the Rajah of Sikkim, or the subjects of either, that such differences shall be referred to the arbitration of the British Government, by whose award the Rajah of Nipal engages to abide.

Article 7

The Rajah of Nipal hereby engages never to take or retain in his service any British subject, nor the subject of any European and American State, without the consent of the British Government.

Article 8

In order to secure and improve the relations of amity and peace hereby established between the two States, it is agreed that accredited Ministers from each shall reside at the Court of the other.

Article 9

This Treaty, consisting of nine Articles, shall be ratified by the Rajah of Nipal within fifteen days from this date, and the ratification shall be delivered to Lieut.-Colonel Bradshaw, who engages to obtain and deliver to the Rajah the ratification of the Governor-General within twenty days, or sooner, if practicable.

Done at Segowlee, on the 2nd day of December 1815.

Received this treaty from Chunder Seekur Opedeea, Agent on the part of the Rajah of Nipal, in the valley of Muckwaunpoor, at half-past two o'clock P.M., on the 4th of March 1816, and delivered to him the Counter-part Treaty on behalf of the British Government.

D.D. OCHTERLONY
Agent, Governor-General

Memorandum for the approval and acceptance of the Rajah of Nipal, presented on the 8th of December 1816

Adverting to the amity and confidence subsisting with the Rajah of Nipal, the British Government proposes to suppress, as much as is possible, the execution of certain Articles in the Treaty of Segowlee, which bear hard upon the Rajah, as follows:

2. With a view to gratify the Rajah in a point which he has much at heart, the British Government is willing to restore the Terai ceded to it by the Rajah in the Treaty, to wit, the whole Terai lands lying between the Rivers Coosa and Gunduck, such as appertained to the Rajah before the late disagreement; excepting the disputed lands in the Zillahs of Tirhoot and Sarun, and excepting such portions of territory as may occur on both sides for the purpose of settling a frontier, upon investigation by the respective Commissioners; and excepting such lands as may have been given in possession to any one by the British Government upon ascertainment of his rights subsequent to the cession of Terai to that Government. In case the Rajah is desirous of retaining the lands of such ascertained proprietors, they may be exchanged for others, and let it be clearly understood that, notwithstanding the considerable extent of the lands in the Zillah of Tirhoot, which have for a long time been a subject of dispute, the settlement made in the year of 1812 of Christ, corresponding with the year 1869 of Bikramajeet, shall be taken, and everything else relinquished, that is to say, that the settlement and negotiations, such as occurred at that period, shall in the present case hold good and be established.

3. The British Government is willing likewise to restore the Terai lying between the Rivers Gunduk and Rapti, that is to say, from the River Gunduk to the western limits of the Zillah of Goruckpore, together with Bootwul and Sheeraj, such as appertained to Nipal previous to the disagreements, complete, with the exception of the disputed places in the Terai, and such quantity of ground as may be considered mutually to be requisite for the new boundary.

4. As it is impossible to established desirable limits between the two States without survey, it will be expedient that Commissioners be appointed on both sides for the purpose of arranging in concert a well defined boundary on the basis of the preceding terms, and of establishing a straight line of frontier, with a view to the distinct separation of the respective territories of the British Government to the south and of Nipal to the

north; and in case any indentations occur to destroy the even tenor of the line, the Commissioners should effect an exchange of lands so interfering on principles of clear reciprocity.

5. And should it occur that the proprietors of lands situated on the mutual frontier, as it may be rectified, whether holding of the British Government or of the Rajah of Nipal, should be placed in the condition of subjects of both Governments, with a view to prevent continual dispute and discussion between the two Governments, the respective Commissioners should effect in mutual concurrence and co-operation the exchange of such lands, so as to render them subject to one dominion alone.

6. Whensoever the Terai should be restored, the Rajah of Nipal will cease to require the sum of two lakhs of Rupees per annum, which the British Government agreed the advance for the maintenance of certain Barahdars of his Government.

7. Moreover, the Rajah of Nipal agrees to refrain from prosecuting any inhabitants of the Terai, after its revertance to his rule, on account of having favoured the cause of the British Government during the war, and should any of those persons, excepting the cultivators of the soil, be desirous of quitting their estates, and of retiring within the Company's territories, he shall not be liable to hindrance.

8. In the event of the Rajah's approving the foregoing terms, the proposed arrangement for the survey and establishment of boundary marks shall be carried into execution, and after the determination in concert of the boundary line, Sunnuds conformable to the foregoing stipulations, drawn out and sealed by the two States, shall be delivered and accepted on both sides.

(Sd.) Edward Gardner
Resident
(A true translation)
(Sd.) G. Wellesley
Assistant

Substance of a Letter under the Seal of the Raja of Nipal, received on the 11th of December 1816

After compliment;

I have comprehended the document under date the 8th of December 1816, or 4th of Poos 1873 Sumbut, which you transmitted relative to the restoration, with a view to my friendship and satisfaction, of the Terai between the Rivers Coosa and Rapti to the southern boundary complete, such as appertained to my estate previous to the war. It mentioned that in the event of my accepting the terms contained in that document, the southern boundary of the Terai should be established as it was held by this Government. I have accordingly agreed to the terms laid down by you, and herewith enclose an instrument of agreement, which may be satisfactory to you. Moreover, it was written in the document transmitted by you, that it should be restored, with the exception of the disputed lands and such portion of land as should, in the opinion of the Commissioners on both sides, occur for the purpose of settling a boundary: and excepting the lands which, after the cessions of the Terai to the Honourable Company, may have been transferred by it to the ascertained proprietors. My friend, all these matters rest with you, and since it was also written that a view was had to my friendship and satisfaction with respect to certain Articles of the Treaty of Segowlee, which bore hard upon me, and which could be remitted, I am well assured that you have at heart the removal of whatever may tend to my distress, and that you will act in a manner corresponding to the advantage of this State and the increase of the friendly relations subsisting between the two Governments.

Moreover I have to acknowledge the receipt of the orders under the red seal of this State, addressed to the officers of Terai between the Rivers Gunduk and Rapti, for the surrender of that Terai, and their retiring from thence, which was given to you at Thankote, according to your request, and which you have now returned for my satisfaction.

(A true translation)
(Sd.) G. Wellesley
Assistant

Substance of a Document under the Red Seal, received from the Durbar, on the 11th of December 1816

With regard to friendship and amity, the Government of Nipal agrees to the tenor of the document under the 8th of December 1816 or 4th Poos 1873 Sumbut which was received by the Darbar from the Honourable Edward Gardner on the part of the Honourable Company, respecting the revertance of the Terai between the Rivers Coosa and Rapti to the former southern boundary, such as appertained to Nipal previous to the war, with exception of the disputed lands.

Dated the 7th of Poos 1873 Sumbat.

(A true translation)
(Sd.) G. WELLESLEY
Assistant

Appendix IV
Treaty with Nipal, 1 November 1860.

During the disturbances which followed the mutiny of the Native army of Bengal in 1857, the Maharaja of Nipal not only faithfully maintained the relations of peace and friendship established between the British Government and the State of Nipal by the Treaty of Segowlee, but freely placed troops at the disposal of the British authorities for the preservation of order in the Frontier Districts, and subsequently sent a force to cooperate with the British Army in the re-capture of Lucknow and the final defeat of the rebels. On the conclusion of these operations, the Viceroy and Governor-General in recognition of the eminent services rendered to the British Government by the State of Nipal, declared his intention to restore to the Maharaja the whole of the lowlands lying between the River Kali and the District of Goruckpoer, which belonged to the State of Nipal in 1815, and were ceded to the British Government in that year by the aforesaid Treaty. These lands have now been identified by Commissioners appointed for the purpose by the British Government, in the presence of Commissioners deputed by the Nipal Darbar; masonry pillars have been erected to mark the future boundary of the two States, and the territory has been formally delivered over to the Nipalese Authorities. In order the more firmly to secure the State of Nipal in the perpetual possession of this territory, and to mark in a solemn way the occasion of its restoration, the following Treaty has been concluded between the two States:

Article 1

All Treaties and Engagements now in force between the British Government and the Maharajah of Nipal, except in so far as they may be altered by the Treaty, are hereby confirmed.

Article 2

The British Government hereby bestows on the Maharajah of Nipal in full sovereignty, the whole of the lowlands between the Rivers Kali and Raptee, and the whole of the lowlands lying between the River Raptee and the District of Goruckpore, which were in the possession of the Nipal State in the year 1815, and were ceded to the British Government by Article III of the Treaty concluded at Segowlee on the 2nd of December in that year.

Article 3

The boundary line surveyed by the British Commissioners appointed for the purpose extending eastward from the River Kali or Sardah to the foot of the hills north of Bagowra Tal, and marked by pillars, shall henceforth be the boundary between the British Province of Oudh and the Territories of the Maharajah of Nipal.

This Treaty, signed by Lieutenant-Colonel George Ramsay, on the part of His Excellency the Right Honourable Charles John, Earl Canning, G.C.B., Viceroy and Governor-General of India, and by Maharajah Jung Bahadoor Rana, G.C.B., on the part of Maharajah Dheraj Soorinder Vikram Sah Bahadoor Shumshere Jung, shall be ratified, and the ratifications shall be exchanged at Khatmandoo within thirty days of the date of signature.

Signed and sealed at Khatmandoo, this First day of November, AD one thousand eight hundred and sixty corresponding to the third day of Kartick Budee, Sumbut Nineteen Hundred and Seventeen.

(Sd.) G. RAMSAY, *Lieut.-Colonel*
Resident at Nipal

(Sd.) CANNING
Viceroy and Governor-General

This Treaty was ratified by His Excellency the Governor-General, at Calcutta, on the 15th of November 1860.

(Sd.) A.R. YOUNG
Deputy Secretary to the Government of India

Appendix V
1920 Sarada Barrage Project Agreement between British India and Nepal

23rd August 1920

My dear Colonel Kennion,

With reference to your letter No. 3351/4550–73 dated the 29th July 1920 enclosing copy of a letter from the Chief Secretary to the United Provinces Government for sanction to the survey party to finally demarcate the land required for the Sarada canal work and the irrigation branch staff entering on it to start necessary work of construction, order has been issued to the Bada Hakim of Kailali-Kanchanpur Goswara, to permit the said parties to enter Nepalese territory for the purposes mentioned. Please arrange that an intimation a fortnight in advance of their coming be sent to the said Bada Hakim at Billouri specifying the dates when and on the points where they would enter Nepalese territory so that he may appoint a Nepalese officer to meet the parties and be with them during the demarcation work. In order that the intimation may reach the Bada Hakim without fail it is requested that it be sent by post as well as by messenger, as the delivery from the post office, which is Puranpir, (about 28 miles) during the dry season and Palia Kalan (about 36 miles) during the dry season and rains is not very certain.

In connection with this Sarada canal project, the construction of the head works etc. and exchange of land relating there to it is understood that it is agreed that:

(1) The Nepal Government will have a right for a supply of 460 cusecs of water and, provided the surplus is available, for a supply of up to 1000 cusecs when cultivation grows at any future time from the Sarada canal Head work during the Kharif, i.e. from 15th May to 15th October; and of 150, cusecs during Rabi, i.e. from the 15th of October to 15th May, the canal head being in the latter period alternately closed and opened for 10 days at a time running 300 cusecs whenever the canal is open.

(2) That is order to give those supplies all necessary works such as the canal head with regulating gates, quarters for the canal staff be on the left bank of the river and also under-sluices for the purpose of

maintaining an open channel from the river to the canal head will be done by the Government of India at their own expense on the understanding that they shall retain full and entire control of the work with this undertaking that they shall supply to Nepal the quantity of water agreed to free of any charge.

(3) That the Nepal Government would transfer necessary land for the construction and maintenance of canal works which is provisionally estimated at 4000 acres and would receive land equal in area from the British Government. The land to be taken from Nepalese territory will, after demarcation, be measured and then land equal in area to it will be given to Nepal by the said Government.

I would ask to be kindly informed whether the Government of India has to make any proposal with regard to the disposal of timber obtained from trees felled in the course of demarcation and when the land so demarcated to be taken will be taken and land to be given in lieu thereof will be measured and given also whether they wish that valuable trees standing on the lands to be exchanged are to be given and taken along with those lands.

I am, with kind regards,
Yours very sincerely,
(Sd.) CHANDRA

Reply of the British Government
No. 4725/4550–78 of 20.

The British Legation, Nepal
21st October 1920.

My dear Maharaja,

With reference to your letter dated the 23rd August 1920, I write to inform Your Excellency that I communicated the contents thereof to the United Provinces Government and enclose herewith a copy of their reply for your Excellency's information.

With kind regards,
Yours very sincerely,
(Sd.)

To

General His Excellency
Maharaja Sir Chandra Shumshere Jung
Bahadur Rana, G.C.B., G.C.S.I., G.C.M.G.,
G.C.V.O., D.C.L.,
Prime Minister and Marshal of Nepal.

Copy of a letter No. 2984, dated the 12th October 1920, from the Chief Secretary to the Government of the United Provinces, to the British Envoy at the Court of Nepal.

1. With reference to your letter No. 3789, dated the 25th August 1920, I am directed to say that the land to be acquired in Nepal in connection with the Sarada-Kitcha feeder project, is 4093.88 acres. The land this Government is offering the Nepal Government in exchange is noted in the margin.

Division	*District*	*Site*	*Area in Acres*
1. Lucknow	Kheri	Sumerpur	2914
2. Fyzabad	Bahraich	Border	569
3. Do	Gonda	Near Koela Basa	65.3
4. Do	Bahraich	Border	516.2
5. Do	Do	Do	29.38

Orders have been issued to the British authorities concerned for the demarcation, on site, of this land and arrangements for the exchange will be made as soon as the land in Nepal and British territory has been demarcated.

2. The summary of the terms regarding the supply of water from the canal to the Nepal Government as given in His Excellency the Prime Minister of Nepal's letter is correct.

3. As regards the ownership of the trees felled in demarcating the land in Nepal, I am to say that as it will be necessary to cut up and remove these trees so as to clear the line, this Government would suggest that to avoid delay, the trees should be regarded as belonging to the Irrigation Branch of this province, who could then arrange to the Irrigation-Branch of this province to dispose of them immediately. Similarly the trees felled in demarcating the land in British India for transfer to Nepal, may be regarded as belonging to the Durbar if it will arrange to clear them away without delay. This arrangement seems to be simple and equitable as it is probable that the trees felled in demarcating the land in Nepal will balance the number of trees felled in demarcating the land in British territory.

4. I am to add that the remaining trees on the land will be exchanged along with the land. The Nepal Durbar is not likely to lose by the exchange as the land which this Government is offering in exchange comprises valuable forest and grazing ground.

Appendix VI
Treaty of Friendship between Great Britain and Nepal, Kathmandu, 21 December 1923

WHEREAS peace and friendship have now existed between the British Government and the Government of Nepal since the signing of the Treaty of Segowlie on the 2nd day of December 1815, and whereas since that date the Government of Nepal has ever displayed its true friendship for the British Government and the British Government has as constantly shown its goodwill towards the Government of Nepal; and whereas the Governments of both the countries are now desirous of still further strengthening and cementing the good relations and friendship which have subsisted between them for more than a century; the two High Contracting Parties having resolved to conclude a new Treaty of Friendship have agreed upon the following Articles:

Article I

There shall be perpetual peace and friendship between the Governments of Great Britain and Nepal, and the two Governments agree mutually to acknowledge and respect each other's independence, both internal and external.

Article II

All previous treaties, agreements and engagements, since and including the Treaty of Segowlie of 1815, which have been concluded between the two Governments are hereby confirmed, except so far as they may be altered by the present Treaty.

Article III

As the preservation of peace and friendly relations with the neighbouring States whose territories adjoin their common frontiers is to the mutual interests of both the High Contracting Parties, they hereby agree to inform each other of any serious friction or misunderstanding with those States likely to rupture such friendly relations, and each to exert its good offices as far as may be possible to remove such friction and misunderstanding.

Article IV

Each of the High Contracting Parties will use all such measures as it may deem practicable to prevent its territories being used for purposes inimical to the security of the other.

Article V

In view of the longstanding friendship that has subsisted between the British Government and the Government of Nepal and for the sake of cordial neighbourly relations between them, the British Government agrees that the Nepal Government shall be free to import from or through British India into Nepal whatever arms, ammunition, machinery, warlike material or stores may be required or desired for the strength and welfare of Nepal, and that this arrangement shall hold good for all time as long as the British Government is satisfied that the intentions of the Nepal Government are friendly and that there is no immediate danger to India from such importations. The Nepal Government, on the other hand, agrees that there shall be no export of such arms, ammunition, etc., across the frontier of Nepal either by the Nepal Government or by private individuals.

If, however, any Convention for the regulation of the Arms Traffic, to which the British Government may be a party, shall come into force, the right of importation of arms and ammunition by the Nepal Government shall be subject to the proviso that the Nepal Government shall first become a party to that Convention, and that such importation shall only be made in accordance with the provisions of that Convention.

Article VI

No Customs duty shall be levied at British Indian ports on goods imported on behalf of the Nepal Government for immediate transport to that country provided that a certificate from such authority as may from time to time be determined by the two Governments shall be presented at the time of importation to the Chief Customs Officer at the port of import setting forth that the goods are the property of the Nepal Government, are required for the public services of the Nepal Government, are not for the purpose of any State monopoly or State trade, and are being sent to Nepal under orders of the Nepal Government.

The British Government also agrees to grant the in respect of all trade goods, imported at British Indian ports for immediate transmission to Kathmandu without breaking bulk *en route*, of a rebate of the full duty paid, provided that in accordance with arrangements already agreed to, between the two Governments, such goods may break bulk for repacking at the port of entry under Customs supervision in accordance with such rules as may from time to time be laid down in this behalf. The rebate may be claimed on the authority of a certificate signed by the said authority that the goods have arrived at Kathmandu with the customs seals unbroken and otherwise untampered with.

Article VII

This Treaty signed on the part of the British Government by Lieutenant-Colonel W.F.T. O'Connor, C.I.E., C.V.O., British Envoy at the Court of Nepal, and on the part of the Nepal Government by General His Highness Maharaja Sir Chandra Shumshere Jung Bahadur Rana, G.C.B., G.C.S.I., G.C.M.G., G.C.V.O., D.C.I., Thong-lin Pimma-Kokang-Wang-Syan, Prime Minister and Marshal of Nepal, shall be ratified and the ratification shall be exchanged at Kathmandu as soon as practicable.[1]

Signed and sealed at Kathmandu this the twenty-first day of December in the year one thousand nine hundred and twenty-three *Anno Domini* corresponding with the sixth Paush, Sambat Era one thousand nine hundred and eighty.

W.F.T. O'CONNOR, LT.-COL.
British Envoy at the Court of Nepal

(Under Vernacular Translation of Treaty)

CHANDRA SHAMSHERE
Prime Minister and Marshal of Nepal

[1] Ratifications exchanged in Kathmandu on 8 April 1925.

APPENDIX VII

Treaty of Peace and Friendship between India and Nepal, Kathmandu, 31 July 1950

THE Government of India and the Government of Nepal, recognizing the ancient ties which have happily existed between the two countries for centuries;

Desiring still further to strengthen and develop these ties and to perpetuate peace between the two countries;

Have resolved therefore to enter into a Treaty of Peace and Friendship with each other and have, for this purpose, appointed as their plenipotentiaries the following persons, namely,

The Government of India:

His Excellency Shri Chandreshwar Prasad Narain Singh, Ambassador of India in Nepal.

The Government of Nepal:

Maharaja Mohun Shamsher Jang Bahadur Rana, Prime Minister and Supreme Commander-in-Chief of Nepal, who, having examined each other's credentials and found them good and in due form have agreed as follows:

Article I

There shall be everlasting peace and friendship between the Government of India and the Government of Nepal. The two Governments agree mutually to acknowledge and respect the complete sovereignty, territorial integrity and independence of each other.

Article II

The two Governments hereby undertake to inform each other of any serious friction or misunderstanding with any neighbouring state likely to cause any breach in the friendly relations subsisting between the two Governments.

Article III

In order to establish and maintain the relations referred to in Article I the two Governments agree to continue diplomatic relations with each other by means of representatives with such staff as is necessary for the due performance of their functions.

The representatives and such of their staff as may be agreed upon shall enjoy such diplomatic privileges and immunities as are customarily granted by international law on a reciprocal basis:

Provided that in no case shall these be less than those granted to persons of a similar status of any other State having diplomatic relations with either Government.

Article IV

The two Governments agree to appoint Consuls-General. Consuls, Vice-Consuls and other consular agents, who shall reside in towns, ports and other places in each other's territory as may be agreed to.

Consuls-General, Consuls, Vice-Consuls and consular agents shall be provided with exequaturs or other valid authorization of their appointment. Such exequatur or authorization is liable to be withdrawn by the country which issued it, if considered necessary. The reasons for the withdrawal shall be indicated wherever possible.

The persons mentioned above shall enjoy on a reciprocal basis all the rights, privileges, exemptions and immunities that are accorded to persons of corresponding status of any other State.

Article V

The Government of Nepal shall be free to import, from or through the territory of India, arms, ammunition or warlike material and equipment necessary for the security of Nepal. The procedure for giving effect to this arrangement shall be worked out by the two Governments acting in consultation.

Article VI

Each Government undertakes, in token of the neighbourly friendship between India and Nepal, to give the nationals of the other, in its territory, national treatment with regard to participation in industrial and economic development of such territory and to the grant of concessions and contracts relating to such development.

Article VII

The Governments of India and Nepal agree to grant, on a reciprocal basis, to the nationals of one country in the territories of the other the same privileges in the matter of residence, ownership of property, participation in trade and commerce, movement and other privileges of a similar nature.

Article VIII

So far as matters dealt with herein are concerned, this Treaty cancels all previous treaties, agreements and arrangements entered into on behalf of India between the British Government and the Government of Nepal.

Article IX

This Treaty shall come into force from the date of signature by both Governments.

Article X

This Treaty shall remain in force until it is terminated by either party by giving one year's notice.

[At a Press Conference in New Delhi on 3 December 1959 Prime Minister Mr Jawaharlal Nehru disclosed that letters were exchanged along with the signing of the Treaty which have been kept secret—*Editor*]

(*Foreign Policy of India, Text of Documents*; Lok Sabha Secretariat, New Delhi: 1966; 56–8)

Done in duplicate at Kathmandu this 31st day of July, 1950.

(Sd.)	(Sd.)
CHANDRESHWAR PRASAD NARAIN SINGH	MOHUN SHAMSHER JANG BAHADUR RANA
For the Government of India	*For the Government of Nepal*

Letter Exchanged with the Treaty

KATHMANDU
Dated the 31st July 1950.

Excellency,

In the course of our discussions of the Treaties of Peace and Friendship and the Trade and Commerce which have been happily concluded between the Government of India and the Government of Nepal, we agreed that certain matters of detail be regulated by an exchange of letters. In pursuance of this understanding, it is here by agreed between the two Governments:

(1) Neither Government shall tolerate any threat to the security of the other by a foreign aggressor. To deal with any such threat, the two Governments shall consult with each other and devise effective countermeasures.

(2) Any arms, ammunition or warlike material and equipment necessary for the security of Nepal that the Government of Nepal may import through the territory of India shall be so imported with the *assistance and agreement* of the Government of India. The Government of India will take steps for the smooth and expeditious transport of such arms and ammunition through India.

(3) In regard to Article 6 of the Treaty of Peace and Friendship which provides for national treatment, the Government of India recognize that it may be necessary for some time to come to afford the Nepalese nationals in Nepal protection from unrestricted competition. The nature and extent to this protection will be determined as and when required by mutual agreement between the two Governments.

(4) If the Government of Nepal should decide to seek foreign assistance in regard to the development of the natural resources of, or of any industrial project in Nepal, the Government of Nepal shall give first preference to the Government or the nationals of India, as the case may be, provided that the terms offered by the Government of India or Indian nationals, as the case may be, are not less favourable to Nepal than the terms offered by any other Foreign Government or by other foreign nationals.

Nothing in the foregoing provision shall apply to assistance that the Government of Nepal may seek from the United Nations Organization or any of its specialized agencies.

(5) Both Governments agree not to employ any foreigners whose activity

may be prejudicial to the security of the other. Either Government may make representations to the other in this behalf, as and when occasion requires.

Please accept Excellency, the assurances of my highest consideration.

(Sd.)
MOHUN SHAMSHER JANG
BAHADUR RANA
Maharaja, Prime Minister
and Supreme Commander-
in-Chief of Nepal

To

HIS EXCELLENCY, SHRI CHANDRESHWAR PRASAD NARAIN SINGH,
Ambassador Extraordinary and Plenipotentiary of India at
the Court of Nepal, Indian Embassy, Kathmandu

Appendix VIII
The 1954 Agreement on the Koshi Project (as revised in 1966)

Amended agreement between His Majesty's Government of Nepal (hereinafter referred to as 'HMG') and the Government of India (hereinafter referred to as the 'Union') concerning the Koshi Project.

WHEREAS the Union was desirous of constructing a barrage, headworks and other appurtenant works about three miles upstream of Hanuman Nagar town on the Koshi River with afflux and flood banks, and canals and protective works on land lying within the territories of Nepal for the purpose of flood control, irrigation, generation of hydro-electric power and prevention of erosion of Nepal areas on the right side of the river, upstream of the barrage (hereinafter referred to as the 'Project').

AND WHEREAS HMG agreed to the construction of the said barrage, headworks and other connected works by and at the cost of the Union, in consideration of the benefits arising therefrom and a formal document incorporating the terms of the Agreement was brought into existence on the 25th April, 1954 and was given effect to;

AND WHEREAS in pursuance of the said Agreement various works in respect of the Project have been completed by the Union while others are in various stages of completion for which HMG has agreed to afford necessary facilities;

And whereas HMG has suggested revision of the said Agreement in order to meet the requirements of the changed circumstances, and the Union, with a view to maintaining friendship and good relation subsisting between Nepal and India, has agreed to the revision of Agreement.

NOW, THEREFORE, THE PARTIES AGREE AS FOLLOWS:

1. DETAILS OF THE PROJECT: (i) The barrage is located about 3 miles upstream of Hunuman Nagar town.

(ii) The general layout of the barrage, the areas within afflux banks, flood embankments, and other protective works, canals, power house and the lines of communication are shown in the amended plan annexed to this agreement as Amended Annexure A.[1]

[1]Not reproduced here.

(iii) Any construction and other undertaking by the Union in connection with this Project shall be planned and carried out in consultation with HMG,

Provided that such works and undertakings which, pursuant to any provision of this Agreement require the prior approval of HMG shall not be started without such prior approval;

And further provided that in situation described in Clause 3(iii) and Clause 3(iv) intimation to HMG shall be sufficient.

(iv) For the purpose of Clauses 3 and 8 of this Agreement the land under the ponded areas and boundaries as indicated by the plan specified in sub-clause (ii) above, shall be deemed to be submerged.

2. INVESTIGATION AND SURVEYS: (i) Whenever the Chief Engineer of Koshi Project, Government of Bihar may consider any survey or investigation to be required in connection with the said Project, HMG shall, if and in so far as HMG has approved such survey or investigation, authorize and give necessary facilities to the concerned officers of the Union or other persons acting under the general or special orders of such officers to enter upon such land as necessary with such men, animals, vehicles, equipment, plant, machinery and instruments as necessary to undertake such surveys and investigations. Such surveys and investigations may comprise aerial and ground surveys, hydraulic, hydrometic, hydrological and geological surveys including construction of drill holes for surface and sub-surface exploration, investigations for communications and for materials of construction; and all other surveys and investigations necessary for the proper design, construction and maintenance of the barrage and all its connected works mentioned under the Project. However, investigations and surveys necessary for the general maintenance and operation of the Project, inside the project area, may be done by the Union after due intimation to HMG.

In this Agreement, the 'Project Area' shall mean the area acquired for the Project.

(ii) The provisions of sub-clause (i) of this clause shall also apply to surveys and investigations of storage dams or detention dams on the Koshi, soil conservation measures, such as check dams, afforestation, etc., required for a complete solution of the Koshi problems in the future.

(iii) The surveys and investigations referred to in sub-clauses (i) and (ii) shall be carried in co-operation with HMG.

(iv) All data, maps, specimens, reports and other results of surveys and investigations carried out by or on behalf of the Union in Nepal pursuant to the provisions of this clause, shall be made available to HMG freely and without delay. In turn, HMG shall, upon request by the Union, make available to the Union all data, maps, specimens, reports, and other results of surveys and investigations carried out by or on behalf of HMG in Nepal in respect of the Koshi river.

3. AUTHORITY FOR EXECUTION OF WORKS AND USE OF LAND AND OTHER PROPERTY: (i) Provided that any major construction work not envisaged in the amended plan (Amended Annexure–A) referred to in clause 1(ii) shall require the prior approval of HMG, HMG shall authorize the Union to proceed with the execution of the said project as and when the project or a part of the project receives sanction of the said Union and notice has been given by the Union to HMG of its intention to commence work on the respective constructions and shall permit access by the Engineer and all other officers, servants, and nominees of the Union, with such men, animals, vehicles, plant, machinery, equipment and instruments as may be necessary for the direction and execution of the respective constructions, to all such lands and places, and shall permit the occupation, for such period as may be necessary, of all such lands and places as may be required for the proper execution of the respective constructions.

(ii) The land required for the purposes mentioned in Clause 3(i) above shall be acquired by HMG and compensation thereof shall be paid by the Union in accordance with the provisions of clause 8 hereof.

(iii) HMG shall, upon prior *notification*, authorize officers of the Union to enter on land outside the limits or boundaries of the barrage and its connected works in case of any accident happening or being apprehended to any of the said works and to execute all works which may be necessary for the purpose of repairing or preventing such damage. Compensation, in every case, shall be tendered by the Union through HMG to the owners of the said land for all accidents done to the same in order that compensation may be awarded in accordance with clause 8 hereof.

(iv) HMG will permit the Union to quarry the construction materials required for the project from the various deposits at Chatra, Dharan Bazar or other places in Nepal.

4. USE OF WATER AND POWER: (i) HMG shall have every right to withdraw for irrigation and for any other purpose in Nepal water from the Koshi river and from the Sun-Koshi river or within the Koshi basin from any other tributaries of the Koshi river as may be required from time to

time. The Union shall have the right to regulate all the balance of supplies in the Koshi river at the barrage site thus available from time to time and to generate power in the Eastern Canal.

(ii) HMG shall be entitled to obtain for use in Nepal any portion up to 50 per cent of the total hydro electric power generated by any Power House situated within a 10-mile radius from the barrage site and constructed by or on behalf of the Union, as HMG shall from time to time determine and communicate to the Union:

Provided that:

HMG shall communicate to the Union any increase or decrease in the required power supply exceeding 6800 KW at least three months in advance.

(iii) If any power to be supplied to Nepal pursuant to the provisions of this sub-clause is generated in a power house located in Indian territory, the Union shall construct the necessary transmission line or lines to such points at the Nepal-Indian border as shall be mutually agreed upon.

(iv) The tariff rates for electricity to be supplied to Nepal pursuant to the provisions of this clause shall be fixed my mutual agreement.

5. LEASE OF THE PROJECT AREAS: (i) All the lands acquired by HMG under the provisions of clause 3 hereof as of the date of signing of these amendments shall be leased by HMG to the Union for a period of 199 years from the date of signing of these amendments at an annual Nominal Rate.

(ii) The rent and other terms and conditions on which lands for Western Koshi Canal shall be leased by HMG to the Union pursuant to this Agreement shall be similar to those as under sub-clause (i).

(iii) The rent and other terms and conditions of any other land to be leased by HMG to the Union pursuant to this Agreement shall be fixed by mutual agreement.

(iv) At the request of the Union, HMG may grant renewal of the leases referred to in sub-clauses (i), (ii) and (iii) on such terms and conditions as may be mutually agreed upon.

(v) The sovereignty rights and territorial jurisdiction of HMG, including the application and enforcement of the law of Nepal on and in respect of the leased land shall continue unimpaired by such lease.

6. ROYALTIES: (i) HMG will receive royalty in respect to power generated and utilized in the Indian Union at rates to be settled by agreement hereafter:

Provided that no royalty will be paid on the power sold to Nepal.

(ii) HMG shall be entitled to receive payment of royalties from the Union in respect of stone, gravel and ballast obtained from Nepal territory and used in the construction and future maintenance of the barrage and other connected works at rates to be settled by agreement hereafter.

(iii) The Union shall be at liberty to use and remove clay, sand and soil without let or hindrance from lands leased by HMG to the Union.

(iv) Use of timber from Nepal forests, required for the construction, shall be permitted on payment of compensation. Provided that no compensation will be payable to HMG for such quantities of timber as may be agreed upon by HMG and the Union to be necessary for the use in the spurs and other river training works required for the prevention of caving and erosion of the right bank in Nepal.

Provided likewise that no compensation will be payable to the Union for any timber obtained from the forest lands leased by HMG to the Union.

7. CUSTOMS DUTIES: HMG shall charge no customs duty or duty of any kind, during construction and subsequent maintenance, on any articles and materials required for the purpose of the Project and the work connected therewith.

8. COMPENSATION FOR LAND PROPERTY AND FOR LAND REVENUE: (i) For assessing the compensation to be awarded by the Union to HMG in cash:

(a) Lands required for the execution of various works as mentioned in clause 3(ii) and clause 9(i); and

(b) Submerged lands will be divided into the following classes:

1. Cultivated lands.
2. Forest lands.
3. Village lands and houses and other immovable property standing on them.
4. Waste lands.

All lands recorded in the register of lands in the territory of Nepal as actually cultivated shall be deemed to be cultivated lands for the purpose of this clause.

(ii) The Union shall pay compensation:

(a) to HMG for the loss of land revenue as at the time of acquisition in respect of the area required, and

(b) to whomsoever it may be due for the lands, houses and other immovable property acquired for the Project and leased to the Union.

The assessment of such compensation and the manner of payment shall be determined hereafter by mutual agreement between HMG and the Union.

(iii) All lands required for the purposes of the Project shall be jointly measured by the duly authorized officers of HMG and the Union respectively.

9. COMMUNICATIONS: (i) HMG agrees that the Union may construct and maintain roads, tramways, railways, ropeways, etc., required for the Project in Nepal and shall provide land for these purposes on payment of compensation as provided in clause 8. Provided that the construction of any roads, tramways, railways, ropeways, etc., outside the Project area shall require the prior approval of HMG.

(ii) Any restrictions, required in the interest of construction, maintenance and proper operation of the Project, regarding the use of the roads, etc., referred to in sub-clause (i) by commercial or private vehicles may be mutually agreed upon. In case of threatened breach or erosion of the structures on account of the river, the officers of the Project may restrict public traffic under intimation to HMG.

(iii) HMG agrees to permit, on the same terms as for other users, the use of all roads, waterways and other avenues of transport and communication in Nepal for *bona fide* purposes of the construction and maintenance of the barrage and other connected works.

(iv) The bridge over Hanuman Nagar barrage shall be open to public traffic. With prior approval of HMG, the Union shall have the right to close the traffic over the bridge temporarily if and in so far as required for technical or safety reasons. In such cases, the Union shall take all measures required for the most expeditious reopening of the bridge.

(v) HMG agrees to permit installation of telegraph, telephone and radio communications in Nepal for the *bona fide* purposes of the construction and maintenance of the Project:

Provided that the Union shall agree to the withdrawal of such facilities which HMG may in this respect provide in future.

Further provided that the Union agrees to permit the use of internal telephone and telegraph in the Project area to authorized servants of HMG for business in emergencies provided such use does not in any way interfere with the construction and operation of the Project.

10. NAVIGATION RIGHTS: All navigation rights in the Koshi River in Nepal shall rest with HMG. Provision shall be made for suitable arrangements at or around the site of the barrage for free and unrestricted navigation in

the Koshi River, if technically feasible. However, the use of any watercraft like boast, launches and timber rafts within two miles of the barrage and headworks shall not be allowed on grounds of safety, except by special permits to be issued by the competent authority of HMG in consultation with the Executive Engineer, Barrage. Any unauthorized water-craft found within this limit shall be liable to prosecution.

11. FISHING RIGHTS: All the fishing rights in the Koshi River in Nepal shall continue to rest with HMG. However, no fishing shall be permitted within two miles of the barrage and headworks except under special permits to be issued by the competent authority of HMG in consultation with the Executive Engineer, Barrage. While issuing the special permits within two miles, HMG shall keep in view the safety of the headworks and the permitholders.

12. USE OF NEPALI LABOUR: The Union shall give preference to Nepali labour, personnel and contractors to the extent available and in its opinion suitable for the construction of the Project but shall be at liberty to import labour of all classes to the extent necessary.

13. CIVIC AMENITIES IN THE PROJECT AREA: Subject to the prior approval of HMG, the Union may, in the Project area, establish schools, hospitals, water-supply systems, electric supply systems, drainage and other civic amenities for the duration of the construction of the Project. On completion of construction of the project, any such amenities shall, upon request by HMG, be transferred to HMG, and that, in any case, all functions of public administration shall, pursuant to the provisions of clause 5(v) be exercised by HMG.

14. ARBITRATION: (i) Any dispute or difference arising out of or in any way touching or concerning the construction, effect or meaning of this Agreement, or of any matter contained herein or the respective rights and liabilities of the parties hereunder, if not settled by discussion shall be determined in accordance with the provisions of this clause.

(ii) Any of the parties may by notice in writing inform the other party of its intention to refer to arbitration any such dispute or difference mentioned in sub-clause (i); and within 90 days of the delivery of such notice, each of the two parties shall nominate an arbitrator for jointly determining such dispute or difference and the award of the arbitrators shall be binding on the parties.

(iii) In case the arbitrators are unable to agree, the parties hereto may consult each other and appoint an Umpire whose award shall be final and binding on them.

15. ESTABLISHMENT OF INDO-NEPAL KOSHI PROJECT COMMISSION: (i) For the discussion of problems of common interest in connection with the Project and for the purposes of co-ordination and co-operation between the two Governments with regard to any matter covered in this Agreement, the two Governments shall at an early date establish a joint 'Indo-Nepal Koshi Project Commission'. The rules for the composition, jurisdiction, etc., of the said Commission shall be mutually agreed upon.

(ii) Until the said Joint Commission shall be constituted the 'Co-ordination Committee for the Koshi Project' shall continue to function as follows:

(a) The committee shall consist of four representatives from each country to be nominated by the respective Governments.

(b) The Chairman of the committee shall be a Minister of HMG, and the Secretary shall be the Administrator of the Koshi Project.

(c) The committee shall consider among other such matters of common interest concerning the project as land acquisition by HMG for lease to the Union, rehabilitation of displaced population, maintenance of law and order.

(iii) As soon as the said Joint Commission shall be constituted, the Co-ordination Committee for the Koshi Project shall be dissolved.

16. (i) This present Agreement shall come into force from the date of signatures of the authorized representatives of HMG and the Union respectively and thereafter, it shall remain valid for a period of 199 years.

(ii) This present Agreement shall supersede the Agreement signed between the Government of Nepal and the Government of India on the 25th April, 1954 on the Koshi Project.

IN WITNESS WHEREOF the undersigned being duly authorized thereto by their respective Governments have signed the present Amended Agreement.

Done at Kathmandu, in quadruplicate, this day, the 19th of December, 1966.

For the Government of India

SHRIMAN NARAYAN
Ambassador of India in Nepal

For His Majesty's Government of Nepal

Y.P. PANT
Secretary, Ministry of Economic Planning and Finance

Appendix IX

Agreement Between His Majesty's Government of Nepal and the Government of India on the Gandak Irrigation and Power Project, Kathmandu, 4 December 1959

PREAMBLE: WHEREAS His Majesty's Government of Nepal and the Government of India consider that it is in the common interests of both Nepal and India to construct a barrage, canal head regulators and other appurtenant works about 1000 feet below the existing Tribeni canal head regulator and of taking out canal systems for purposes of irrigation and development of power for Nepal and India (hereinafter referred to as 'the Project').

AND WHEREAS in view of the common benefits, His Majesty's Government have agreed to the construction of the said barrage, canal head regulators and other connected works as shown in the Plan annexed[1] to this Agreement to the extent that they lie within the territory of Nepal, by and at the cost of the Government of India.

NOW THE PARTIES AGREE AS FOLLOWS

1. INVESTIGATION AND SURVEYS: His Majesty's Government authorize the Project Officers and other persons acting under the general or special orders of such officers to move in the area indicated in the said Plan with men, material and equipment as may be required for the surveys and investigations in connection with the Project, before, during and after construction, as may be found necessary from time to time. These surveys include ground, aerial, hydraulic, hydrometric, hydrological and geological surveys; investigations for communication and for the alignment of canals and for materials required for the construction and maintenance of the Project.

2. AUTHORITY FOR THE EXECUTION OF WORKS AND THEIR MAINTENANCE: (i) His Majesty's Government authorize the Government of India to proceed with the execution of the Project and for this purpose His Majesty's Government shall acquire all such lands as the Government of India may require and will permit the access to, the movement within and the residence in the area indicated in the Plan of officers and field staff with labour force, draught animals, vehicles, plants, machinery, equipment and instruments

[1]Not reproduced here.

as may be necessary for the execution of the Project and for its operation and maintenance after its completion.

(ii) In case of any apprehended danger or accident to any of the structures, the officers of the Government of India will execute all works which may be necessary for repairing the existing works or preventing such accidents and/or danger in the areas indicated in the Plan. If any of such works have to be constructed on lands as may be necessary for the purpose. In all such cases the Government of India shall pay reasonable compensation for the lands so acquired as well as for damage, if any, arising out of the execution of these works.

3. LAND ACQUISITION: (i) His Majesty's Government will acquire or requisition, as the case may be, all such lands as are required by the Government of India for the Project, i.e., for the purpose of investigation, construction and maintenance of the Project and the Government of India shall pay reasonable compensation for such lands acquired or requisitioned.

(ii) His Majesty's Government shall transfer to the Government of India such lands belonging to His Majesty's Government as are required for the purpose of the Project on payment of reasonable compensation by the Government of India.

(iii) Lands requisitioned under paragraph (i) shall be held by the Government of India for the duration of the requisition and lands acquired under sub-clause (i) or transferred under sub-clause (ii) shall vest in the Government of India as proprietor and subject to payment of land revenue (Malpot) at the rates at which it is leviable on agricultural lands in the neighbourhood.

(iv) When such land vesting in the Government of India or any part thereof ceases to be required by the Government of India for the purposes of the Project, the Government of India will reconvey the same to His Majesty's Government free of charge.

4. QUARRYING: His Majesty's Government shall permit the Government of India on payment of reasonable royalty to quarry materials such as block stones, boulders, shingle and sand required for the construction and maintenance of the Project from the areas indicated in the said Plan.

5. COMMUNICATIONS: (i) His Majesty's Government shall allow the Government of India to construct and maintain such portion of the main Western Canal which falls in the Nepal territory and to construct and maintain communications for the construction and maintenance of

the Project. The roads will be essentially departmental roads of the Project and their use by commercial and non-commercial vehicles of Nepal will be regulated as mutually agreed upon between His Majesty's Government and the Government of India.

(ii) The bridge over the Gandak Barrage will be open to public traffic, but the Government of India shall have the right to close the traffic over the bridge for repair, etc.

(iii) The Government of India agree to provide locking arrangements for facility of riverine traffic across the Barrage free from payment of any tolls whatever, provided that this traffic will be regulated by the Project staff in accordance with the rules mutually agreed upon between His Majesty's Government and the Government of India.

(iv) His Majesty's Government agree to permit installations of telegraph, telephone; and radio communications as approximately indicated in the Plan for the *bona fide* purpose of the construction, maintenance and operation of the Project.

(v) The Government of India shall permit the use of internal telegraph, telephone and radio communications as indicated in the Plan to the authorized servants of His Majesty's Government in emergencies, provided such use does not interfere with the construction, maintenance and operation of the Project.

6. Ownership, operation and maintenance of works: Subject to the provisions of sub-clause (v) of clause 7, all works connected with the Project in the territory of Nepal will remain the property of and be operated and maintained by the Government of India.

7. Irrigation for Nepal: (i) The Government of India shall construct at their own cost the Western Nepal Canal including the distributary system thereof down to a minimum discharge of 20 cusecs for providing flow irrigation in the gross commanded area estimated to be about 40,000 acres.

(ii) The Government of India shall construct the Eastern Nepal Canal from the tail end of the Don Branch Canal up to river Bagmati including the distributary system down to a minimum discharge of 20 cusecs at their own cost for providing flow irrigation in Nepal for the gross commanded area estimated to be 1,03,500 acres.

(iii) His Majesty's Government shall be responsible for the construction of channels below 20 cusecs capacity for irrigation in Nepal but the Government of India shall contribute such sum of money as they may consider reasonable to meet the cost of construction.

(iv) The Nepal Eastern Canal and the Nepal Western Canal shall be completed, as far as possible, within one year of the completion of the barrage.

(v) The canal systems including the service roads situated in Nepal territory except the main Western Canal, shall be handed over to His Majesty's Government for operation and maintenance at their cost.

8. Power development and reservation for Nepal: (i) The Government of India agree to construct one Power House with an installed capacity of 15,000 KW in the Nepal territory on the Main Western Canal.

(ii) The Government of India also agree to construct a transmission line from the Power House in Nepal to the Bihar border near Bhaisalotan and from Sagauli to Raxaul in Bihar in order to facilitate supply of power on any point in the Bihar Grid up to and including Raxaul.

(iii) The Government of India shall supply power to His Majesty's Government at the Power House and/or at any point in the Grid up to and including Raxaul to an aggregate maximum of 10,000 KW up to 60 per cent load factor at power factor not below 0.85. The charges for supply at the Power House shall be the actual cost of production, and on any point on the Grid up to Raxaul it shall be the cost of production *plus* the cost of transmission on such terms and conditions as may be mutually agreed upon.

(iv) His Majesty's Government will be responsible for the construction at their own cost of the transmission and distribution system for supply of power within Nepal from the Power House or from any point on the Grid up to and including Raxaul.

(v) The ownership and management of the Power House shall be transferred to His Majesty's Government on one year's notice in writing given by them to the Government of India after the full load of 10,000 KW at 60 per cent load factor has been developed in Nepal from this Power House.

(vi) The ownership of the transmission system constructed by the Government of India at its cost shall remain vested in the Government of India, but, on transfer of the Power House, the Government of India shall continue the arrangements for transmission of power, if so desired by His Majesty's Government, on payment of the cost of transmission. Provided that His Majesty's Government shall have the right to purchase the transmission system from the Power House to Bhaisalotan situated in the Nepal territory on payment of the original cost *minus* depreciation.

(vii) The Government of India shall be free to regulate the flow into or close the Main Western Canal Head Regulator temporarily, if such works are found to be necessary in the interest of the efficient maintenance and operation of the Canal or the Power House, provided that in such situations the Government of India agree to supply the minimum essential power from the Bihar Grid to the extent possible on such terms and conditions as may be mutually agreed upon.

9. PROTECTION OF NEPAL'S RIPARIAN RIGHTS: His Majesty's Government will continue to have the right to withdraw for irrigation or any other purpose from the river or its tributaries in Nepal such supplies of water as may be required by them from time to time and His Majesty's Government agree that they shall not exercise this right in such manner as is likely, in the opinion of the parties hereto prejudicially to affect the water requirements of the Project as set out in the schedule annexed hereto.

10. PRO RATA REDUCTION OF SUPPLIES DURING PERIOD OF SHORTAGE: Whenever the supply of water available for irrigation falls short of the requirements of the total area under the Project for which irrigation has to be provided the shortage shall be shared on *pro rata* basis between the Government of India and His Majesty's Government.

11. SOVEREIGNTY AND JURISDICTION: Nothing in this Agreement shall be deemed to derogate from the sovereignty and territorial jurisdiction of His Majesty's Government in respect of lands acquired by His Majesty's Government and made available to the Government of India for investigation, execution and maintenance of the Project.

12. ARBITRATION: (1) Any dispute or difference arising out of or in any way touching or concerning the construction, effect or meaning of this Agreement, or of any matter contained herein or the respective rights and liabilities of the parties hereunder, if not settled by discussion, shall be determined in accordance with the provisions of this clause.

(2) Any of the parties may by notice in writing inform the other party of its intention to refer to arbitration any such dispute or difference mentioned in sub-clause (1) and within 90 days of the delivery of such notice, each of the two parties shall nominate an arbitrator for jointly determining such dispute or difference and the award of the arbitrators shall be binding on the parties.

(3) In case the arbitrators are unable to agree, the parties hereto may consult each other and appoint an Umpire whose award shall be final and binding on them.

13. This Agreement will come into force with effect from the date of signatures of the authorized representatives of His Majesty's Government and the Government of India respectively.

IN WITNESS WHEREOF the undersigned being duly authorized thereof by their respective Governments have signed the present AGREEMENT in Nepali, Hindi and English in duplicate, all three texts being equally authentic, at Kathmandu this 19th day of Magh Sambut 2016 corresponding to December 4, 1959. For purposes of interpretation the English text shall be used.

For the Government of India
For and on behalf of the
President of India

BHAGWAN SAHAY
Ambassador of India

On behalf of
His Majesty's Government
of Nepal

SUBARNA SHAMSHERE
Deputy Prime Minister

Appendix X
The 1965 'Secret' Arms Agreement between Nepal and India

Foreign Secretary
Government of India, New Delhi
His Excellency Shri Yadu Nath Khanal
The Royal Nepalese Ambassador to India
New Delhi

Royal Nepalese Embassy
Barakhamba Road
New Delhi (India)
January 30, 1965

Excellency,

I wrote to acknowledge the receipt of your letter of today's date, which reads as follows:

During his visit to Delhi in August, 1963 His Majesty the King of Nepal had raised the question of the reorganization and modernization of the Nepalese Army. The Government of India expressed their willingness to provide the necessary assistance, and discussions took place in Delhi in December 1963 between a delegation of His Majesty's Government and representatives of the Government of India, with a view to determining the details of the assistance required by His Majesty's Government for the reorganization and modernization of the Nepalese Army. During these discussions the Nepalese delegation had proposed that the Government of India should assist His Majesty's Government in the raising and equipping a new brigade group.

2. The Government of India have given full and detailed consideration to the proposals made by His Majesty's Government. In view of the close and traditional bonds of friendship between our two countries, the Government of India are anxious to give all possible assistance to His Majesty's Government with the object of strengthening the security and independence of Nepal.

3. In the furtherance of these objectives it is hereby agreed that; (a) The Government of India undertake to supply arms, ammunition and equipment for the entire Nepalese Army on the basis of a total strength

of about 17,000 men, comprising four reorganized brigades. This will be inclusive of the existing Himal troops, home guards, household troops, militia companies, etc.

(b) The Government of India further undertake to replace the existing Nepalese stock by modern weapons as soon as available and also to provide the maintenance of and replacement for the equipment to be supplied by them.

(c) The Government of India undertake to provide all training facilities required for the Nepalese Armed Forces personnel in the training establishments in India, as necessary, and also by sending training personnel to Nepal at the request of His Majesty's Government. During their training in India adequate funds will be made available by the Government of India to enable them to meet expenses on a parity basis as incurred by the Indian military personnel of equivalent rank. The Government of India will also bear the expenses on account of lodging, including water charges and electricity, of such personnel. During the period of training, Nepalese officers will be given an allowance to enable them to defray the cost of incidental expenses, while other ranks will be provided with free messing.

(d) The Government of India will give full assistance to His Majesty's Government for the procuring in India, on payment, of olive green drill and other items of clothing and general stores, such as boots and webbing, etc., which are required for officers and men of the Nepalese Army.

(e) The existing programme of supplies of military equipment on a credit basis having been completed, the military assistance to be provided by the Government of India under this letter will be on a grant basis.

(f) The equipment and other assistance to be provided by the Government of India will be for the use of the Nepalese Army only, and shall not be diverted to any third party.

(g) The supplies under this programme of assistance will commence as soon as the composition and schedules of supply and the details of pattern and equipment have been agreed upon between the defence authorities of India and Nepal.

4. The Government of India understand that the Government of the UCS and the UK have also agreed to furnish some defence assistance to His Majesty's Government with a view to supplementing assistance from India. The Governments of the UK and the USA have given the Government of India to understand that if there are any shortfalls in the supply of arms

and equipment by the Government of India, these two Governments will fill the gaps to the extent of their ability. At an appropriate time, the details can be suitably co-ordinated.

5. The arrangements envisaged above shall have no bearing on the independent foreign policy on either Government. The Government of Nepal shall be free to import from or through the territory of India arms, ammunition or warlike material and equipment necessary for the security of Nepal. The procedures for giving effect to this arrangement shall be worked out by the two Governments acting in consultation.

6. The arrangements envisaged in this note may be reviewed from time to time by consultations between the Government of India and His Majesty's Government of Nepal.

7. I shall be grateful if your Excellency would kindly confirm that the above correctly sets out the understanding reached between us, and that this letter together with your Excellency's reply will constitute an agreement between His Majesty's Government of Nepal and the Government of India, which will come into force on the date of your Excellency's reply.

I confirm that the foregoing correctly sets out the understanding reached between us and that your Excellency's letter of January 30, 1965 together with this reply constitutes an agreement between His Majesty's Government of Nepal and the Government of India which comes into force from today, January 30, 1965.

Please accept, excellency, the assurances of my highest consideration and esteem.

(Sd.) Y.N. Khanal
Royal Nepalese Ambassador
His Excellency Mr Y. D. Gundevia
Foreign Secretary to the Government of India,
New Delhi.

Appendix XI
Nepal-India Joint Communiqué of 1990

[The following is the full text of the Nepal-India Joint Communiqué signed by the Prime Minister, Mr Krishna Prasad Bhattarai, and the Prime Minister of India, Mr Vishwanath Pratap Singh, in New Delhi on Sunday, June 10, 1990.]

Shri K. P. Bhattarai, the Prime Minister of Nepal, visited India from 8–10 June, 1990 at the invitation of the Prime Minister of India, Shri V.P. Singh. The two leaders held talks on bilateral, regional, and international issues of mutual concern. The talks were held in the most cordial and friendly atmosphere, characterizing the age-old ties and shared values of the two countries in the economic, social, cultural and religious spheres.

The Prime Minister of India applauded the success of the movement for democracy in Nepal and the commencement of the process of the establishment of a multi-party system with a constitutional monarchy and with the people of Nepal as the repository of power. The two leaders reaffirmed their desire promptly to normalize the unique, friendly and brotherly relations between their two peoples, impart them new dimensions and dynamism and elevate them to ever-rising levels of cordiality.

The two leaders reiterated their Governments' adherence to and respect for the principles of sovereign equality, territorial integrity, national independence, non-use of force, non-interference in each other's internal affairs and peaceful settlement of all disputes. They agreed that Nepal and India will fully respect each other's security concerns. In this context, neither side will allow activities in its territory prejudicial to the security of the other. The two countries shall have prior consultations with a view to reaching mutual agreement on such defence related matters which, in the view of either country, could pose a threat to its security.

Pending the finalization of a comprehensive arrangement covering all aspects of bilateral relations, the two Prime Ministers agreed to restore status quo ante to April 1, 1987 in the relations between the two countries. The two Governments will take all necessary steps, such as the issue of administrative orders, notifications, legislations of ordinances etc. in order to ensure that the status quo ante to April 1, 1987 is restored by July 1, 1990. Illustrative lists of action to be completed by the two Governments are given in Annexure I (India) and Annexure II (Nepal). It was further agreed that the above arrangements would not be altered by either side without mutual consultations.

The two leaders declared their solemn intention to usher in a new era of cooperation between the two countries—particularly in the spheres of industrial and human resources development, for the harnessing of the waters of the common rivers for the benefit of the two peoples and for the protection and the management of the environment.

During his visit, the Prime Minister of Nepal called on the President of India, Shri R. Venkataraman and on the Vice-President of India, Dr S. D. Sharma. He also visited Rajghat and Shantivana and laid wreaths in honour of Mahatma Gandhi and Pandit Jawaharlal Nehru.

The Prime Minister of Nepal extended a cordial invitation to the Prime Minister of India to visit Nepal. The invitation was accepted with pleasure.

NEW DELHI
JUNE 10, 1990.

Annexure I
Action To Be Taken By Government Of India

Trade

1. Import of primary products from Nepal to be exempted from basic customs duties as well as from quantitative restrictions.

2. Provide access, free of basic customs duties and quantitative restrictions, for all manufactured articles containing not less than 65 per cent of Nepalese materials or Nepalese and Indian materials, on a case by case basis, keeping in mind the need for expeditious clearance.

3. Allow 50 per cent tariff concession on MFN rate of import duty, where value of Nepalese and Indian materials and labour added in Nepal is at least 40 per cent of the ex-factory price, on a case by case basis, keeping in mind the need for expeditious clearance.

4. Export to Nepal of quota good, namely those that are either restricted or canalized for export from India.

5. The refund of Indian excise duty to Nepal under the Duty Refund Procedure should be such as to cover, but not to exceed, the basic and additional customs duties levied on similar goods imported from third countries.

6. Supplies of coke and coal to Nepal under quota will be resumed. Prices and supply schedules will be subject to agreement between MMTC and Nepal Coal Limited.

7. Canalizing of exports of POL products to Nepal through IOC, and agreement between IOC and NOC for product exchange between the two organizations.

8. Restoration of the Standby Credit Facility to Nepal at the enhanced level of Indian Rupees 35 crores.

Transit

9. Notification under Section 7 of the Customs Act 1962 restoring the 22 border points covered under GOI Notification No. 73/Customs/ F. no. 552/58/78-LCI and 238/Customs dated 15.12.1979 and 149/84 Customs dated 19.5.1984, and the routes specified therein as Land Customs Stations for the movement of goods between India and Nepal.

10. The 15 points earlier designated as transit point for Nepal's transit trade, through India, with third countries be reinstated.

Others

11. Restoration of the movement of the Nepalese trucks to and from the nearest railway heads/terminal.

12. Once a joint venture is approved by the two Governments, the Government of India would allow movement of capital as per the terms agreed upon in the joint venture.

13. Restoration of the three earlier immigration points on the Indo-Nepal border for the movement of tourists.

Annexure II

Action To Be Taken By His Majesty's Government of Nepal

Trade

1. Restoration of tariff preferences to Indian goods by, inter alia, exemption of additional customs duty.

2. Exemption of basic customs duty on imports of primary products from India as provided for similar products from Nepal imported to India.

3. Tariff preferences for third country goods should not be such as to be detrimental to the tariff regime for Indian exports.

4. Valuation of Indian goods exported under DRP for assessment of basic customs duty will be made on the basis of ex-factory/ex-depot price, excluding any element of refundable Indian duties and taxes, but including transport and insurance charges, wherever applied.

Indian Nationals

5. Removal of Indian nationals from the ambit of the Work Permit scheme.

6. Indian nationals employed in schools in Nepal will be placed on the same footing as Nepalese nationals as regards terms and conditions of employment.

Other Matters

7. Removal of restrictions on the movement of Indian currency between Nepal and India on the basis of reciprocity.

8. Restoration of facilities for Indian nationals to have their vehicles registered in Nepal on the basis of reciprocity.

Appendix XII
Treaty Between His Majesty's Government of Nepal and the Government of India Concerning the Integrated Development of the Mahakali River Including Sarada Barrage, Tanakpur Barrage, and Pancheshwar Project

His Majesty's Government of NEPAL and the Government of INDIA (thereinafter referred to as the 'Parties'),

Reaffirming the determination to promote and strengthen their relations of friendship and close neighbourliness for the co-operation in the development of water resources;

Recognizing that the Mahakali River is a boundary river on major stretches between the two countries;

Realizing the desirability to enter into a treaty on the basis of equal partnership to define their obligations and corresponding rights and duties thereto in regard to the waters of the Mahakali River and its utilization;

Noting the Exchange of Letters of 1920 through which both the Parties had entered into an arrangement for the construction of the Sarada Barrage in the Mahakali River, whereby Nepal is to receive some waters from the said Barrage;

Recalling the decision taken in the Joint Commission dated 4–5 December, 1991 and the Joint Communiqué issued during the visit of the Prime Minister of India to Nepal on 21st October, 1992 regarding the Tanakapur Barage which India has constructed in a course of the Mahakali River with a part of the eastern afflux bund at Jimuwa and the adjoining pondage area of the said Barrage lying in the Nepalese territory;

Noting that both the Parties are jointly preparing a Detailed Project Report of the Pancheshwar Multipurpose Project to be implemented in the Mahakali River;

Now, therefore, the Parties hereto hereby have agreed as follows:

Article 1

1. Nepal shall have the right to a supply of 28.35 m3/s (1000 cusecs) of water from the Sarada Barrage in the wet season (i.e. from 15th May to 15th October) and 4.25m3/s (150 cusecs) in the dry season (i.e. from 16th October to 14th May).

2. India shall maintain a flow of not less than 10 m3/s (350 cusecs) downstream of the Sarada Barrage in the Mahakali River to maintain and preserve the river eco-system.

3. In case the Sarada Barrage become non-functional due to any cause:

(a) Nepal shall have the right to a supply of water as mentioned in Paragraph 1 of this Article, by using the head regulator(s) mentioned in Paragraph 2 of Article 2 herein. Such a supply of water shall be in addition to the water to be supplied to Nepal pursuant to Paragraph 2 of Article 2.

(b) India shall maintain the river flow pursuant to Paragraph 2 of this Article from the tailrace of the Tanakpur Power Station downstream of the Sarada Barrage.

Article 2

In continuation of the decisions taken in the Joint Commission dated 4–5 December, 1991 and the Joint Communiqué issued during the visit of the Prime Minister of India to Nepal on 21st October, 1992, both the Parties agree as follows:

1. For the construction of the eastern afflux bund of the Tanakpur Barrage, at Jimuwa and tying it up to the high ground in the Nepalese territory at EL 250 M, Nepal gives its consent to use a piece of land of about 577 metres in length (an area of about 2.9 hectares) of the Nepalese territory at the Jimuwa Village in Mahendranagar Municipal area and a certain portion of the No-Man's Land on either side of the border. The Nepalese land consented to be so used and the land lying on the west of the said land (about 9 hectares) up to the Nepal-India border which forms a part of the pondage area, including the natural resources endowment lying within that area, remains under the continued sovereignty and control of Nepal and Nepal is free to exercise all attendant rights thereto.

2. In lieu of the eastern afflux bund of the Tanakpur Barrage, at Jimuwa thus constructed, Nepal shall have the right to:

(a) a supply of 28.35 m3/s (1000 cusecs) of water in the wet season (i.e. from 15th May to 15th October) and 8.50 m3/s (300 cusecs) in the dry season (i.e. from 16th October to 14th May) from the date of the entry into force of this Treaty. For this purpose and for the purposes of Article 1 herein, India shall construct the head regulator(s) near the left undersluice of the Tanakpur Barrage and also the waterways of the required capacity upto the Nepal–India border. Such head regulator(s) and waterways shall be operated jointly.

(b) a supply of 70 millions kilowatt-hour (unit) of energy on a continuous basis annually, free of cost, from the date of the entry into force of this Treaty. For this purpose, India shall construct a 132 KV transmission line up to the Nepal-India border from the Tanakpur Power Station (which has, at present, an installed capacity of 120,000 kilowatt generating 448.4 millions kilowatt-hour of energy annually on 90 per cent dependable year flow).

3. Following arrangements shall be made at the Tanakpur Barrage at the time of development of any storage project(s), including Pancheshwar Multipurpose Project upstream of the Tanakpur Barrage:

(a) Additional head regulator and the necessary waterways, as required, up to the Nepal-India border shall be constructed to supply additional water to Nepal. Such head regulator and waterways shall be operated jointly.

(b) Nepal shall have additional energy equal to half of the incremental energy generated from the Tanakpur Power Station, on a continuous basis from the date of augmentation of the flow of the Mahakali River and shall bear half of the additional operation cost and, if required, half of the additional capital cost at the Tanakpur Power Station for the generation of such incremental energy.

Article 3

Pancheshwar Multipurpose Project (hereinafter referred to as the 'Project') is to be constructed on a stretch of the Mahakali River where it forms the boundary between the two countries and hence both the Parties agree that they have equal entitlement in the utilization of the waters of the Mahakali River without prejudice to their respective existing consumptive uses of the waters of the Mahakali River. Therefore, both the Parties agree to implement the Project in the Mahakali River in accordance with the Detailed Project Report (DPR) being jointly prepared by them. The Project shall be designed and implemented on the basis of the following principles:

1. The Project shall, as would be agreed between the Parties, be designed to produce the maximum total net benefit. All benefits accruing to both the Parties with the development of the Project in the forms of power, irrigation, flood control etc., shall be assessed.

2. The Project shall be implemented or caused to be implemented as an integrated project including power stations of equal capacity on each side of the Mahakali River. The two power stations shall be operated in an integrated manner and the total energy generated shall be shared equally between the Parties.

3. The cost of the Project shall be borne by the Parties in proportion to the benefits accruing to them. Both the Parties shall jointly endeavour to mobilize the finance required for the implementation of the Project.

4. A portion of Nepal's share of energy shall be sold to India. The quantum of such energy and its price shall be mutually agreed upon between the Parties.

Article 4

India shall supply 10 m3/s (350 cusecs) of water for the irrigation of Dodhara–Chandani area of Nepalese Territory. The technical and other details will be mutually worked out.

Article 5

1. Water requirements of Nepal shall be given prime consideration in the utilization of the waters of the Mahakali River.

2. Both the Parties shall be entitled to draw their share of waters of the Mahakali River from the Tanakpur Barrage and/or other mutually agreed points as provided for in this Treaty and any subsequent agreement between the Parties.

Article 6

Any project, other than those mentioned herein, to be developed in the Mahakali River, where it is a boundary river, shall be designed and implemented by an agreement between the Parties on the principles established by this Treaty.

Article 7

In order to maintain the flow and level of the waters of the Mahakali River, each Party undertakes not to use or obstruct or divert the waters of the Mahakali River adversely affecting its natural flow and level except by an agreement between the Parties. Provided, however, this shall not preclude the use of the waters of the Mahakali River by the local communities living along both sides of the Mahakali River, not exceeding five (5) per cent of the average annual flow at Pancheshwar.

Article 8

This Treaty shall not preclude planning, survey, development and operation of any work on the tributaries of the Mahakali River, to be carried out independently by each Party in its own territory without adversely affecting the provision of Article 7 of this Treaty.

Article 9

1. There shall be a Mahakali River Commission (hereinafter referred to as the 'Commission'). The Commission shall be guided by the principles of equality, mutual benefit and no harm to either Party.

2. The Commission shall be composed of equal number of representatives from both the Parties.

3. The functions of the Commission shall, inter alia, include the following:

(a) To seek information on and, if necessary, inspect all structures included in the Treaty and make recommendations to both the Parties to take steps which shall be necessary to implement the provisions of this Treaty,

(b) To make recommendations to both the Parties for the conservation and utilization of the Mahakali River as envisaged and provided for in this Treaty,

(c) To provide expert evaluation of projects and recommendations thereto,

(d) To co-ordinate and monitor plans of actions arising out of the implementation of this Treaty, and

(e) To examine any differences arising between the Parties concerning the interpretation and application of this Treaty.

4. The expenses of the Commission shall be borne equally by both the Parties.

5. As soon as the Commission has been constituted pursuant to Paragraphs 1 and 2 of this Article, it shall draft its rules of procedure which shall be submitted to both the Parties for their concurrence.

6. Both the Parties shall reserve their rights to deal directly with each other on matters which may be in the competence of the Commission.

Article 10

Both the Parties may form project specific joint entity/ies for the development, execution and operation of new projects including Pancheshwar Multipurpose Project in the Mahakali River for their mutual benefit.

Article 11

1. If the Commission fails under Article 9 of this Treaty to recommend its opinion after examining the differences of the Parties within three (3) months of such reference to the Commission or either Party disagrees with the recommendation of the Commission then a dispute shall be deemed to have been arisen which shall then be submitted to arbitration for decision. In so doing either Party shall give three (3) months prior notice to the other Party.

2. Arbitration shall be conducted by a tribunal composed of three arbitrators. One arbitrator shall be nominated by Nepal, one by India, with neither country to nominate its own national, and the third arbitrator shall be appointed jointly, who, as a member of the tribunal, shall preside over such tribunal. In the even that the Parties are unable to agree upon the third arbitrator within ninety (90) days after receipt of a proposal, either Party may request the Secretary-General of the Permanent Court of Arbitration at the Hague to appoint such arbitrator who shall not be a national of either country.

3. The procedures of the arbitration shall be determined by the arbitration tribunal and the decision of a majority of the arbitrators shall be the decision of the tribunal. the proceedings of the tribunal shall be conducted in English and the decision of such a tribunal shall be in writing. Both the Parties shall accept the decision as final, definitive and binding.

4. Provision for the venue of arbitration, the administrative support of the arbitration tribunal and the remuneration and expenses of its

arbitrators shall be as agreed in an exchange of notes between the Parties. Both the Parties may also agree by such exchange of notes on alternative procedures for settling differences arising under this Treaty.

Article 12

1. Following the conclusion of this Treaty, the earlier understandings reached between the Parties concerning the utilization of the waters of the Mahakali River from the Sarada Barrage and the Tanakpur Barrage, which have been incorporated herein, shall be deemed to have been replaced by this Treaty.

2. This Treaty shall be subject to ratification and shall enter into force on the date of exchange of instruments of ratification. It shall remain valid for a period of seventy-five (75) years from the date of its entry into force.

3. This Treaty shall be reviewed by both the Parties at ten (10) years interval or earlier as required by either Party and make amendments thereto, if necessary.

4. Agreements, as required, shall be entered into by the Parties to give effect to the provisions of this Treaty.

IN WITNESS WHEREOF the undersigned being duly authorized thereto by their respective governments have hereto signed this Treaty and affixed thereto their seals in two originals each in Hindi, Nepali and English languages, all the texts being equally authentic. In case of doubt, the English text shall prevail.

Done at New Delhi, India, on the twelfth day of February of the year one thousand nine hundred ninety six.

SHER BAHADUR DEUBA
Prime Minister
His Majesty's Government of Nepal

P.V. NARASIMHA RAO
Prime Minister of India

Letter Exchanged with the Treaty

KATHMANDU
NEPAL

The Prime Minister

February 12,1996

Excellency,

I have the honour to refer to the Treaty concluded between us concerning the Integrated Development of the Mahakali River including Sarada Barrage, the Tanakpur Barrage and Pancheswar Project (Treaty). At this juncture, may I also recall for Your Excellency the decisions taken in the Joint Commission dated 4–5 December, 1991 and the Joint Communiqué issued during your visit to Nepal on 21st October, 1992.

In order to give effect to the desires expressed by our respective Governments, I have the honour to make the following proposals on the basis of the provisions of the said understandings and the said Treaty.

1. The all-weather link road connecting the Tanakpur Barrage to the East–West Highway at Mahendranagar in Nepal shall be completed by India within one (1) year from the date of the entry into force of the Treaty.

2. The supply of 20 millions kilowatt-hour of energy annually, free of cost, to Nepal from the Tanakpur Power Station as indicated in the said Joint Communiqué from the date of commissioning of the Tanakpur Power Station in July 7, 1992 till the start of the supply of 70 millions kilowatt-hour (unit) of energy annually, free of cost, to Nepal as provided for in the Treaty, shall be reconciled with the energy procured or to be procured by Nepal from India under the existing power exchange arrangement.

3. Regarding Pancheshwar Multipurpose Project (Project), the following principles shall be adopted and arrangements made for finalization of the Detailed Project Report (DPR) completion of negotiation and implementation of the Project:

(a) The DPR shall be finalized by both the countries within six (6) months from the date of the entry into force of the Treaty. For this purpose, necessary data and reports shall be exchanged expeditiously. While assessing the benefits from the Project during the preparation of the DPR, net power benefit shall be assessed on the basis of, inter alia, saving in costs to the beneficiaries as compared with the relevant alternatives available. Irrigation benefit shall be assessed on the basis of incremental and additional benefits due to augmentation of river flow and flood control benefit shall be assessed on the basis of the value of works saved and damages avoided.

(b) It is understood that Paragraph 3 of Article 3 of the Treaty precludes the claim, in any form, by either Party on the unutilized portion of the shares of the waters of the Mahakali River of that Party without affecting the provision of the withdrawal of the respective shares of the water of the Mahakali River by each Party under this Treaty.

(c) Agreement for the financing and implementation of the Project, including the proposal for the establishment of the Pancheshwar Development Authority shall be negotiated and finalized by both the countries within one (1) year from the finalization of the DPR.

(d) In order to expedite the implementation of the Project, field investigation and detailed design including tender document preparation shall start immediately after the finalization of the DPR and run parallel to the negotiation on agreement for implementation of the Project. For this purpose, a separate financing arrangement for such activities shall be agreed upon by both the countries.

(e) The Project shall be aimed to be completed within eight (8) years from the date of the agreement for its implementation, subject to the provision of the DPR.

I shall be grateful if Your Excellency will kindly confirm that the above correctly sets out the understanding reached between our two Governments. This letter and Your Excellency's reply confirming the understanding will constitute an agreement between our two Governments which also shall come into force on the date of exchange of instruments of ratification between the Parties as set forth in Paragraph 2 of Article 12 of the Treaty.

Please accept, Your Excellency, the assurances of my highest considerations.

SHER BAHADUR DEUBA

H.E. MR P.V. NARASIMHA RAO
Prime Minister of India
New Delhi

Appendix XIII
Agreement of Friendship and Commerce between Nepal and the United States

Exchange of notes at Kathmandu April 25, 1947
Entered into force April 25, 1947

The Chief of the United States Special Diplomatic Mission to the Prime Minister and Supreme Commander-in-Chief of Nepal

UNITED STATES SPECIAL DIPLOMATIC
MISSION TO THE KINGDOM OF NEPAL
KATHMANDU, April 25, 1947

YOUR HIGHNESS:

I have the honour to make the following statement of my Government's understanding of the agreement reached through recent conversations held at Kathmandu by representatives of the Government of the United States of America and the Government of the Kingdom of Nepal with reference to diplomatic and consular representation, juridical protection, commerce and navigation. These two Governments, desiring to strengthen the friendly relations happily existing between the two countries, to further mutually advantageous commercial relations between their peoples, and to maintain the most-favoured-nation principle in its unconditional and unlimited form as the basis of their commercial relations, agree to the following provisions:

1. The United States of America and the Kingdom of Nepal will establish diplomatic and consular relations at a date which shall be fixed by mutual agreement between the two Governments.

2. The diplomatic representatives of each Party accredited to the Government of the other Party shall enjoy in the territories of such other Party the rights, privileges, exemptions and immunities accorded under generally recognized principles of international law. The consular officers of each Party who are assigned to the Government of the other Party, and are duly provided with exequaturs, shall be permitted to reside in the territories of such other Party at the places where consular officers are permitted by the applicable laws to reside; they shall enjoy the honorary privileges and the immunities accorded to officers of their rank by general

international usage; and they shall not, in any event, be treated in a manner less favourable than similar officers of any third country.

3. All furniture, equipment and supplies intended for official use in a consular or diplomatic office of the sending state shall be permitted entry into the territory of the receiving state free of all customs duties and internal revenue or other taxes whether imposed upon or by reason of importation.

4. The baggage and effects and other articles imported exclusively for the personal use of consular and diplomatic officers and employees and the members of their respective families and suites, who are nationals of the sending state and are not nationals of the receiving state and are not engaged in any private occupation for gain in territory of the receiving state, shall be exempt from all customs duties and internal revenue or other taxes whether imposed upon or by reason of importation. Such exemption shall be granted with respect to property accompanying any person entitled to claim an exemption under this paragraph on first arrival or on any subsequent arrival and with respect to property consigned to any such person during the period the consular or diplomatic officer or employee, for or through whom the exemption is claimed, is assigned to or is employed in the receiving state by the sending state.

5. It is understood, however, (a) that the exemptions provided by paragraph 4 of this Agreement shall be accorded in respect of employees in a consular office only when the names of such employees have been duly communicated to the appropriate authorities of the receiving state; (b) that in the case of the consignments to which paragraph 4 of the Agreement refers, either state may, as a condition to the granting of the exemption provided, require that a notification of any such consignment be given in such manner as it may prescribe; and (c) that nothing herein shall be construed to permit the entry into the territory of either state of any article the importation of which is specifically prohibited by law.

6. Nationals of the Kingdom of Nepal in the United States of America and nationals of the United States of America in the Kingdom of Nepal shall be received and treated in accordance with the requirements and practices of generally recognized international law. In respect of their persons, possessions and rights, such nationals shall enjoy the fullest protection of the laws and authorities of the country, and shall not be treated in any manner less favourable than the nationals of any third country.

7. In all matters relating to customs duties and charges of any kind imposed on or in connection with importation or exportation or

otherwise affecting commerce and navigation, to the method of levying such duties and charges, to all rules and formalities in connection with importation or exportation, and to transit, warehousing and other facilities, each Party shall accord unconditional and unrestricted most-favoured-nation treatment to articles the growth, produce or manufacture of the other Party, from whatever place arriving, or to articles destined for exportation to the territories of such other Party, by whatever route. Any advantage, favour, privilege or immunity with respect to any duty, charge or regulation affecting commerce or navigation now or hereafter accorded by the United States of America or by the Kingdom of Nepal to any third country shall be accorded immediately and unconditionally to the commerce and navigation of the Kingdom of Nepal and of the United States of America, respectively.

8. There shall be excepted from the provisions of paragraph 7 of this Agreement advantages now or hereafter accorded: (a) by virtue of a customs union of which either Party may become a member; (b) to adjacent countries in order to facilitate frontier traffic; (c) to third countries which are parties to a multilateral economic agreement of general applicability, including a trade area of substantial size, having as its objective the liberalization and promotion of international trade or other international economic intercourse and open to adoption by all the United Nations; and (d) by the United States of America or its territories or possessions to one another, to the Republic of Cuba, to the Republic of the Philippines, or to the Panama Canal Zone. Clause (d) shall continue to apply in respect of any advantages now or hereafter accorded by the United States of America or its territories or possessions to one another irrespective of any change in the political status of any such territories or possessions.

9. Nothing in this Agreement shall prevent the adoption or enforcement by either Party; (a) of measures relating to fissionable materials, to the importation or exportation of gold and silver, to the traffic in arms, ammunitions and implements of war, or to such traffic in other goods and materials as is carried on for the purpose of supplying a military establishment; (b) of measures necessary in pursuance of obligations for the maintenance of international peace and security or necessary for the protection of the essential interests of such Party in time of national emergency; or (c) of statutes in relation to immigration.

10. Subject to the requirement that, under like circumstances and conditions, there shall be no arbitrary discrimination by either Party

against the nationals, commerce or navigation of the other Party in favour of the nationals, commerce or navigation of any third country, the provisions of this Agreement shall not extend to prohibitions or restrictions: (a) imposed on moral or humanitarian grounds; (b) designed to protect human, animal, or plant life or health; (c) relating to prison-made goods; or (d) relating to the enforcement of police or revenue laws.

11. The provisions of this Agreement shall apply to all territory under the sovereignty or authority of either of the parties, except the Panama Canal Zone.

12. This Agreement shall continue in force until superseded by a more comprehensive commercial agreement, or until thirty days from the date of a written notice of termination given by either Party to the other Party, whichever is the earlier. Moreover, either Party may terminate paragraphs 7 and 8 on thirty days' written notice.

If the above provisions are acceptable to the Government of the Kingdom of Nepal this note and the reply signifying assent thereto shall, if agreeable to that Government, be regarded as constituting an agreement between the two Governments which shall become effective on the date of such acceptance.

Please accept, Your Highness, the renewed assurances of my highest consideration.

JOSEPH C. SATTERTHWAITE

To,
His Highness
The Maharaja
PADMA SHUM SHERE JUNG BAHADUR RANA
Prime Minister and Supreme Commander-in-Chief
Nepal

The Prime Minister and Supreme Commander-in-Chief of Nepal to the Chief of the United States Special Diplomatic Mission

YOUR EXCELLENCY,

I have the honour to acknowledge the receipt of your note dated 25th April 1947, in which there is set forth the understanding of your Government of the agreement reached through recent conversations held at Kathmandu between the representatives of the Government of the United States of America and the representatives of the Government of the Kingdom of Nepal, in the following terms:

The Government of the United States of America and the Government of the Kingdom of Nepal, desiring to strengthen the friendly relations happily existing between the two countries, to further mutually advantageous commercial relations between their peoples, and to maintain the most-favoured-nation principle in its unconditional and unlimited form as a basis of their commercial relations, agree to the following provisions:

The Government of the Kingdom of Nepal approves the above provisions and is prepared to give effect thereto beginning with the date of this reply note.

Please accept Your Excellency the renewed assurance of high consideration with which I remain,

Your Excellency's sincerely,

PADMA SHUM SHERE JUNG R.B.

KATHMANDU
Dated the 25th APRIL 1947.

To,
His Excellency
THE HON'BLE MR JOSEPH C. SATTERTHWAITE
Chief, United States Special
Diplomatic Mission to the Kingdom of Nepal
Kathmandu.

Appendix XIV
1947 Tripartite Agreements Between Nepal, India, and the United Kingdom after Partition to Retain Gurkha Services in the British and Indian Armies

Memorandum of Agreement

1. At a meeting held at Kathmandu on 1st May 1947 between representatives of His Majesty's Government in the United Kingdom; the Government of India and Government of Nepal, His Highness the Prime Minister and Supreme Commander-in-Chief of Nepal stated that he would welcome the proposals to maintain the Gurkha connection with the armies of the United Kingdom and India on the following basis 'If the terms and conditions at the final stage do not prove detrimental to the interest or dignity of the Nepalese Government, my Government will be happy to maintain connections with both armies, provided men of the Gurkha Regiments are willing so to serve (if they will not be looked upon as distinctly mercenary)'.

2. Discussions have taken place in Delhi between representatives of His Majesty's Government in the United Kingdom and of the Government of the Dominion of India and the points of agreement are embodied in the Memorandum dated 7 November 1947 a copy of which forms Annexure I of this document. Necessary financial adjustments between the two Governments are still under consideration.

3. Further discussions between the representatives of the three Governments have taken place at Kathmandu during which the Government of Nepal have put forward certain pertinent observations on the memorandum of Agreement referred to in the proceeding paragraph which are set out in Annexure II. In regard to these points, the representatives of His Majesty's Government in the United Kingdom and of the Government of the Dominion of India have replied as follows:

(a) Location of the Recruiting Depots.

The use of the existing depots at Gorakhpur and Chum has been sought by His Majesty's Government in the United Kingdom for a temporary period only pending establishment of their own depots in Nepal. The wishes of the Government of Nepal have been noted and arrangements for the establishment in India of the Recruiting Depots required to meet the needs of the Gurkha units of the British Army will be settled between the United Kingdom and Indian Governments.

(b) Desire of the Government of Nepal that the total number of Gurkha Units to be employed in the Armies of the United Kingdom and or India shall be limited and brought down to the peace-time strength of 20 Battalions out of which 8 Battalions will be allotted to the British Army.

The representatives of His Majesty's Government in the United Kingdom and of the Government of Dominion of the India have taken note of the wishes of the Government of Nepal.

The representative of His Majesty's Government in the United Kingdom has explained that the long term planning of the British Post-War Army has proceeded on the assumption that the Government of Nepal would be prepared to furnish sufficient men to establish the equivalent of an Infantry Division in South-East Asia and he has received an assurance from the Government of Nepal that a final decision on the question of recruitment of Gurkhas in excess of 8 Battalions at peace-time strength shall be left open until His Majesty's Government in the United Kingdom have had an opportunity of considering the views of the Government of Nepal.

As regards the reduction of the Gurkha Units in the Indian Army the Government of Nepal have informed the representative of the Government of the Dominion of India that the reduction should not be carried out immediately in view of the existing political situation in India.

(c) Arrangements for the import of the foreign currency belonging to the Gurkha units of the 8 Battalions service overseas.

It is noted that the Government of the Dominion of India has agreed to afford all normal facilities in regard to the import of foreign currency belonging to these men (Annexure 1, item 10). A reply to the specific point raised in this connection will be sent to the Government of Nepal in due course.

4. The Government of Nepal being generally satisfied in regard to the terms and conditions of employment of Gurkhas troops and taking note of the agreement dated 7th November 1947 reached between His Majesty's Government in the United Kingdom and of the Government of Dominion of India hereby signify their agreement to the employment of Gurkha troops in the armies of the United Kingdom and of India.

5. In addition to the observations referred to above the Government of Nepal have put forward certain suggestions connected with the employment of Gurkhas in the armies of the United Kingdom and of India. These suggestions are contained in Annexure III of this document and the views of the two Governments thereon will be communicated to the Government of Nepal in due course.

6. Note has been taken of the desire of His Majesty's Government in United Kingdom that prompt action be taken to ascertain the wishes of the personnel of the 8 Gurkha Battalions concerned as to whether they desire to be transferred for service under the United Kingdom Government. With this object in view a questionnaire and a Memorandum embodying terms and conditions of service have been prepared by the representatives of His Majesty's Government in the United Kingdom. These documents are acceptable to the Governments of India and Nepal. They will be issued to the personnel of the 8 units concerned as soon as possible. In accordance with the wishes of the Government of Nepal as well as those of the Government of India it is agreed that their representatives will be present with the 8 units while the referendum is being taken.

7. The representatives of the three Governments desire to place on record that their deliberations have been conducted in an atmosphere of cordiality and goodwill and are confident that the friendly relations which have existed in the past will be further cemented as a result of the arrangements which have been agreed for the continued employment of Gurkha soldiers in the armies of the United Kingdom and of India.

8. Signed in triplicate at Kathmandu this 9th day of November 1947.

For the Government of the United Kingdom

For the Government of the Dominion of India

For the Government of Nepal.

Annexure I

Memorandum of Government of the Dominion of India and His Majesty's Government in the United Kingdom of 7 November 1947

1. That all volunteers from Regular battalions of each of the Second, Sixth, Seventh and Tenth Gurkha Rifles, together with personnel of their Regimental Centres, shall be transferred to H.M. British Army, subject to the negotiation of terms and conditions with the Government of Nepal.

2. That the personal arms and equipment of those units if required by H.M. Government will be issued on payment, and removed overseas with the units.

3. That H.M. Government may for the present continue to use the existing recruiting depots at Gurakhpur and Ghum, and that the British and Gurkha Military personnel serving in them may wear uniform.

4. That the plans of H.M. Government for recruiting in Nepal up to a possible strength of a Division (say 25,000 men), shall not in any way interfere with recruitment to the Gurkha units in the Indian Army.

5. That Gurkha Officers, recruits, soldiers, ex-soldiers and pensioners of Gurkha units serving H.M. Government, and their dependants, shall be permitted to travel freely between Nepal and an Indian port on their lawful occasions, provided mufti is worn in transit through India; the stipulation regarding dress shall not apply to the four Regiments named 2nd GR (the Sirmoor Rifles); 6th GR; 7th GR; and 10th GR.

6. That the normal road and rail transport facilities in India shall be available, at the public rates prevailing from time to time, to all British Officers serving with Gurkhas, Gurkha Officers and their families, Gurkha other ranks and their families and the necessary maintenance stores and baggage of such personnel in the service of H.M. Government; and that such staging facilities as may be required shall be provided at the expense of H.M. Government.

7. That India's postal, money-order and telegraphic services to and from Nepal shall be available to H.M. Government, and Gurkhas serving H.M. Government, at the normal rates prescribed from time to time.

8. That the Government of India shall make available annually to H.M. Government, for the use of Gurkha soldiers, the following quantities of foodstuffs:

Atta	2200 tons.
Ghee	750 tons.
Dhal	1200 tons.
Condiment powder 150 tons.	

provided H.M. Government arrange to supply the Government of India with 2200 tons of wheat in replacement of the atta supplied to them.

9. That the Government of India shall make available to H.M. Government such Indian currency as may be necessary for purposes connected with their employment of Gurkha soldiers, provided that the sterling equivalent thereof shall be credited to the Government of India Sterling Account One.

10. That Gurkha Officers, soldiers, ex-soldiers, pensioners and their dependants shall have the right to send or take Indian money back to Nepal subject only to such Indian currency regulations of general application as may be in force from time to time; foreign currencies imported into India shall be subject to the general Indian currency regulations obtaining from time to time.

11. That the basic rates of pay admissible to Gurkha officers and soldiers serving H.M. Government shall approximate to those laid down in the present Indian Pay Code, at which rates personnel serving at the recruiting depots in Gorakhpur and Ghum shall be paid; and that a special allowance, to compensate for permanent service overseas and high cost of living, shall in addition be admissible to Gurkha officers and soldiers serving H.M. Government, overseas.

12. After the 8 Battalions have been asked to opt for service under H.M. Government, Government of India will try to make up the deficiency caused by those who do not wish to serve with H.M. Government, by asking other soldiers who have completed their existing engagement and who do not wish to continue to serve in the Indian Army Units. If the required number can not thus be made good the deficiency will be made up by H.M. Government by direct recruitment.

For the Government of the Dominion of India
For His Majesty's Government in the United Kingdom

Kathmandu
7th November 1947

Annexure II
Nepalese reaction to 'Points of Agreement between Government of India and H.M.G.'

1. *Para (4)* It appears that the arrangements of having recruiting Depots at Gorakhpur and Ghum for the British Gurka Regiments has as an after-thought been made of a temporary character. Nepal Government feels that it would definitely be more convenient to all three parties, if the recruiting is carried on for both Indian and British armies at the present depots or any other places in India.
2. *Para (5)* In view of our long-standing friendship the Government of Nepal had agreed to raise the strength of the Gurkha Regiments during the period of the last war. But she feels that the continuation of this emergency measure will be too much of a drain on the man-power of the country. So she desires that the total be limited and brought down to the peace-time strength of 20 battalions to be divided between the Indian and British Armies, as already arranged.
3. *Para (11)* Nepal Government desires that the foreign currency brought by the personnel of the Gurkha Regiments serving abroad be credited to the Nepal Government account in any bank (to be settled afterwards); the Government of Nepal providing Indian Currency therefore at the prevailing market rate.

Annexure III

Nepal Government's position on the tripartite and bilateral agreements to retain Gurkha troops in the British and the Indian armies

1. In all matters of promotion, welfare and other facilities the Gurkha troops should be treated on the same footing as the other units in the parent army so that the stigma of 'mercenary troops' may for all time be wiped out. These troops should be treated as a link between two friendly countries.

2. The Gurkha troops should be given every facility so that it might be officered by their own men and they should be eligible to commissioned

ranks with no restrictions whatsoever to the highest level to which qualified officers may be promoted.

3. The Gurkha troops should not be used against Hindu or any other unarmed mobs.

4. To avoid any clash between the Gurkhas themselves, Gurkha troops should not be used if any contingency of their having to serve in opposite camps arises.

5. To enable us supply better quality men, we request that our following military needs may be met:

(i) A well-equipped arms and ammunition factory producing all modern small arms and ammunitions.

(ii) A few Army transport planes.

(iii) Our requirements of Army Stores and civil supplies could be discussed later on.

6. To establish better liaison between Nepal and the troops, liaison officers would be appointed by the Nepalese Government and would form part of the unit of the Gurkha troops.

7. It is very desirable that the morale of the recruits as well as the armed forces, should remain unimpaired. Therefore all activities prejudicial to the interest and security of one party should be prevented in the territories of the other parties.

8. The Government of Nepal reserves the right to withdraw all Gurkha troops in case Nepal is involved in any war.

9. All facilities for the training of Nepalese officers in the military academies of India and Britain should be provided as and when the Nepal Government wants.

10. As Khukri is the religious and national emblem of the Gurkhas forming also a part of the uniform of the Gurkha Army, the carrying of Khukri by Gurkhas of all categories must not be banned in territories where the Gurkhas reside.

11. When Gurkha troops go on active service, intimation might be given to the Government of Nepal.

12. The above mentioned points are to be incorporated in a treaty and or agreement to be signed between the parties in due course.

Appendix XV
Indo-Bhutan Treaty of Peace and Friendship, 1949

The Government of India on the one part, and His Highness the Druk Gyalpo's Government on the other part, equally animated by the desire to regulate in a friendly manner and upon a solid and durable basis the state of affairs caused by the termination of the British Government's authority in India, and to promote and foster the relations of friendship and neighbourliness so necessary for the well-being of their peoples, have resolved to conclude the following treaty, and have, for this purpose named their representatives, that is to say Sri Harishawar Dayal representing the Government of India, who has full powers to agree to the said treaty on behalf of the Government of India, and Deb Zimpon Sonam Tobgy Dorji, Yang-Lop Sonam, Chho-Zim Thondup, Rin-Zim Tandin and Ha Drung Jigmie Palden Dorji, representing the Government of His Highness the Druk Gyalpo, Maharaja of Bhutan, who have full powers to agree to the same on behalf of the Government of Bhutan.

Article 1

There shall be perpetual peace and friendship between the Government of India and the Government of Bhutan.

Article 2

The Government of India undertakes to exercise no interference in the internal administration of Bhutan. On its part the Government of Bhutan agrees to be guided by the advice of the Government of India in regard to its external relations.

Article 3

In place of the compensation granted to the Government of Bhutan under Article 4 of the treaty of Sinchula and enhanced by the treaty of the eighth day of January 1910 and the temporary subsidy of Rupees one lakh per annum granted in 1942, the Government of India agrees to make an annual payment of Rupees five lakhs to the Government of Bhutan. And it is further hereby agreed that the said annual payment shall be made on the tenth day of January every year, the first payment being made on the tenth day of January 1950. This payment shall continue so long as this treaty remains in force and its terms are duly observed.

Article 4

Further to mark the friendship existing and continuing between the said Governments, the Government of India shall, within one year from the date of signature of this treaty, return to the Government of Bhutan about thirty-two square miles of territory in the area known as Dewangiri. The Government of India shall appoint a competent officer or officers to mark out the area so returned to the Government of Bhutan.

Article 5

There shall, as heretofore, be free trade and commerce between the territories of the Government of India and of the Government of Bhutan; and the Government of India agrees to grant the Government of Bhutan every facility for the carriage, by land and water, of its produce throughout the territory of the Government of India, including the right to use such forest roads as may be specified by mutual agreement from time to time.

Article 6

The Government of India agrees that the Government of Bhutan shall be free to import, with the assistance and approval of the Government of India, from or through India into Bhutan, whatever arms, ammunition, machinery, warlike material or stores may be required or desired for the strength and welfare of Bhutan, and that this arrangement shall hold good for all time as long as the Government of India is satisfied that the intentions of the Government of Bhutan are friendly and that there is no danger to India from such importations. The Government of Bhutan, on the other hand, agrees that there shall be no export of such arms, ammunition, etc., across the frontier of Bhutan either by the Government of Bhutan or by private individuals.

Article 7

The Government of India and the Government of Bhutan agree that Bhutanese subjects residing in Indian territories shall have equal justice with Indian subjects, and that Indian subjects residing in Bhutan shall have equal justice with the subjects of the Government of Bhutan.

Article 8

(1) The Government of India shall, on demand being duly made in writing by the Government of Bhutan, take proceedings in accordance with the provisions of the Indian Extradition Act, 1903 (of which a copy shall be furnished to the Government of Bhutan), for the surrender of all Bhutanese subjects accused of any of the crimes specified in the first schedule of the said Act who may take refuge in Indian territory.

(2) The Government of Bhutan shall, requisition being duly made by the Government of India, or by any officer authorized by the Government of India in this behalf, surrender any Indian subjects, or subjects of a foreign power, whose extradition may be required in pursuance of any agreement or arrangements made by the Government of India with the said power, accused of any of the crimes, specified in the first schedule of Act XV of 1903, who may take refuge in the territory under the jurisdiction of the Government of Bhutan, and also any Bhutanese subjects who, after committing any of the crimes referred to in Indian territory, shall flee into Bhutan, on such evidence of their guilt being produced as shall satisfy the local court of the district in which the offence may have been committed.

Article 9

Any differences and disputes arising in the application or interpretation of this treaty shall in the first instance be settled by negotiation. If within three months of the start of negotiations no settlement is arrived at, then the matter shall be referred to the arbitration of three arbitrators, who shall be nationals of either India or Bhutan, chosen in the following manner:

(1) One person nominated by the Government of India;

(2) One person nominated by the Government of Bhutan;

(3) A Judge of the Federal Court, or of a High Court in India, to be chosen by the Government of Bhutan, who shall be Chairman.

The judgement of this Tribunal shall be final and executed without delay by either party.

Article 10

This treaty shall continue in force in perpetuity unless terminated or modified by mutual consent.

Done in duplicate at Darjeeling this eighth day of August, one thousand nine hundred and forty-nine, corresponding with the Bhutanese date the fifteenth day of the sixth month of the Earth-Bull year.

HARISHWAR DAYAL
Political Officer in Sikkim

DEB ZIMPON SONAM
TOBGYE DORJI
YANG-LOP SONAM
CHHO-ZIM THONDUP
RIN-ZIM TANDIN
HA DRUNG JIGMIE
PALDEN DORJI

Instrument of Ratification

WHEREAS a Treaty relating to the promotion of, and fostering the relations of friendship and neighbourliness was signed at Darjeeling on the 8th day of August 1949 by representatives of the Government of India and of the Government of His Highness the Druk Gyalpo, Maharaja of Bhutan, which Treaty is, word for word as follows:

* * * *

The Government of India, having considered the treaty aforesaid, hereby confirm and ratify the same and undertake faithfully to perform and carry out all the stipulations therein contained.

In witness whereof this instrument of ratification is signed and sealed by the Governor-General of India.

Done at New Delhi, the 22nd day of September 1949.

(Sd.) C. RAJAGOPALACHARI
Governor-General of India

Whereas a Treaty relating to the promotion of, and fostering, relations of friendship and neighbourliness was signed at Darjeeling on the eighth day of August 1949 by Representatives of my Government and of the Government of India which Treaty is, word for word, as follows:

* * * *

My Government, having considered the treaty aforesaid, hereby confirm and ratify the same and undertake faithfully to perform and carry out all the stipulations there contained.

In witness whereof I have signed this instrument of ratification and affixed hereto my seal.

Done at Tongsa the fifteenth day of September, 1949.

(Sd.) J. WANGCHUK
Druk Gyalpo

Seal

Appendix XVI
Indo-Sikkim Treaty of Peace and Friendship, 1950

The President of India and His Highness the Maharaja of Sikkim being desirous of further strengthening the good relations already existing between India and Sikkim, have resolved to enter into a new Treaty with each other, and the President of India has, for the purpose, appointed as his plenipotentiary Shri Harishwar Dayal, Political Officer in Sikkim, and His Highness the Maharaja having examined Shri Harishwar Dayal's credentials and found them good and in due form, the two have agreed as follows:-

Article I

All previous treaties between the British Government and Sikkim which are at present in force as between India and Sikkim are hereby formally cancelled.

Article II

Sikkim shall continue to be a Protectorate of India and, subject to the provisions of this Treaty, shall enjoy autonomy in regard to its internal affairs.

Article III

(1) The Government of India will be responsible for the defence and territorial integrity of Sikkim. It shall have the right to take such measures as it considers necessary for the defence of Sikkim or the security of India, whether preparatory or otherwise, and whether within or outside Sikkim. In particular, the Government of India shall have the right to station troops anywhere within Sikkim.

(2) The measures referred to in paragraph (1) will as far as possible be taken by the Government of India in consultation with the Government of Sikkim.

(3) The Government of Sikkim shall not import any arms, ammunition, military stores or other warlike materials of any description for any purpose whatsoever without the previous consent of the Government of India.

Article IV

(1) The external relations of Sikkim, whether political, economic or financial, shall be conducted and regulated solely by the Government of India; and the Government of Sikkim shall have no dealings with any foreign power.

(2) Subjects of Sikkim travelling to foreign countries shall be treated as Indian protected persons for the purpose of passports, and shall receive from Indian representatives abroad the same protection and facilities as Indian nationals.

Article V

The Government of Sikkim agrees not to levy any import duty, transit duty or other impost on goods brought into, or in transit through, Sikkim; and the Government of India agrees not to levy any import or other duty on goods of Sikkimese origin brought into India from Sikkim.

Article VI

(1) The Government of India shall have exclusive right of constructing, maintaining and regulating the use of railways, aerodromes and landing grounds and air navigation facilities, posts, telegraphs, telephones and wireless installations in Sikkim; and the Government of Sikkim shall render the Government of India every assistance in their construction, maintenance and protection.

(2) The Government of Sikkim may, however, construct, maintain, and regulate the use of railways and aerodroms and landing grounds and air navigation facilities to such extent as may be agreed to by the Government of India.

(3) The Government of India shall have the right to construct and maintain in Sikkim roads for strategic purposes and for the purpose of improving communications with India and other adjoining countries; and the Government of Sikkim shall render the Government of India every assistance in the construction, maintenance and protection of such roads.

Article VII

(1) Subjects of Sikkim shall have the right of entry into, and free movement within, India, and Indian nationals shall have the right of entry into, and free movement within, Sikkim.

(2) Subject to such regulations as the Government of Sikkim may

prescribe in consultation with the Government of India, Indian nationals shall have:

(a) the right to carry on trade and commerce in Sikkim; and

(b) when established in any trade in Sikkim, the right to acquire, hold and dispose of any property, movable or immovable, for the purposes of their trade or residence in Sikkim.

(3) Subjects of Sikkim shall have the same right:

(a) to carry on trade and commerce in India, and to employment therein; and

(b) of acquiring, holding and disposing of property, movable and immovable, as Indian nationals.

Article VIII

(1) Indian nationals within Sikkim shall be subject to the laws of Sikkim and subjects of Sikkim within India shall be subject to the laws of India.

(2) Whenever any criminal proceedings are initiated in Sikkim against any Indian national or any person in the service of the Government of India or any foreigner, the Government of Sikkim shall furnish the Representative of the Government of India in Sikkim (hereinafter referred to as the Indian Representative) with particulars of the charges against such person.

If in the case of any person in the service of the Government of India or any foreigner it is so demanded by the Indian Representative, such person shall be handed over to him for trial before such courts as may be established for the purpose by the Government of India either in Sikkim or outside.

Article IX

(1) The Government of Sikkim agrees to seize and deliver up any fugitive offender from outside Sikkim who has taken refuge therein on demand being made by the Indian Representative. Should any delay occur in complying with such demand, the Indian police may follow the person whose surrender has been demanded into any part of Sikkim, and shall, on showing a warrant signed by the Indian Representative, receive every assistance and protection in the prosecution of their object from the Sikkim officers.

(2) The Government of India similarly agrees, on demand being made by the Government of Sikkim, to take extradition proceedings against,

and surrender, any fugitive offender from Sikkim who has taken refuge in the territory of India.

(3) In this article, 'fugitive offender' means a person who is accused of having committed an extradition offence as defined in the First Schedule to the Indian Extradition Act, 1903, or any other offence which may hereafter be agreed upon between the Government of India and the Government of Sikkim as being an extradition offence.

Article X

The Government of India, having in mind the friendly relations already existing between India and Sikkim and now further strengthened by this Treaty, and being desirous of assisting in the development and good administration of Sikkim, agrees to pay the Government of Sikkim a sum of rupees three lakhs every year so long as the terms of this Treaty are duly observed by the Government of Sikkim.

The first payment under this Article will be made before the end of the year 1950, and subsequent payments will be made in the month of August every year.

Article XI

The Government of India shall have the right to appoint a Representative to reside in Sikkim; and the Government of Sikkim shall provide him and his staff with all reasonable facilities in regard to their carrying out their duties in Sikkim.

Article XII

If any dispute arises in the interpretation of the provisions of this Treaty which cannot be resolved by mutual consultation, the dispute shall be referred to the Chief Justice of India whose decision thereon shall be final.

Article XIII

This treaty shall come into force without ratification from the date of signature by both the parties.

Done in duplicate at Gangtok on this 5th day of December, 1950.

(Sd.) Harishwar Dayal
Political Officer in Sikkim

(Sd.) Tashi Namgyal
His Highness the Maharaja of Sikkim

Appendix XVII
Treaty[1] of Peace and Friendship between the Government of the United Kingdom and the Government of Nepal. Signed at Kathmandu, on 30 October 1950

The Government of the United Kingdom of Great Britain and Northern Ireland and the Government of Nepal;

Recognizing that peace, friendship and goodwill have now happily existed between them since 1815;

Considering that in consequence of the establishment of the two independent States of India and Pakistan certain of the provisions of the Treaty signed at Kathmandu on 21st December, 1923,[2] and of prior treaties are no longer applicable between the Governments of the United Kingdom and Nepal;

Desiring still further to strengthen and confirm their good relations which have so long subsisted; and

Having resolved therefore to conclude a new Treaty for this purpose,

Have agreed as follows:

Article I

There shall be perpetual peace and friendship between the Government of the United Kingdom and the Government of Nepal.

Article II

The two Contracting Parties agree mutually to acknowledge and respect each other's independence both external and internal.

Article III

In order to secure and improve the relations of peace and amity hereby confirmed between the Government of the United Kingdom and the

[1] Came into force on 3 May 1951, by the exchange of the instruments of ratification at Kathmandu, in accordance with Article IX.

[2] League of Nations, *Treaty Series*, vol. XXXVI, p. 357.

Government of Nepal, each of the two countries shall continue to be represented in the other by a diplomatic representative duly accredited, with such staff as is necessary for the due performance of his functions.

Article IV

The two Contracting Parties shall maintain and develop mutually advantageous commercial relations appropriate to their long and cordial friendship and in accordance with the generally recognized principles of international law and practice.

Article V

(a) The nationals of each Contracting Party shall be entitled to enter, travel and reside in, and to leave any territory of the other to which this Article applies so long as they satisfy and observe the conditions and regulations applicable in that territory to the entry, travel, residence and departure of all foreigners. The nationals of each Contracting Party shall furthermore be received and treated in any territory of the other to which this Article applies in accordance with the generally recognized requirements of international law and practice and shall enjoy the fullest protection of the laws and authorities of that territory in respect of their persons, possessions and rights; and in respect of all matters relating to commerce, to industry, to the carrying on of any description of business, to the exercise of professions and occupations, to the acquisition, ownership and disposal of property and to the levying of taxes and requirements relating to the levying of taxes, shall not be treated in any manner less favourable than the nationals of any other foreign country.

(b) For the purposes of this Article, in so far as it refers to treatment accorded by the Government of the United Kingdom to nationals of any other foreign country, the term 'foreign country' means any country not included in the territories enumerated in the following list:

The United Kingdom of Great Britain and Northern Ireland,
Canada,
The Commonwealth of Australia,
New Zealand,
The Union of South Africa,
India,

Pakistan,

Ceylon,

Territories for the international relations of which the Governments of the United Kingdom, the Commonwealth of Australia, New Zealand and the Union of South Africa are responsible at the date of signature of the present Treaty, and The Irish Republic.

(c) The provisions of this Article shall not apply to the advantages now or hereafter accorded by the Government of Nepal to adjacent countries in order to facilitate frontier traffic.

Article VI

(a) The provisions of Article V shall apply:

(i) in relation to the Government of the United Kingdom, to the United Kingdom of Great Britain and Northern Ireland and to any territory to which the provisions of Article V have been extended in accordance with paragraph (b) of this Article;

(ii) in relation to the Government of Nepal, to Nepal.

(b) The Government of the United Kingdom may, at the time of signature or ratification of the present Treaty or at any time thereafter, declare by notification given to the Government of Nepal that Article V thereof shall extend to any of the territories for whose international relations the Government of the United Kingdom are responsible, and Article V shall, from the date of receipt of the notification, extend to the territories named therein.

(c) The Government of the United Kingdom may, at any time after the making of a declaration under paragraph (b) of this Article extending Article V to any territory for whose international relations they are responsible, declare by notification given to the Government of Nepal that Article V shall cease to extend to any territory named in the notification, and Article V shall, from the date of receipt of the notification, cease to extend to such territory.

Article VII

In the present Treaty the term 'nationals' (a) in relation to the Government of the United Kingdom, means:

(i) all citizens of the United Kingdom and Colonies who derive their citizenship from connexion with any territory to which Article V applies;

(ii) all British protected persons who derive their status as such from connexion with any territory to which Article V applies;

(iii) all citizens of Southern Rhodesia if Article V shall have been extended to Southern Rhodesia;

and (b) in relation to the Government of Nepal, means all nationals of Nepal.

Article VIII

All treaties, engagements and agreements between the Government of the United Kingdom and the Government of Nepal concluded prior to 21st December, 1923, and the Treaty signed at Kathmandu on that date, shall cease to have effect from the date on which the present Treaty comes into force in so far as their application between the United Kingdom and Nepal is concerned.

Article IX

The present Treaty shall be ratified and shall come into force on the date on which the instruments of ratification are exchanged. Instruments of ratification shall be exchanged at Kathmandu as soon as possible.

Article X

The present Treaty shall remain in force indefinitely, but subject to termination by one year's notice in writing given by either Contracting Party to the other.

IN WITNESS WHEREOF the undersigned, duly authorized for the purpose by their respective Governments, have signed the present Treaty in English and Nepali both texts being equally authoritative except, in the case of doubt, when the English text shall prevail.

DONE in duplicate at Kathmandu this 30th day of October, 1950 AD corresponding to 14th day of Kartik, 2007 S.E.

[L. S.]

GEORGE FALCONER (Lt. Col.)
His Britannic Majesty's Ambassador
at the Court of Nepal

Appendix XVIII
Treaty of Peace and Friendship between Nepal and China, 28 April 1960

THE Chairman of the People's Republic of China and His Majesty the King of Nepal, desiring to maintain and further develop peace and friendship between the People's Republic of China and the King of Nepal,

Convinced that the strengthening of good-neighbourly relations and friendly co-operation between the People's Republic of China and the Kingdom of Nepal is in accordance with the fundamental interests of the peoples of the two countries and conducive to the consolidation of peace in Asia and the world,

Have decided for this purpose to conclude the present Treaty in accordance with the Five Principles of peaceful co-existence jointly affirmed by the two countries, and have appointed as their respective Plenipotentiaries:

The Chairman of the People's Republic of China: Premier Chou En-lai of the State Council,

His Majesty the King of Nepal: Prime Minister Bishweshwar Prasad Koirala.

The above-mentioned Plenipotentiaries, having examined each other's credentials and found them in good and due form, have agreed upon the following:

Article I

The Contracting Parties recognize and respect the independence, sovereignty and territorial integrity of each other.

Article II

The Contracting Parties will maintain and develop peaceful and friendly relations between the People's Republic of China and the Kingdom of Nepal. They undertake to settle all disputes between them by means of peaceful negotiation.

Article III

The Contracting Parties agree to develop and further strengthen the economic and cultural ties between the two countries in a spirit of friendship and co-operation, in accordance with the principles of equality and mutual benefit and of non-interference in each other's internal affairs.

Article IV

Any difference or dispute arising out of the interpretation or application of the present Treaty shall be settled by negotiation through normal diplomatic channels.

Article V

This present Treaty is subject to ratification and the instruments of ratification will be exchanged in Peking as soon as possible.

The present Treaty will come into force immediately on the exchange of the instruments of ratification[1] and will remain in force for a period of ten years.

Unless either of the Contracting Parties gives to the other notice in writing to terminate the Treaty at least one year before the expiration of this period, it will remain in force without any specific time limit, subject to the right of either of the Contracting Parties to terminate it by giving to the other in writing a year's notice of its intention to do so.

Done in duplicate in Kathmandu on the twenty-eighth day of April 1960, in the Chinese, Nepali and English languages, all texts being equally authentic.

Plenipotentiary of the People's Republic of China	*Plenipotentiary of the Kingdom of Nepal*
(Sd.) CHOU EN-LAI	(Sd.) B.P. KOIRALA

[1] The instruments of ratification were exchanged in Peking on 13 Nov. 1961.

Appendix XIX
Draft
Agreement between the Government of India and His Majesty's Government of Nepal on Mutual Cooperation*

The Government of India and His Majesty's Government of Nepal (hereinafter also referred to as the 'Contracting Parties'),

Recalling the unique, aged-old and traditional friendship between the peoples of India and Nepal based on the bonds of history, geography, and of shared social and cultural values,

Reaffirming their adherence to the Treaty of Peace and Friendship between the Governments of India and Nepal of 1950, which has ever since been and remains the cornerstone of Indo-Nepal relations,

Keen to sustain and further strengthen the bonds of friendship, good neighbourliness and mutually beneficial cooperation between the two countries and peoples,

Determined to strengthen economic cooperation between them,

Desiring to develop their economies in their own and common interest,

Convinced of the benefits of mutual sharing of scientific and technical knowledge and experience to promote trade between them,

Have agreed as follows:

Part I
Treatment of Each Others' Nationals in Their Respective Territories

Article I

Subject to such exceptions as may be mutually agreed upon, the Contracting Parties undertake not to enact and to repeal any laws, rules, regulations, and Government orders which restrict the rights and privileges of the nationals of one Contracting Party in the territory of the other in matters of residence, ownership of property, employment, participation in trade and commerce, movement, participation in industrial and economic development of such territory and the grant of concessions and contracts

*'Secret' Agreement proposed by India during 1989/90 Crisis.

relating to such development and other privileges of similar nature as enjoined by the Treaty of Peace and Friendship between the Government of India and the Government of Nepal of 1950 and the letters exchanged along with the Treaty.

Article II

Each Contracting Party shall have the freedom to bring to the notice of the other any laws, rules, regulations, and Government orders of the other Contracting Party which may restrict such rights and privileges of its nationals in the territory of the other.

Part II
Defence Cooperation

Article I

In the interest of strengthening their defence capabilities, the Contracting parties have agreed to cooperate with each other in the military field. To this end, His Majesty's Government of Nepal shall consult and enter into suitable protocols with the Government of India concerning the acquisition by Nepal of arms, ammunition and other materials and equipment necessary for the security of Nepal.

Article II

Such cooperation between the Contracting Parties in the military field shall include assistance by the Government of India by providing arms, ammunition, other materials and equipment and in coordinating training to raise additional formations and units for the Royal Nepalese Army on the basis of the details to be mutually determined by the representatives of the Contracting Parties.

Article III

The cooperation between the Contracting Parties in the military field shall also include cooperation in the training of Nepalese Armed Forces' personnel.

Article IV

The Contracting Parties undertake not to enter into any military alliance with any other state against each other. His Majesty's Government of Nepal, in this respect, agrees not to enter into any arrangements concerning the matters mentioned in Articles I to III above with any other state or organization without prior consultation and agreement with the Government of India

Article V

The arrangements envisaged in Article I to IV above shall have no bearing on the independent foreign policy of either Contracting Party.

Part III
Trade

(Agreed Articles on Trade to be included in this Part)

Part IV
Transit

(Agreed Articles on Transit to be included in this Part)

Part V
Cooperation to Control Unauthorized Trade

(Agreed Articles on Cooperation to control Unauthorized Trade to be included in this Part)

Part VI
Economic, Industrial, and Water Resources Cooperation

Article I

In the traditional spirit of friendly cooperation between India and Nepal and for the benefit and welfare of the people of Nepal, the Government of India undertakes to provide, at the request of His Majesty's Government of Nepal, such developmental assistance as may be mutually determined by the Contracting Parties from time to time.

Article II

Should His Majesty's Government of Nepal decide to seek foreign assistance for the development of the natural resources of Nepal or for any industrial project in Nepal, they shall give first preference to the Government or the nationals of India, as the case may be, provided that the terms offered by the Government of India or Indian nationals, as the case may be, are not less favourable to Nepal than the terms offered by any other state or its nationals or by any international organization or agency.

Article III

The two Contracting Parties being equally desirous of attaining complete and satisfactory utilization of the waters of the commonly shared rivers, undertake to, (i) plan new uses or projects subject to the protection of the existing uses on the rivers, and (ii) cooperate with each other to formulate and modify the planned new uses or projects taking into consideration the water requirements of the Parties.

Article IV

The Contracting Parties agree to jointly plan, construct, and manage projects of mutual benefit. In this regard, the involvement of a third party, where felt to be necessary and in the common interest, shall be subject to mutual consent.

Part VII
Final Clauses

Article I

To facilitate the effective and harmonious implementation of this Agreement, the Contracting Parties shall consult each other regularly, and review the implementation of this Agreement, within the forum of India–Nepal Joint Commission. They shall meet for this purpose at least once every twelve months.

Article II

For the purpose of this Agreement, the various Parts specified therein are interrelated and shall be considered as a whole.

Article III

Part I of this Agreement shall remain in force for the same duration of time for which the Treaty of Peace and Friendship between the Government of India and the Government of Nepal of 1950 shall be in force.

Part II of the Agreement shall remain in force for a period of ten years, and it may be renewed for further periods of ten years by mutual consent, subject to such modifications as may be agreed upon.

Part III of the Agreement shall remain in force for a period of ... years, and it may be renewed for further periods of ... years by mutual consent, subject to such modifications as may be agreed upon.

Part IV of the Agreement shall remain in force for a period of ... years, and it may be renewed for further periods of ... years by mutual consent, subject to such modifications as may be agreed upon.

Part V of the Agreement shall remain in force for a period of ... years, and it may be renewed for further periods of ... years by mutual consent, subject to such modifications as may be agreed upon.

Part VI of the Agreement shall remain in force for a period of ... years, and it may be renewed for further periods of ... years by mutual consent, subject to such modifications as may be agreed upon.

Article IV

This Agreement shall come into force on ... 1990 and remain valid for the same duration of time for which the Treaty of Peace and Friendship between the Government of India and the Government of Nepal of 1950 shall be in force.

Done at Kathmandu on ... day of ... One Thousand Nine Hundred and Ninety in two originals each in Hindi, Nepali, and English languages, all of them being equally authentic. In case of doubt the English text shall prevail.

For His Majesty's Government of Nepal For the Government of India

Appendix XX
Proposed Model Draft Treaty of Peace and Friendship between Nepal and India

Preamble

The Republic of India and the Kingdom of Nepal (hereinafter referred to as 'the High Contracting Parties');

Being desirous of expanding and consolidating the existing relations of sincere friendship between them;

Believing that the further development of friendship and cooperation fulfils the basic national interests of enduring peace in the region and the world;

Adhering firmly to the basic tenets of non-alignment, peaceful coexistence, mutual cooperation, non-interference in the internal affairs of each other, and respect for territorial integrity and sovereignty;

Reaffirming their determination to abide by the purposes and principles of the Charter of the United Nations and the Charter of the South-Asian Association for Regional Cooperation;

Having resolved to conclude the present Treaty, for which purpose the following Plenipotentiaries have been appointed:

On behalf of the Republic of India

...

On behalf of the Kingdom of Nepal

...

Who, having presented their credentials, which are found to be in proper form and due order

Have agreed as follows:

Article 1

(1) The High Contracting Parties solemnly declare that there shall be enduring peace and friendship between their two countries and their peoples, each shall respect the complete independence, sovereignty, and territorial integrity of the other and refrain from interfering in the internal affairs of the other.

(2) The High Contracting Parties shall further develop and strengthen the relations of friendship, good-neighbourliness, and cooperation existing

between them on the basis of the above mentioned principles as well as the principles of equality and mutual benefit.

Article 2

The High Contracting Parties shall continue to strengthen and widen their mutually advantageous cooperation in the economic, scientific, and technical fields. The high Contracting Parties shall develop mutual cooperation in the fields of trade, transport, communication, environment, and various development projects concerning, inter alia, irrigation, river basin development, flood control, and the development of hydroelectric power between them on the basis of the principles of equality and mutual benefit.

Article 3

The High Contracting Parties shall promote mutual relations in the fields of art, literature, education, culture, sports, and health.

Article 4

(1) The Kingdom of Nepal shall have freedom of transit through the territory of the Republic of India by all means of transport and the right of free access to and from the sea under international law.

(2) The Kingdom of Nepal shall, in exercise of the freedom of transit and the right of free access, be free to import from or through the territory of the Republic of India arms, ammunition, or warlike material and equipment necessary for the security of the Kingdom of Nepal.

(3) Details of the terms and modalities for exercising freedom of transit and the right of free access to and from the sea by Nepal shall be agreed between the two High Contracting parties through a separate bilateral transit treaty.

(4) The Republic of India, in exercise of its sovereignty over its territory, shall have the right to take all indispensable measures, compatible with the provisions of bilateral treaties existing between the two High Contracting Parties and the principles of international law, to ensure that the freedom of transit accorded by it on its territory to the Kingdom of Nepal does not in any way infringe its legitimate interests.

Article 5

The High Contracting Parties shall maintain regular contacts with each other on major international and regional problems affecting the interests of both states, through meetings and exchanges of views at all levels.

Article 6

(1) In accordance with the traditional friendship subsisting between them, the High Contracting Parties undertake not to enter into or participate in any military alliance directed against each other.

(2) The High Contracting Parties shall not resort to the use or threat of force against each other or allow any hostile activities of any form in their territories which are directed against the other Party or which might endanger the peace and security of the other Party.

Article 7

The nationals of either High Contracting Party shall have privileges in matters of residence, movement from one country to the other, and participation in trade, commerce, and industrial ventures in the territory of the other as determined by the laws prevailing in their respective countries.

Article 8

Each of the High Contracting Parties solemnly declares that it shall not undertake any commitment, secret or open, towards one or more states which may be incompatible with the present Treaty.

Article 9

(1) Any differences and disputes arising in the application or interpretation of this Treaty shall in the first place be settled amicably in a spirit of mutual respect and understanding. If within three months of the start of negotiations no settlement is arrived at, then the matter shall, at the request of either party, be referred to the arbitration of three arbitrators chosen in the following manner:

(a) One person nominated by His Majesty's Government of Nepal;
(b) One person nominated by the Government of India;

(c) One person, who shall be the Chairperson, chosen in common agreement between the two High Contracting Parties.

If the Parties fail to agree on the designation of the third member within a period of three months, the third member shall be appointed by the president of the International Court of Justice. In case any of the Parties fail to make an appointment within a period of three months the president of the International Court of Justice shall fill the remaining vacancy.

(2) The arbitration tribunal shall decide on the matters placed before it by simple majority and its decisions shall be final and binding on the Parties.

Article 10

This Treaty shall come into force from the date of exchange of instruments of ratification between the High Contracting Parties.

Article 11

(1) This Treaty shall remain in force for a period of 20 years and be automatically renewed for further periods of 20 years unless it is amended under clause (2) or terminated under clause (3) of this Article.

(2) At the end of each 20 years' period this Treaty may, at the request of either party, be reviewed jointly by the High Contracting Parties and if necessary be amended by mutual agreement.

(3) This Treaty may be terminated by either High Contracting Party by giving one year's prior notice in writing to the other.

Article 12

This Treaty shall replace the Treaty of Peace and Friendship of 31 July 1950 together with the letters exchanged thereunder and cancel the Arms Assistance Agreement of 30 January 1965, and the arrangements made through the Joint Communiqué of 10 June 1990 between the two countries.

Done at New Delhi on ... day of ... Two thousand and ... in two originals each in the Nepali, Hindi, and English languages all of them being equally authentic. However, in case of divergence between these texts the English text shall prevail.

For the Kingdom of Nepal *For the Republic of India*

Bibliography

Books

Aitchison, C.U., *Treaties and Engagements Relating to Nepal*, Pt. II (Calcutta: Govt. of India Printing Dept., 1909).

Akehurst, M.A., *A Modern Introduction to International Law* (London/New York: Routledge, 1984).

Allocok, J.B., *Border and Territorial Disputes*, 3rd edn (London: Longman Current Affairs, 1992).

Amarsinghe, C.F., *State Responsibility for Injuries to Aliens* (Oxford: Clarendon Press, 1967).

Anand, R.P. (ed.), *Law of The Sea: Caracas and Beyond*, vol. 3 (The Hague/ Boston/London: Martinus Nijhoff Publishers, 1980).

Anaya, S.J., *Indigenous People in International Law* (New York: Oxford University Press, 1996).

Attard, D., *The Exclusive Economic Zone in International Law* (Oxford: Oxford University Press, 1987).

Baral, L.R., 'Nepal in the Non-Aligned Movement', in G.R. Agrawal et al., *Fundamentals of Nepalese Foreign Policy* (Kathmandu: CEDA, Tribhuvan University, 1985).

Baral, D.B. (ed.), *Tanakpur: From the Beginning to the End* (Kathmandu: Pairavi Publications, 1993).

Barth, A., *The Religions of India*, authorized trans. Rev. J. Wood (Delhi: S. Chand & Co., 1969).

Bhattacharjee, G.P., *India and the Politics of Modern Nepal* (Calcutta: Minerva Associates, 1970).

Bhasin, A.S., *Documents on Nepal's Relations with India and China 1946–66* (Bombay: Academic Books, 1970).

Bista, D.B., *Fatalism and Development: Nepal's Struggle for Modernization* (Calcutta: Orient Longman, 1991).

Bogdanovic, S., *International Law of Water Resources: Contribution of the International Law Association (1954–2000)* (London/The Hague/Boston: Kluwer Law International).

Bowman, M.J. and Harris, D.J., *Multilateral Treaties, Index and Current Status* (London: Butterworths, 1984).

Brown, C., *Sovereignty, Rights and Justice: International Political Theory Today* (USA: Blackwell Publishers Inc. 2002).

Brown, E.D., *Sea-Bed Energy and Minerals: The International Legal Regime*, vol. 1 (Dordrecht/Boston/London: Martinus Nijhoff Publishers, 1992).

Brownlie, I., *African Boundaries: A Legal and Diplomatic Encyclopaedia* (London: C. Hurst & Co Publishers Ltd, 1979).

Bruhacs, J., *The Law of Non-Navigational Uses of International Watercourses* (Dordrecht/Boston/London: Martinus Nijhoff Publishers 1993).

Buchanan, A., *Justice, Legitimacy, and Self-Determination: Moral Foundation for International Law* (Oxford: Oxford University Press, 2004).

Buchheit, L.C., *Secession: The Legitimacy of Self-Determination* (New Haven/London: Yale University Press, 1978).

Caflisch, L., 'Regulation of the Uses of International Watercourses', in S.A. Salman and L. B. de Chazournes (eds), *International Watercourses: Enhancing Co-operation and Managing Conflict* (Washington D.C: The World Bank, 1998).

______. 'The Law of International Waterways and its Sources', in R. Macdonald (ed.), *Essays in Honour of Wang Tieya* (Dordrecht: Martinus Nijhoff, 1994).

Caponera, D.A., *National and International Water Law and Administration* (The Hague/London/New York: Kluwer Law International, 2003).

Casesse, A., *Self-Determination of Peoples: A Legal Reappraisal* (Cambridge: Cambridge University Press 1995).

Chauhan, R.S., *Political Development in Nepal, 1950–70* (New Delhi: Associated Publishing House, 1970).

Churchill, R.R., and A.V. Lowe, *The Law of the Sea* (Manchester: Manchester University Press, 1985).

Colombos, C.J., *The International Law of the Sea* (London: Longman Green & Co. 1967).

Eagleton, C., *The Responsibility of States in International Law* (New York: New York University Press, 1928).

Ewing, T., *Between the Hammer and the Anvil?* (Bloomington, IN: Indiana University Press, 1980).

Flanz, Gisbert H. (ed.), *Constitutions of the Countries of the World: Nepal*, vol x (Dobbs Ferry, New York: Oceana Publications, 1985).

Fueton, T.W., *The Sovereignty of the Sea* (Edinburgh and London: William Blackwood Sons, 1911).

GATT Secretariat, *The Result of the Uruguay Round of Multinational Trade Negotiations: Legal Texts* (Geneva: Cambridge University Press, 1994).

Glassner, M.I., *Access to the Sea for Developing Land-locked States* (The Hague: Martinus Nijhoff, 1970).

———. *Bibliography on Land-Locked States: Fourth Revised and Enlarged Edition* (Dordrecht/ Boston/London: Martinus Nijhoff, 1995).

———. *The United Nations at Work* (London: Praeger Publishers, 1998).

Hodder, D., S.J. Lloyd, K. McLachlan, *Land-Locked States of Africa and Asia* (London/Portland: Frank Cass, 1998).

Husain, S.A., *Politics and Society in Bangladesh 1921–37: A Legislative Perspective* (Dhaka: Dhaka University, 1980).

Imam, Z., *Towards a Model Relationship: A Study of Soviet Treaties with India and Other Third World Countries* (New Delhi: ABC Publishers, 1983).

Iyer, R., and B.G. Verghese, *Harnessing the Eastern Himalayan Rivers: Regional Co-operation in South Asia* (New Delhi: Konark Publishers Pvt. Ltd., 1993).

Khanal, Y.N., *Reflections on Nepal–India Relations* (Delhi: Rakesh Press, 1964).

King, A., 'Modes of Executive–Legislature Relations', in P. Norton (ed.), *Legislatures* (Oxford: Oxford University Press, 1990).

Kohli, A., *Democracy and Discontent, India's Growing Crisis of Governability* (Cambridge: Cambridge University Press, 1990).

Kwiatkowska, B., *The 200 Mile Exclusive Economic Zone in the New Law of the Sea* (The Hague: Kluwer Academic Publishers, 1989).

Lauterpacht, H., *The Development of International Law by the International Court* (London: Stevens, 1958).

Ma, Y., *Legal Problems of Seabed Boundary Delimitation in the East China Sea* (Baltimore: Occasional Papers/Reprints Series in Contemporary Asian Studies Inc, 1984).

McCaffrey, S.C., *The Law of International Watercourses: Non-Navigational Uses* (Oxford: Oxford University Press, 2001).

Mehra, P., *Negotiating with the Chinese 1846–1987: Problems and Perspectives* (New Delhi: Reliance Publishing House, 1989).

Mehta, J.S., 'Opportunity Costs of Delay in Water Resources Management Between Nepal, India, and Bangladesh', in D. J. Easton, (ed.), *The Ganges–Brahmaputra Basin: Water Resources Co-operation between Nepal, India and Bangladesh* (Austin, Texas: Lyndon B. Johnson School of Public Affairs, the University of Texas at Austin 1992).

Meyers, C.J., 'The Colorado Basin', in A.H. Garreston, et al. (eds), *The Law of International Drainage Basins*, Published for the Institute of International Law, New York University School of Law (Dobbs Ferry, New York: Oceana, 1967).

Mojumdar, K., *Political Relations between India and Nepal (1877–1923)* (Delhi: Munshiram Manoharlal, 1973).
Morris-Jones, W.H., *The Government and Politics of India* (London: Hutchinson University Library, 1964).
Muni, S.D., *Foreign Policy of Nepal* (New Delhi: National Publishing House, 1973).
Nepal and India: Facts and Chronology of the Problem (Kathmandu: Govt. of Nepal, Ministry of Communications, 1989).
Norton, P., and N. Ahmed, *Parliaments in Asia* (England: Frank Cass 1999).
O'Connell, D.P., *State Succession in Municipal Law and International Law*, vols. 1 &11 (Cambridge: Cambridge University Press, 1967).
______. (I.A. Shearer, ed.), *The International Law of the Sea*, vol. 1 (Oxford: Clarendon Press, 1982).
Pemble, J., *The Invasion of Nepal: John Company at War* (Oxford: Oxford University Press, 1971).
Prescott, J.R.V., *The Maritime Political Boundaries of the World* (London: Methuen & Co. Ltd., 1985).
Platzoder, R. (ed.), *The United Nations Conference on the Law of the Sea, Documents*, vol. I–XVIII (New York: Oceana, 1982–88).
Ragachari, R., K.B.S. Rasheedd and B.G. Verghese (ed. Adhikari et al.), *Cooperation on Eastern Himalayan Rivers: Opportunities and Challenges* (New Delhi: Konarak Publishers Pvt. Ltd., 2000).
Ranganathan, C.V., and V.C. Khanna, *India and China: The Way Ahead After 'Mao's India War'* (New Delhi: Har-Anand, 2000).
Rashiduzzaman, M., *The Central Legislature in British India: 1921–47* (Dhaka: Mullick Brothers, 1965).
Reed, H.B., and M.I. Reed, *Nepal in Transition: Educational Innovation* (University of Pittsburgh Press, 1968).
Regmi, S.C., *The Peace Zone Proposal of Nepal* (Kathmandu: Regmi Publications, 1985).
Rozakis, C., *The Conventional Arrangements on Hydroeconomy between Greece and Bulgaria–Turkey–Yugoslavia* in *The Legal Regime of International Rivers and Lakes*, ed. R. Zacklin and L. Caflisch (USA/Canada : Kluwer Boston, Inc. 1981).
Schrijver, N., *Sovereignty Over Natural Resources: Balancing the Rights and Duties* (Cambridge: Cambridge University Press, 1997).
Sen, A., 'Equality or What?', in *The Tanner Lectures on Human Values*, vol. I (Cambridge: Cambridge University Press, 1980).
Shaha, R., *Nepali Politics: Retrospect and Prospect* (Delhi: Oxford University Press, 1978).
______. *Nepal and the World.* 3rd edn (Kathmandu: Naya Nepal Prakashan, 1962).
______. *Politics in Nepal: 1980–1991* (New Delhi: Manohar, 1993).

Shalowitz, A.L., *Shore and Sea Boundaries*, vol. 1 (Washington: United States Government Printing Office, 1962).

Sharma, C. K., *A Treatise on Water Resources of Nepal* (Kathmandu: Ms Sangeeta Sharma, Bishal Nagar 1997).

Sharma, J., *Nepal : Struggle For Existence* (Kathmandu: Communications Inc. 1986).

Sharma, S.P., *Territorial Acquistion, Dispute and International Law*, vol. 26 (The Netherlands: Kluwer Law International, 1997).

Shaw, M., *Title to Territory in Africa: International Legal Issues* (New York: Oxford University Press, 1986).

Shrestha, H.L., *Some Unequal Treaties* (Kathmandu: Jhilko Publication, 1980).

Shrestha, H.M., and L.M. Singh, 'The Ganges Brahmaputra System: A Nepalese Perspective in the Context of Regional Co-operation', in Biswas, A.K. and T. Hasimoto (eds), *Asian International Waters: From Ganges–Brahmaputra to Mekong* (Bombay: Oxford University Press, 1996).

Shrivastava, L.P.S., *Nepal at the Crossroads* (New Delhi: Allied Publishers, 1996).

Sinjela, A.M., *Land-Locked States and the UNCLOS Regime* (London, Rome and New York: Oceana, 1983).

Smith, R.W., *Exclusive Economic Zone Claims: An Analysis and Primary Documents* (The Haugue, Kluver Academic Publishers, 1989).

Stern, B., 'How to Regulate Globalization?', in M. Byers (ed.), *The Role of Law In International Politics* (New York: Oxford University Press, 2000).

Subedi, S.P., *Contemporary Issues in International Law: A Collection of the Josephine Onoh Memorial Lectures*, edited collection with Professors David Freestone and Scott Davidson (The Hague/London: Kluwer Law International, 2002).

———. The United Nations and the Trade and Transit Problems of Land-locked States', in Martin Glassner (ed.), *The United Nations at Work* (Praeger: Greenwood Publishing, Inc., Westport, Conn., 1998).

———. 'Indo-Nepal Relations: The Causes of Conflict and their Resolution', in Subrata K. Mitra and Dietmar Rothermund (eds), *Legitimacy and Conflict in South Asia* (New Delhi Branch of Heidelberg University & Manohar, 1997).

———. *Land and Maritime Zones of Peace in International Law* (Oxford: Clarendon Press, 1996).

———. *Land- Locked Nepal and International Law* (Kathmandu: Kokila Guatam, 1989).

Swarztrauber, S.A., *The Three-Mile Limit of Territorial Seas* (Annapolis, Maryland: Naval Institute Press, 1972).

Symmons, C.R., *The Maritime Zones of Islands in International Law* (The Hague: Martinus Nijhoff Publishers, 1979).

Tomuschat, C. (ed.), *Modern Law of Self-Determination*, vol. 16 (The Netherlands: Martinus Nijhoff Publishers, 1993).

Umozurike, U.O., *Self-Determination in International Law* (Connecticut: The Shoe String Press published as an Archon Book, 1972).

Upreti, B.C., *Politics of Himalayan River Waters: An Analysis of the River Water Issues of Nepal, India and Bangladesh* (New Delhi: Nirala Publications, 1993).

Uprety, K., and S.M.A. Salman, *Conflict and Cooperation on South Asia's International Rivers: A Legal Perspective* (London/The Hague/New York: Kluwer Law International, 2002).

Vasciannie, S.C., *Land-locked and Geographically Disadvantaged States in the International Law of the Sea* (New York: Oxford University Press, 1990).

Wood, R., *From Marshall Plan to Debt Crisis: Foreign Aid and Development Choices in The World Economy* (Berkeley and Los Angeles: University of California Press, 1986).

Yearbook of the International Law Commission, 1957, United Nations, New York.

Yong Leng, L., *Southeast Asia and the Law of the Sea* (Singapore: Singapore University Press, 1980).

Younger, P., *Introduction to Indian Religious Thoughts* (Philadelphia, PA: Westminster Press, 1972).

Articles

Acharya, T., 'Nepal's Fight for Freedom', *India Today*, 1, no. 12 (1952).

Allen-Mills, T., 'Nepal Suffers But is Standing Firm', *Independent*, 11 April 1989.

Anand, R.P., 'The Politics of a New Legal Order for Fisheries', II, *Ocean Development and International Law* (1982), 265–9.

______. 'Legal Continental Shelf and What it Includes', 5, *Institute for Defence Studies Analysis Journal* (1973), 358ff.

______. 'Limits of National Jurisdiction in the Sea-Bed', 29, *Indian Quarterly* (1973), 77.

Ayoob, M., 'India and Nepal: Politics of Aid and Trade', *Institute for Defence Studies and Analyses Journal*, vol. 3, no. 2 (1970).

Benvenisti, E., 'Collective Action in the Utilization of Shared Freshwater: The Challenges of International Water Resources Law', *American Journal of International Law*, vol. 90 (1996), 384–415.

Berreman, G., 'People and Cultures of the Himalaya', *Asian Survey*, III, no. 6 (1963).

Biswas, A. K., 'Indus Water Treaty: The Negotiation Process', in *Water International*, vol. 17 (1992), 209.

Brown, M., 'The Diplomatic Development of Nepal', *Asian Survey*, XI no. 7 (1971).

Caflisch, L., 'Land-locked States and Their Access to and from the Sea', *British Yearbook of International Law*, vol. 49, (1978), 71–100

Chadwick, D. H., and W., Thompson, 'At the Crossroads of Kathmandu', 172(1) *National Geographic* (1987), 32.

Chakravarty, S., 'Indo-Bangladesh Treaty on Sharing of Ganga Waters', *Mainstream,* 11 January 1997, 32.

Clad, J., 'GDP Set to Slump in Wake of Transit Dispute: Gasping for Breath', *Far Eastern Economic Review*, 8 March 1990, 25–7.

Copes, P., 'The Impact of UNCLOS III on Management of the World's Fisheries' *Marine Policy* (1981), 217.

Dahbour, O., 'Self-Determination in Political Philosophy and International Law', *History of European Ideas,* 16 (1993), 879–84.

Datta- Ray, S.K. 'Living with Nepal: Must Busybodies Queer the Pitch? *Statesman Weekly* (Calcutta), 17 Feb. 1990, 11.

D'Amato, A. 'On Consensus' VIII, *The Canadian Yearbook of International Law*, (1970), 104, 108.

Desai, B., 'Sharing of International Water Resources: The Ganges and Mahakali River Treaties', *Asia Pacific Journal of Environmental Law,* vol. 3, Issue 2 (1998), 172–7.

Dhungel, H., 'Risks and Reward of Mega Projects: The Political Economy of Paraguayan Hydropower', in *Water Nepal,* vol., 7 (1999), 25–6.

Driver, P.A., 'International Fisheries' in R.P. Barstan and P. Birnie (eds.) *The Maritime Dimension* (London: Allen & Unwin, 1980).

Dubey, M., 'International Law relating to the Transit Trade of Land-locked Countries', XIV, *Indian Yearbook of International Affairs* (1965).

Fawcett, J., 'Trade and Finance in International Law, *Hague Recueil Des Cours*, 1 (1968).

Franck, T., 'The Emerging Right to Democratic Governance', *American Journal of International Law* 86 (1992), 46–91.

Fried, J.H.E., 'The 1965 Convention on Transit Trade of Land-locked States', *Indian Journal of International Law,* vol. 6 (1966), 9–30.

Fuentes, X., 'The Criteria for the Equitable Utilization of International Rivers', 69, *British Year Book of International Law* (1998), 337–412.

Gardam, J.G., 'Proportionality and Force in International Law', *American Journal of International Law*, vol. 87 (1993), no. 3.

Ghori, K., 'Nepal and its Neighbours', *Pakistan Horizon*, vol. 17(1964), no. 4.

Govindraj, V. C., 'Land-locked States and their Right of Access to the Sea', *Indian Journal of International Law* (1974), 190.

James, B., 'Nepalese United in Adversity as Indian Blockade Bites', *The Times* (London) (1989).

Kashyap, S.C., 'A New Parliament Initiative: Subject Based Standing Committee of Parliament', *Economic and Political Weekly*, Oct. 1990.

Karl, D.E., 'Islands and the Delimitation of Continental Shelf: A Framework for Analysis', *American Journal of International Law,* vol. 71 (1977), 642.

Kent, H.S.K., 'The Historical Origins of the Three-mile Limit', *American Journal of International Law,* vol. 48 (1954), 534.

Kingsbury, B., 'Sovereignty and Inequality', *European Journal of International Law,* vol. 9 (1998), 599–625.

Koudstall, R., 'The Water Resources System in Bangladesh and the Netherlands', *Daily Star*, Dhaka, 30 April 2001, 18.

Kumar, D. P., 'Chinese Anti-Aircraft Guns: Nepal Violated Secret Agreement with India', *Statesman* (Delhi), 27 May 1989.

Larson, D.L., 'Forward', 11, *Ocean Development and International Law* (1982), 1.

Lauterpacht, E., 'Freedom of Transit in International Law', *Grotius Society Transactions for the Year* 1958 and 1959, vol. 44, 313–56.

Law of the Sea: Rights of Access of Land-Locked States to and from the Sea and Freedom of Transit (New York: United Nations, 1994)

Lowe, A.V., 'Reflections on the Waters: Changing Conceptions of Property Rights in the Law of the Sea', 1, *International Journal of Estuarine and Costal Law* (1986).

Malla, B.C., 'Nepal a Zone of Peace: National Perspective' in G.R. Agrawal et al, *Fundamentals of Nepalese Foreign Policy* (Kathmandu: CFDA, Tribhuvan University, 1985).

Mendelson, M.H., & Hutton, S.C., 'The Iraq-Kuwait Boundary' 64 *British Yearbook of International Law*, (1993), 135.

Mirvahabi, F., 'The Rights of the Land-locked and Geographically Disadvantaged States in Exploitation of Marine Fisheries', *Netherlands International Law Review,* vol. 26, no. 2, (1979), 130–62.

Moellendorf, D., 'Constructing the Law of People', *Pacific Philosophical Quarterly,* 77 no. 2, (1996), 132–54.

Moore, G., 'National Legislation for the Management of Fisheries under Costal State Jurisdiction', 11(2), *Journal of Maritime Law and Commerce* (1982), 153, 160.

Mukerjee, D., 'India, Nepal Accord on Military Tie', *Times of India*, 21 Oct. 1970, 1

_____. 'Himalayan Stalemate Indian: Stake in Nepali Goodwill', *Times of India,* 4 April 1989, 1.

Oda, S., 'Fisheries Under the United Nations Convention on the Law of the Sea', 77, *American Journal of International Law* (1983), 739.

Pun, S.B., ' *The Evolving Role of the Public and Private Institutions in the Nepalese*

Power Sector', in Annual Report of Water and Energy Commission Secretariat, Adm./060799/1/1, Seq.041, 38–49.

Ramakant, 'Indo-Nepal Relations: Geopolitical Compulsions', *South Asian Studies*, vol. 6, no.1 (1971).

Rama Rao, T.S., 'The Himalayan Frontier Policy of India- A Historical Perspective', XV-XVI, *Indian Yearbook of International Affairs* (1966–7), 558.

Rana, P.S.J.B., 'The Prospect of Water Resources of Nepal and the Mahakali River Integrated Development Treaty', *Nepal Council of World Affairs*, 16 Aug. 1996. (a copy of this paper is on file with me).

Sagnier, T., 'Educating the Most Beautiful Children in the World' in *UN Chronical*, vol. XXIV, no. 4, Nov. 1987, 74.

Sanders, D., 'The Re-emergence of Indigenous Questions in International Law', *Canadian Human Rights Yearbook* 3 (1983), 12–30.

Sarup, A., 'Transit Trade of Land-locked Nepal', 21, *International and Comparative Law Quarterly* (1972), 287, 294.

Shaha, R., 'Himalayan Impasse: Need for New Perspectives', *The Times of India* 7 June 1989.

Shaha, P., 'Nepal as a Zone of Peace', *Pacific Community*, vol. 8, no. 1 (1976).

Shrestha, G.D., 'Himalayan Waters: Need for Positive Indo-Nepal Co-operation', in *Water Nepal*, vol., 4, no. 1 (1994), 272.

Singh, N.K., 'An Agenda for Talks with Mr Bhattarai', *Times of India*, 7 June 1990.

Slaughter, A., 'International Law and International Relations Theory: A Dual Agenda', *American Journal of International Law* , 87 (1993), 205–39.

Slaughter, A., 'International Law in a World of Liberal States', *European Journal of International Law* 6 (1995), 503–38.

Smith, C., 'Nepal Suffers to Fend off the New Raj', *Observer* (1986).

Subedi, S.P., 'The Himalayan Frontier Policy of British-India and the Significance of the 1923 Treaty of Friendship between Great Britain-Nepal', 27, *Journal of the Britain-Nepal Society*, London (Dec. 2003), 35–9.

———. 'Resolution of International Water Disputes: Challenges for the 21st Century', *in* International Bureau of the Permanent Court of Arbitration, *Resolution of International Water Disputes,* vol. 6 in the PCA Peace Palace Papers series, The Hague, Kluwer Law International (2003), 33–47.

———. 'The Concept in Hinduism of "Just War"', *Journal of Conflict and Security Law* Oxford University Press, vol. 8 (2) (2003), 339–61.

———. 'The Legal Regime Concerning the Utilization of the Water Resources of the River Ganges Basin', 46 *German Yearbook of International Law* (2003), 452–93.

———. 'Regulation of Shared Water Resources in International Law: The Challenge of Balancing Competing Demands', *Nepal Law Review* (Faculty of Law, Tribhuvan University), vol. 15 (1 & 2), July 2002, 1–14.

_____. 'Incorporation of the Principle of Sustainable Development into the Development Policies of the Asian Countries', *Environmental Policy and Law* (International Council of Environmental Law, Bonn), vol. 32 (2), April 2002, 85–90.

_____. 'Hydro-diplomacy in South Asia: The Conclusion of the Ganges and the Mahakali River Treaties', 93 (4), *American Journal of International Law* (Oct. 1999), 631–40.

_____. 'Constitutional Accommodation of Ethnicity and National Identity in Nepal', *International Journal on Minority and Group Rights* (Kluwer Law International, The Hague), vol. 6, no.1/2 (1999), 121–47.

_____. 'Environmental Inputs into the Planning Process and Access to Justice', in *Environmental Policy and Law* (International Council of Environmental Law, Bonn), vol. 28, no. 2 (May 1998), 96–103.

_____. 'Transit Arrangements between Nepal and India: A Study in International Law', in *Geopolitics and International Boundaries*, vol. 2 (1) (Frank Cass: London, 1997), 175–96.

_____. 'When is a Treaty a Treaty in Law? An Analysis of the Views of the Supreme Court of Nepal on a Bilateral Water Agreement between Nepal and India', 5 *Asian Yearbook of International Law* (1996), 201–10.

_____. 'India–Nepal Security Relations and the 1950 Peace and Friendship Treaty: Time for New Perspectives', *Asian Survey* (University of California Press), vol. 34, no. (3) (1994), 273–84.

_____. 'Obligations and Responsibilities of Transit and Land-Locked States in the Absence of a Transit Treaty', *Rising Nepal*, 20 May 1989, 2.

_____. 'The Marine Fishery Rights of Land-locked States with Particular Reference to the EEZ', *International Journal of Estuarine and Coastal Law*, vol. 2, no 4 (1987), 227–39.

Thapa, Dhruba B.S., 'India–Nepal Relations, Perspectives on Present Problem: a Legal Approach', Paper Presented at a Seminar on 'Transit' Organized by the Nepal University Teachers Association, Kathmandu, May 1989.

Weissberg, G., 'Maps as Evidence in International Boundary Dispute', *American Journal of International Law*, vol. 57 (1963).

Wijkman, A.M., 'The UNCLOS and the Redistribution of Ocean Wealth', 16, *Journal of World Trade Law* (1982)

Wouters, P.K., 'Allocation of the Non-Navigational Uses of International Watercourses: Efforts at Codification and the Experience of Canada and the United States', *Canadian Yearbook of International Law* (1992), 43–88.

Index